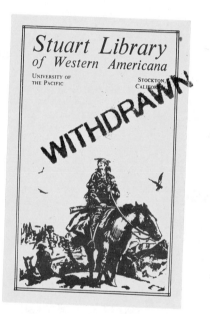

# The

An index

# Pacific

to people and places

# Northwest

in books

Joseph
Gerald
Drazan

The Scarecrow Press, Inc.
Metuchen, N.J., & London          1979

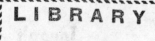
Library of Congress Cataloging in Publication Data

Drazan, Joseph Gerald, 1943-
  The Pacific Northwest.

  Bibliography: p.
  1. Northwest, Pacific--Indexes. 2. Alaska--
Indexes. 3. Yukon Territory--Indexes. 4. Northwest,
Pacific--Biography--Indexes. 5. Alaska--Biography--
Indexes. 6. Yukon Territory--Biography--Indexes.
I. Title.
Z1251.N7D7 [F851]    979.5'0016    79-16683
ISBN 0-8108-1234-7

for Deanna

# TABLE OF CONTENTS

Preface                                        vii

How to Use This Index                           xi

Bibliography of Sources Indexed                  1

The Index to People and Places                  27

v

# PREFACE

Having been a reference librarian, I am acutely aware
of the scarcity of local and regional reference tools at the
librarian's or researcher's disposal for locating information
about a person or place. This book should help fill that gap
for the Pacific Northwest in that one should not have to
flounder around quite so noticeably in an attempt to find
source material for the seemingly obvious or for the obscure,
unusual, or odd bit of data.

Few libraries in the Pacific Northwest will own all of
the source books indexed here, but every library, even the
smallest, can benefit from this content analysis by knowing
where to find the information, and then pursuing it through
loan channels if desired.

This index, then, is designed as a simple reference
tool with which to locate information about 6830 people, and
2100 cities, towns, and forts in the Pacific Northwest. It
is a selective master index to 320 English-language books,
each of which has its own index, whose contents are solely--
or nearly so--concerned either with the Northwest as a regional unit or with smaller areas within that region.

For my purposes the Pacific Northwest is defined as
encompassing the states of Alaska, Washington, Oregon,
Idaho, Montana, and the Province of British Columbia, and
the Yukon Territory. Some of the source books cover only
a single state or perhaps only a county or area within a

state, but taken as a whole collection, and as a project starting point, they altogether provide a very comprehensive survey of the total region.    Furthermore these source books include many subjects; obviously most are related to history,
but the fields of education, economics, politics, the arts,
and even medicine are all reflected in the present index.
No books containing indexes are excluded because of publication date or time period covered.

The present work is a selective index in that each of
the source book indexes was gleaned for the most substantive
and useful entries.    Many source books actually contribute
only a few entries to the total index, while many contribute
scores or hundreds, especially those major historical com-
pilations from the turn of the century that are rich in de-
tailed biographical entries.

Total indexing would have given a reference book ten
times this size, and it is my opinion this would be unneces-
sary in light of probable use.    So many vagaries exist from
one source book's index to another, especially in subject indexing, that it was decided for practical purposes to try to
index those relatively absolute entries that consist of personal and geographic names.    Probably not even half the personal names encountered were used, either because many are
not Northwesterners (and this was verified by referring to the
book's contents when any doubt existed), or because many index entries in the source books are simply of the "in pass-
ing" type.    Those entries verified as too brief and/or mean-
ingless have been nearly totally avoided so that the user will
find something of substance about the person or place, maybe
not exactly what he had in mind, but at least some facts or
information to make the look-up more than useless.

EXCLUSIONS

Some major persons have been selected out, such as
John McLoughlin and Lewis and Clark, because there is just
too much information in this group of source books to make
the entries usable. This is true with metropolitan cities,
too: excluded are Seattle, Spokane, Tacoma, Vancouver (BC),
Victoria, Portland, Eugene, Helena, Butte, Boise, Fairbanks,
Juneau, and Anchorage, because virtually every book concerned
with their respective states has entries that would overwhelm
the scope of this work. At the other extreme, I had to re-
ject many small towns because there was simply no information in the text to back up the index entry in the source book.

Defining a "Northwesterner" for this index of course
is a dangerous thing to do, even somewhat impossible; however, I have played it loose while trying to avoid transients.
It is safe to say that most persons named in this index were
at least residents or settlers for some length of time. In
some cases it may have only been for a few years, and in
many instances it would be impossible to determine anyway,
but at least at that point in that particular work, the person,
through a check of the book's contents appeared to be a
"legitimate" Northwesterner. Right now it should be stated
that hundreds of "nobodies" are listed in concert with the
knowns and the renowned. Therefore this index should be
very useful to genealogists as well as local historians.

Many errors and misspellings were encountered in the
individual indexes. These have been corrected for my listing when possible. It is true, though, that errors can exist
in these indexes which were not perceived or detected, and
therefore were transferred to my integrated index. I expect
and hope that these are few, and if discovered can somehow

be brought to my attention.

I noted previously that the source books used were only a starting point; this is the type of project that can never be complete.    Of over 1000 relatively available indexed books known to me at this point, I chose to use this group as a fairly comprehensive and representative sample.    It might appear to be slanted towards Washington and Oregon, but probably more indexed books on those two states have been produced.    Also, I keep discovering new finds that lengthen my list of knowns that could be used to expand or supplement this work.    And, of course, each year a few dozen more candidates are published.    Books printed through the end of 1977 are the most recent included in this index.

The most distressing aspect of this undertaking was to see how many important and worthwhile books on the Northwest there are that lack an index; hundreds of them, and for this they have excluded themselves.    A project of this kind might stimulate publishers to include indexes in more books to promote a more lasting value for them.

Finally, I will repeat that this is only a beginning in what I hope will be an ongoing effort, simultaneously indexing books selectively as published, while a retrospective venture is undertaken, to aim for absolute comprehensiveness.

The largest debt of gratitude is due the library of Whitman College, which also just happens to have an extensive Northwest collection of many fine materials.

Joseph Drazan
Walla Walla, Washington
August 1978

## HOW TO USE THIS INDEX

The first part of this book is a listing by author of the sources used. Some cross-referencing is employed, especially from co-authors to the primary author. Each entry in this section is preceded by a reference number from 1 to 320.

The main body of the book is the master index with all entries in a single alphabet. The numbers following the indexed entry that are separated by a colon refer the user to the correct source book, and indicate on how many pages in that book one can expect to find some information on the subject desired. For example:

Emerson, George Harvey  150:1  266:3

Information about Emerson appears only in these two source books, numbers 150 and 266, and in the former his name appears only on one page, while in the latter it shows on three pages. Note also that source numbers are always given sequentially after each index entry for convenience.

Obviously a most important feature about this index is that it tells one where not to look. Revealing the number of pages in each, however, can be somewhat misleading in that the one-page entry could be a lengthy biography, while the three-page entry could provide less information because Emerson may not actually fill the three pages, but only a paragraph or sentence about him on each. As I remarked

earlier, though, a laborious effort was made to avoid insig-
nificant entries.  A primary reason for stating the number
of pages is to make it a guide for the user in choosing from
a number of source books in some cases.  One may wish to
limit the search accordingly when a large group of sources
are presented.  Also, in requesting photocopies, one will
know in advance the amount of paper to expect in return.

To use the index the searcher must know with some
precision who or what is wanted.  For example, Walter
Clark is a common name to search, but when it is linked
with its source book, it might immediately end the search
since that book is a 1968 work on Alaska while the interest
might have been in an Idahoan of that name.

Like place names follow the personal name list, for
example, Clark, MT follows all persons surnamed Clark.  I
have underscored place names so that they will stand out
and so they will not be confused with personal names-plus-
initials since I have elected to use two-letter codes for the
states' abbreviations.

SEE and SEE ALSO references have been liberally
used, mostly to tie together place names that are treated
differently in the various indexes.  Such are the Forts; they
are indexed here as they are in the source books, sometimes
under Fort, and sometimes under the name itself with cross-
references added by me.  The Dalles, OR is a good example;
some index it under The, and some under Dalles.  Therefore I use both as found to aid the user when the source
books are confronted.

Many towns are included that are not on today's maps;
these are ghost towns or ones that have changed names--
some more than once.  Again, cross-references are provided
for these cases.

# BIBLIOGRAPHY OF SOURCES INDEXED

1 Abbott, Newton C. Montana in the Making, 6th ed. Billings, MT: Gazette Printing Co., 1931. 544pp.

2 Adams, W. Claude. History of Dentistry in Oregon. Portland, OR: Binfords & Mort, 1956. 343pp.

3 Akrigg, G. P. V., and Helen B. Akrigg. British Columbia Chronicle, 1847-1871; Gold and Colonists. Vancouver, BC: Discovery Press, 1977. 439pp.

4 Allen, Opal Sweazea. Narcissa Whitman; An Historical Biography. Portland, OR: Binfords & Mort, 1959. 325pp.

5 Allison, Susan. A Pioneer Gentlewoman in British Columbia; The Recollections of Susan Allison, ed. by Margaret A. Ormsby. Vancouver: University of British Columbia, 1976. 210pp.

6 American West. The Great Northwest; The Story of a Land and Its People. Palo Alto, CA: American West, 1973. 285pp.

7 Anderson, Eva G. Chief Seattle. Caldwell, ID: Caxton, 1943. 390pp.

8 Anderson, Hobson Dewey, and Walter C. Eells. Alaska Natives; A Survey of Their Sociological and Educational Status. Stanford, CA: Stanford University, 1935. 472pp.

9 Andrews, Ralph W. Heroes of the Western Woods. New York: Dutton, 1960. 192pp.

10 Arctander, John W. The Apostle of Alaska; The Story of William Duncan of Metlakahtla. New York: Fleming H. Revell, 1909. 395pp.

1

11  Arnold, Royal Ross.  Indian Wars of Idaho.  Caldwell,
    ID:  Caxton, 1932.  268pp.

12  Ashworth, William.  Hell's Canyon; The Deepest Gorge
    on Earth.  New York:  Hawthorn, 1977.  246pp.

13  Athearn, Robert G.  Thomas Francis Meagher; An Irish
    Revolutionary in America.  New York:  Arno, 1976.
    182pp.

14  Atwood, A.  Glimpses in Pioneer Life on Puget Sound.
    Seattle:  Denny-Coryell Co., 1903.  483pp.

15  Avery, Mary W.  Government of Washington State, rev
    ed.  Seattle:  University of Washington, 1973.  329pp.

16  _____.  Washington; A History of the Evergreen State.
    Seattle:  University of Washington, 1965.  362pp.

17  Babcock, Chester D.  Our Pacific Northwest; Yesterday
    and Today.  New York:  McGraw-Hill, 1963.  444pp.

18  Badlam, Alexander.  The Wonders of Alaska.  San Fran-
    cisco:  Bancroft Co., 1890.  152pp.

19  Bancroft, Hubert Howe.  History of Alaska.  (His Works,
    vol. 33.)  San Francisco:  Bancroft Co., 1886.
    775pp.

20  _____.  History of British Columbia.  (His Works,
    vol. 32.)  San Francisco:  History Co., 1887.  792pp.

21  Barbeau, Marius.  Pathfinders in the North Pacific.
    Caldwell, ID:  Caxton, 1958.  235pp.

22  Barker, Burt Brown.  The McLoughlin Empire and Its
    Rulers.  Glendale, CA:  Arthur Clark, 1959.  370pp.

23  Barrett, Glen.  Idaho Banking, 1863-1976.  Boise, ID:
    Boise State University, 1976.  312pp.

24  _____.  Small Town Banking in the Good Ol' Days.
    Boise, ID:  Boise State University, 1976.  110pp.

25  Barsness, Larry.  Gold Camp; Alder Gulch and Virginia
    City, Montana.  New York:  Hastings House, 1962.
    312pp.

Barth, Gunter  SEE  Bensell, Royal A.

26  Beal, Merrill D.  "I Will Fight No More Forever"; Chief Joseph and the Nez Perce War.  Seattle:  University of Washington, 1963.  366pp.

27  Becher, Edmund T.  Spokane Corona; Eras and Empires. Spokane, WA:  E. T. Becher, 1973.  319pp.

28  Becker, Ethel A.  A Treasury of Alaskana.  Seattle: Superior Publishing Co., 1969.  183pp.

29  Beckett, Paul L.  From Wilderness to Enabling Act; The Evolution of a State of Washington.  Pullman:  Washington State University, 1968.  111pp.

30  Bensell, Royal A.  All Quiet on the Yamhill; The Civil War in Oregon; The Journal of Corporal Royal A. Bensell, ed. by Gunter Barth.  Eugene:  University of Oregon, 1959.  226pp.

Bibb, Thomas W.  SEE  Bolton, Frederick E.

31  Binns, Archie.  Northwest Gateway; The Story of the Port of Seattle.  Garden City, N.Y.:  Doubleday, Doran, 1941.  313pp.

32  _____.  Sea in the Forest.  Garden City, N.Y.: Doubleday, 1954.  256pp.

33  Bird, Annie Laurie.  Boise; The Peace Valley.  Caldwell, ID:  Caxton, 1934.  408pp.

34  Bischoff, William N.  Jesuits in Old Oregon, 1840-1940. Caldwell, ID:  Caxton, 1945.  258pp.

_____  SEE  Kelly, Plympton J.

35  Blair, Harry C., and Rebecca Tarshis.  Lincoln's Constant Ally; The Life of Colonel Edward D. Baker. Portland:  Oregon Historical Society, 1960.  233pp.

36  Blankenship, William Russell.  And There Were Men. New York:  Knopf, 1942.  300pp.

37  Boge, Lila V. Cooper.  Tillamook History; Sequel to Tillamook Memories.  Tillamook, OR:  Tillamook County Pioneer Association, 1975.  262pp.

38   Bolton, Frederick E. , and Thomas W. Bibb. History
       of Education in Washington. (Department of the In-
       terior Bulletin No. 9, 1934. ) Washington, DC:  U. S.
       Government Printing Office, 1935.   448pp.

39   Bond, Rowland.  Early Birds in the Northwest.  Nine
       Mile Falls, WA:  Spokane House Enterprises, 1973.
       248pp.

     Bone, Hugh A.  SEE   Ogden, Daniel M.

40   Bowes, Gordon E.  Peace River Chronicles.  Vancouver,
       BC:  Prescott Publishing Co. , 1963.   557pp.

41   Brier, Howard M.  Sawdust Empire;  The Pacific North-
       west.  New York:  Knopf, 1958.   269pp.

42   Brogan, Phil F.  East of the Cascades.  Portland, OR:
       Binfords & Mort, 1964.   304pp.

43   Brosnan, Cornelius J.  History of the State of Idaho.
       New York, Scribner's, 1918.   237pp.

44   _____.  Jason Lee; Prophet of the New Oregon.   New
       York, Macmillan, 1932.   348pp.

45   Brown, Jennie B.  Fort Hall on the Oregon Trail.   Cald-
       well, ID:  Caxton, 1934.   466pp.

     Brown, John A.  SEE   Ruby, Robert H.

46   Brown, Kimberly.  Historical Overview of the Dillon
       District.  Boulder, CO: WICHE [Western Interstate
       Commission for Higher Education], 1975.   177pp.

47   Bryan, Liz.  Backroads of British Columbia.  Vancou-
       ver, BC:  Sunflower Books, 1976.   156pp.

48   Burlingame, Merrill G.  Montana Frontier.  Helena,
       MT:  State Publishing Co. , 1942.   418pp.

49   Burton, Robert E.  Democrats of Oregon;  The Pattern
       of Minority Politics, 1900-1956.  Eugene:  Univer-
       sity of Oregon, 1970.   158pp.

50   Cantwell, Robert.  The Hidden Northwest.  Philadelphia:
       Lippincott, 1972.   335pp.

51   Carey, Charles Henry, ed.  The Oregon Constitution and
     Proceedings and Debates of the Constitutional Conven-
     tion of 1857.  Salem: State of Oregon, 1926.  543pp.

52   Carrighar, Sally.  Moonlight at Midday.  New York:
     Knopf, 1958.  392pp.

53   Chaffee, Eugene B.  Boise College;  An Idea Grows.
     Boise, ID:  E. Chaffee, 1970.  273pp.

54   Chasan, Daniel J.  Klondike '70; The Alaskan Oil Boom.
     New York:  Praeger, 1971.  184pp.

55   Clark, Henry W.  Alaska;  The Last Frontier, 2nd ed.
     New York:  Grosset & Dunlap, 1930.  246pp.

56   Clark, Keith, and Lowell Tiller.  Terrible Trail; The
     Meek Cutoff, 1845.  Caldwell, ID:  Caxton, 1966.
     244pp.

57   Clark, Norman H.  Mill Town; A Social History of Ever-
     ett, Washington.  Seattle:  University of Washington,
     1970.  267pp.

58   _____.  Washington; A Bicentennial History.  New
     York:  Norton, 1976.  204pp.

59   Clements, Louis J.  Pioneering the Snake River Fork
     Country.  Rexburg, ID:  Eastern Idaho Publishing
     Co. , 1972.  312pp.

     _____.  SEE  Dubois, Fred

60   Clinch, Thomas A.  Urban Populism and Free Silver in
     Montana.  Missoula:  University of Montana, 1970.
     190pp.

61   Coburn, Walt.  Pioneer Cattleman in Montana.  Norman:
     University of Oklahoma, 1968.  338pp.

62   Cohn, Edwin J.  Industry in the Pacific Northwest and
     the Location Theory.  New York:  Columbia Univer-
     sity, 1954.  214pp.

63   Colby, Merle.  A Guide to Alaska, Last American Fron-
     tier.  (Federal Writers Project. )  New York:  Mac-
     millan, 1959.  427pp.

64 Conant, Roger. Mercer's Belles: The Journal of a Reporter, ed. by Lenna A. Deutsch. Seattle: University of Washington, 1960. 190pp.

65 Cooley, Richard A. Alaska; A Challenge in Conservation. Madison: University of Wisconsin, 1966. 170 pp.

66 Cooper, Bryan. Alaska; The Last Frontier. New York: Morrow, 1973. 248pp.

67 Copper Camp; Stories of the World's Greatest Mining Town, Butte, Montana, compiled by Workers of the Writer's Program of the Works Progress Administration. New York: Hastings House, 1943. 308pp.

68 Corning, Howard M. Willamette Landings; Ghost Towns of the River, 2nd ed. Portland: Oregon Historical Society, 1973. 224pp.

69 Cornish, Nellie C. Miss Aunt Nellie; The Autobiography of Nellie C. Cornish. Seattle: University of Washington, 1964. 283pp.

70 Countryman, Vern. Un-American Activities in the State of Washington; The Work of the Canwell Committee. Ithaca, NY: Cornell University, 1951. 405pp.

71 Covert, James T. A Point of Pride; The University of Portland Story. Portland, OR: University of Portland, 1976. 328pp.

72 Cox, Ross. The Columbia River; or, Scenes and Adventures during a Residence of Six Years on the Western Side of the Rocky Mountains ..., ed. by Edgar and Jane R. Stewart. Norman: University of Oklahoma, 1957. 398pp.

73 Cox, Thomas R. Mills and Markets; A History of the Pacific Coast Lumber Industry to 1900. Seattle: University of Washington, 1974. 332pp.

74 Crawford, Harriet Ann. The Washington State Grange, 1889-1924. Portland, OR: Binfords & Mort, 1940. 334pp.

75 Culp, Edwin D. Stations West; The Story of the Oregon Railways. Caldwell, ID: Caxton, 1972. 265pp.

76  Cushman, Dan.  Montana; The Gold Frontier.  Great
    Falls, MT:  Stay Away Joe, 1973.  293pp.

77  Dall, William H.  Alaska and Its Resources.  Boston:
    Lee & Shepard, 1870.  627pp.

78  Davis, Jean.  Shallow Diggin's; Tales from Montana's
    Ghost Towns.  Caldwell, ID:  Caxton, 1962.  375pp.

79  Demoro, Harre.  The Evergreen Fleet; A Pictorial His-
    tory of Washington State Ferries.  San Marino, CA:
    Golden West, 1971.  136pp.

80  Denny, Arthur A.  Pioneer Days on Puget Sound.  Seat-
    tle:  Harriman Co. , 1908.  103pp.

    Deutsch, Lenna A.  SEE  Conant, Roger

81  DeWindt, Harry.  Through the Gold Fields of Alaska to
    Bering Straits.  New York:  Harper, 1898.  314pp.

82  Dierdorff, John.  How Edison's Lamp Helped Light the
    West; The Story of Pacific Power and Light Company.
    Portland, OR:  Pacific Power & Light Co. , 1971.
    313pp.

83  Dill, Clarence C.  Where Water Falls.  Spokane, WA:
    C. C. Dill, 1970.  276pp.

84  Dobbs, Caroline C.  Men of Champoeg; A Record of the
    Lives of the Pioneers Who Founded the Oregon Gov-
    ernment.  Portland, OR:  Metropolitan Press, 1932.
    219pp.

85  Dodds, Gordon B.  Oregon; A Bicentennial History.  New
    York:  Norton, 1977.  240pp.

86  _____.  The Salmon King of Oregon; R. D. Hume and
    the Pacific Fisheries.  Chapel Hill:  University of
    North Carolina, 1959.  257pp.

87  Donaldson, Thomas.  Idaho of Yesterday.  Caldwell,
    ID:  Caxton, 1941.  406pp.

88  Douglas, William O.  Go East Young Man; The Early
    Years ... Autobiography.  New York:  Random,
    1974.  493pp.

89   Downie, Ralph Ernest.  Pictorial History of the State
     of Washington, 2nd ed. Seattle:  Lowman & Hanford,
     1937.

90   Drucker, Philip.  Cultures of the North Pacific Coast.
     San Francisco:  Chandler, 1965.  243pp.

91   Drury, Clifford M.  A Tepee in His Front Yard; A
     Biography of H. T. Cowley ... .  Portland, OR:
     Binfords & Mort, 1949.  206pp.

92   Dryden, Cecil.  Dryden's History of Washington.  Port-
     land, OR:  Binfords & Mort, 1968.  412pp.

93   _____ .  Give All to Oregon; Missionary Pioneers of
     the Far West.  New York:  Hastings House, 1968.
     256pp.

94   _____ .  Light for an Empire; The Story of Eastern
     Washington State College.  Cheney:  Eastern Wash-
     ington State College, 1965.  369pp.

95   Dubois, Fred T.  The Making of a State [Idaho], ed. by
     Louis J. Clements.  Rexburg;  Eastern Idaho Pub-
     lishing Co. , 1971.  207pp.

96   Dyar, Ralph E.  News for an Empire; The Story of the
     Spokesman-Review of Spokane, Washington, and of
     the Field It Serves.  Caldwell, ID:  Caxton, 1952.
     494pp.

     Eells, Walter C.  SEE  Anderson, Hobson.

97   El Hult, Ruby.  Lost Mines and Treasures of the Pa-
     cific Northwest.  Portland, OR:  Binfords & Mort,
     1964.  257pp.

98   _____ .  Northwest Disaster; Avalanche and Fire.
     Portland, OR:  Binfords & Mort, 1960.  228pp.

99   _____ .  Steamboats in the Timber.  Caldwell, ID:
     Caxton, 1953.  209pp.

100  _____ .  The Untamed Olympics; The Story of a Pen-
     insula.  Portland, OR:  Binfords & Mort, 1954.
     267pp.

101  Elliott, Thomas Coit.  Coming of the White Women,

1836, as Told in the Letters and Journal of Narcissa
Prentiss Whitman. Portland: Oregon Historical Society, 1937.

102  Elsensohn, Alfreda. Pioneer Days in Idaho County,
vol. 1, and:

103  _____. Pioneer Days in Idaho County, vol. 2.
Caldwell, ID: Caxton, 1947. 1145pp.

104  Ernst, Alice H. Trouping in the Oregon Country; A
History of Frontier Theatre. Portland: Oregon Historical Society, 1961. 197pp.

105  Etulain, Richard W. , and Bert W. Marley, eds. The
Idaho Heritage; A Collection of Critical Essays. Pocatello: Idaho State University, 1974. 230pp.

Evans, Ellwood SEE History of the Pacific Northwest.

106  Fahey, John. Ballyhoo Bonanza; Charles Sweeny and
the Idaho Mines. Seattle: University of Washington,
1971. 288pp.

107  _____. Inland Empire; D. C. Corbin and Spokane.
Seattle: University of Washington, 1965. 270pp.

108  Fargo, Lucile F. Spokane Story. New York: Columbia University, 1950. 276pp.

109  Feagans, Raymond J. The Railroad That Ran by the
Tide; Ilwaco Railroad & Navigation Company of the
State of Washington. Berkeley, CA: Howell-North,
1972. 146pp.

Federal Writer's Project SEE 67, 164, 239, 305

110  French, Giles. Cattle Country of Peter French. Portland, OR: Binfords & Mort, 1964. 167pp.

111  _____. Homesteads and Heritages; A History of
Morrow County, Oregon. Portland, OR: Binfords
& Mort, 1971. 127pp.

112  Frenchtown Historical Society. Frenchtown Valley
Footprints. Frenchtown, MT: Frenchtown Historical
Society, 1976. 173pp.

113  Friedheim, Robert L.  Seattle General Strike.  Seattle:  University of Washington, 1964.  224pp.

114  Friedman, Ralph.  Tales Out of Oregon.  Portland, OR:  Pars Publishing Co. , 1967.  248pp.

Fullenwider, Elmer D.  SEE  King, William A.

115  Gardey, Jon.  Alaska; The Sophisticated Wilderness.  New York:  Stein & Day, 1976.  224pp.

116  Gellatly, John A.  A History of Wenatchee.  Wenatchee, WA:  J. A. Gellatly, 1963.  399pp.

117  Gibbs, Rafe.  Beacon for Mountain and Plain; Story of the University of Idaho.  Moscow:  University of Idaho, 1962.  420pp.

118  _____.  Beckoning the Bold; Story of the Dawning of Idaho.  Moscow:  University Press of Idaho, 1976.  266pp.

119  Gilbert, Frank T.  Historic Sketches of Walla Walla, Whitman, Columbia and Garfield Counties, Washington Territory.  Portland, OR:  A. G. Walling, 1882.  447pp.

120  Gough, Barry M.  The Royal Navy and the Northwest Coast of North America, 1810-1914.  Vancouver:  University of British Columbia, 1971.  294pp.

121  Gould, Dorothy Fay.  Beyond the Shining Mountains; 36 Northwest Adventures.  Portland, OR:  Binfords & Mort, 1938.  206pp.

122  Gould, Ed.  Logging; British Columbia Logging History.  Saanichton, BC:  Hancock House, 1975.  221pp.

123  Gould, Jan.  Women of British Columbia.  Saanichton, BC:  Hancock House, 1975.  221pp.

124  Gray, Alfred O.  Not by Might; The Story of Whitworth College, 1890-1965.  Spokane, WA:  Whitworth College, 1965.  279pp.

The Great Northwest  SEE  American West

125  Greely, Adolphus W.  Handbook of Alaska; Its Re-

sources, Products, and Attractions. New York:
Scribner's, 1909. 280pp.

126  Gregson, Harry. A History of Victoria, 1842-1970.
Victoria, BC: Victoria Observer Publishing Co.,
1970. 246pp.

127  Grover, David H. Debaters and Dynamiters; The Story
of the Haywood Trial. Corvallis: Oregon State University, 1964. 310pp.

128  Gruening, Ernest H. The Battle for Alaska Statehood.
College: University of Alaska, 1967. 122pp.

129  _____. Many Battles; The Autobiography of Ernest
Gruening. New York: Liveright, 1973. 564pp.

130  _____. The State of Alaska. New York: Random,
1968. 661pp.

Gruenstein, Peter SEE Hanrahan, John

131  Hacking, Norman R. The Princess Story; A Century
and a Half of West Coast Shipping. Vancouver, BC:
Mitchell Press, 1974. 360pp.

132  Haines, Francis. The Story of Idaho. Boise, ID:
Syms-York Co., 1942. 169pp.

133  Hamilton, James M. History of Montana; From Wilderness to Statehood, 2nd ed. Portland, OR: Binfords
& Mort, 1970. 672pp.

134  Hanley, Mike. Owyhee Trails; The West's Forgotten
Corner. Caldwell, ID: Caxton, 1974. 314pp.

135  Hanna, Warren L. Montana's Many-Splendored Glacier-
land. Seattle: Superior Publishing Co., 1976. 215
pp.

136  Hanrahan, John, and Peter Gruenstein. Lost Frontier;
The Marketing of Alaska. New York: Norton, 1977.
363pp.

137  Harkey, Ira. Pioneer Bush Pilot; The Story of Noel
Wien. Seattle: University of Washington, 1974.
307pp.

138 Harris, Lorraine. Halfway to the Goldfields; A History of Lillooet. Vancouver, BC: J.J. Douglas, 1977. 97pp.

139 Hart, Herbert M. Old Forts of the Northwest. New York: Bonanza Books, 1963. 192pp.

140 Hays, Hoffman R. Children of the Raven; The Seven Indian Nations of the Northwest Coast. New York: McGraw-Hill, 1975. 314pp.

141 Hazard, Joseph T. Companion of Adventure; A Biography of Isaac Ingalls Stevens. Portland, OR: Binfords & Mort, 1952. 238pp.

142 Heffelfinger, C. H. Evergreen Citizen; A Textbook on the Government of the State of Washington. Caldwell, ID: Caxton, 1941. 343pp.

143 Hellenthal, John A. The Alaskan Melodrama. New York: Liveright, 1936. 312pp.

144 Hendricks, Robert J. Bethel and Aurora; An Experiment in Communism as Practical Christianity. New York: Press of the Pioneers, 1933. 324pp.

145 Hendrickson, James E. Joe Lane of Oregon: Machine Politics and the Sectional Crisis, 1849-1861. New Haven, CT: Yale University, 1967. 274pp.

146 Higginson, Ella. Alaska, the Great Country. New York: Macmillan, 1926. 583pp.

147 Hilleary, William M. A Webfoot Volunteer; The Diary of William M. Hilleary, ed. by Herbert B. Nelson and Preston E. Onstad. Corvallis: Oregon State University, 1965. 240pp.

148 Hilscher, Herbert H. Alaska Now, rev. ed. Boston: Little, Brown, 1950. 309pp.

149 Hinckley, Ted C. The Americanization of Alaska, 1867-1897. Palo Alto, CA: Pacific Books, 1972. 285pp.

150 History of the Pacific Northwest; Oregon and Washington ... , 2 vols. , by Elwood Evans, et al. Portland, OR: North Pacific History Co. , 1889.

151   Holbrook, Stewart H.   The Columbia.   New York:
      Rinehart, 1956.   393pp.

152   _____.   Far Corner; A Personal View of the Pa-
      cific Northwest.   New York:   Macmillan, 1952.   270
      pp.

153   Horner, John B.   Oregon History and Early Literature,
      rev. & enl. ed.   Portland, OR:   J. K. Gill Co. , 1931.
      442pp.

154   _____.   A Short History of Oregon.   Portland, OR:
      J. K. Gill Co. , 1924.   201pp.

155   Howard, Helen Addison.   Northwest Trail Blazers.
      Caldwell, ID:   Caxton, 1963.   418pp.

156   Howard, Joseph Kinsey.   Montana; High, Wide, and
      Handsome.   New Haven, CT:   Yale University, 1943.
      347pp.

157   Hull, Lindley M.   History of Central Washington In-
      cluding the Famous Wenatchee, Entiat, Chelan, and
      the Columbia Valleys ... .   Spokane, WA:   Shaw
      and Borden Co. , 1929.

158   Hull, Raymond.   Vancouver's Past.   Seattle:   Univer-
      sity of Washington, 1974.   96pp.

159   Hulley, Clarence C.   Alaska, 1741-1953.   Portland,
      OR:   Binfords & Mort, 1953.   406pp.

      Hult, Ruby El   SEE   El Hult, Ruby.

160   Hunt, William R.   Alaska; A Bicentennial History.   New
      York:   Norton, 1976.   200pp.

161   _____.   Arctic Passage.   New York:   Scribner's,
      1975.   395pp.

162   Hussey, John A.   Champoeg; A Place of Transition.
      Portland:   Oregon Historical Society, 1967.   404pp.

163   Hynding, Alan.   The Public Life of Eugene Semple;
      Promoter and Politician of the Pacific Northwest.
      Seattle:   University of Washington, 1973.   195pp.

164   Idaho; A Guide in Word and Picture, compiled by the

Federal Writers Project. Caldwell, ID: Caxton, 1937. 431pp.

165  Jackman, S. W. Vancouver Island. Harrisburg, PA: Stackpole, 1972. 212pp.

166  James, Bushrod W. Alaska, Its Neglected Past, Its Brilliant Future. Philadelphia: Sunshine Publishing Co. , 1897. 444pp.

167  James, Don. Butte's Memory Book. Caldwell, ID: Caxton, 1975. 295pp.

168  James, James A. The First Scientific Exploration of Russian America and the Purchase of Alaska. Evanston, IL: Northwestern University, 1942. 276pp.

169  Johns, Helen. Twenty-Five Years of the Washington Library Association. Palo Alto, CA: Pacific Books, 1956. 176pp.

170  Johnson, Claudius O. Borah of Idaho. New York: Longman's Green, 1936. 511pp.

171  Johnson, Hugh A. , and Harold T. Jorgenson. The Land Resources of Alaska; A Conservation Foundation Study. New York: University Publications, 1963. 551pp.

172  Johnson, Jalmar. Builders of the Northwest. New York: Dodd, Mead, 1963. 242pp.

173  Johnson, Olga W. Flathead and Kootenay; The Rivers, the Tribes, and the Region's Traders. Glendale, CA: Arthur Clark, 1969. 392pp.

174  Jonasson, Jonas A. Bricks without Straw; The Story of Linfield College. Caldwell, ID: Caxton, 1938. 215pp.

175  Jones, Alden H. From Jamestown to Coffin Rock; A History of Weyerhauser Operations in Southwest Washington. Tacoma, WA: Weyerhauser Co. , 1974. 346pp.

176  Jones, Nard. Evergreen Land; A Portrait of the State of Washington. New York: Dodd, Mead, 1947. 276 pp.

177 _____. The Great Command; The Story of Marcus
      and Narcissa Whitman and the Oregon Country Pi-
      oneers. Boston: Little, Brown, 1959. 398pp.

178 _____. Seattle. Garden City, NY: Doubleday,
      1972. 371pp.

    Jorgenson, Harold T. SEE Johnson, Hugh A.

179 Kelly, Plympton J. We Were Not Summer Soldiers;
      The Indian War Diary of Plympton J. Kelly, with
      introductory essay and annotations by William N.
      Bischoff. Tacoma: Washington State Historical So-
      ciety, 1976. 191pp.

180 King, William A., and Elmer D. Fullenwider. Pacific
      Northwest; Its Resources and Industries. Cincinnati:
      Southwestern Publishing Co., 1938. 390pp.

181 Koelbel, Lenora. Missoula the Way It Was. Missoula,
      MT: Gateway Printing, 1972. 128pp.

182 Krutilla, John V. Columbia River Treaty; The Econ-
      omics of an International River Basin Development.
      Baltimore: Johns Hopkins, 1967. 211pp.

183 Lacey, Richard H. The Montana Militia; A History of
      Montana's Volunteer Forces, 1867-1976, 2nd ed.
      Dillon, MT: Dillon-Tribune Examiner Press, 1976.
      96pp.

184 Landeen, William M. E.O. Holland and the State Col-
      lege of Washington, 1916-1944. Pullman, WA: State
      College of Washington, 1958. 454pp.

185 Large, Richard G. Prince Rupert; A Gateway to Alas-
      ka and the Pacific, 2nd ed. Vancouver, BC: Mitchell
      Press, 1973. 228pp.

186 _____. The Skeena; River of Destiny, 3rd ed. Van-
      couver, BC: Mitchell Press, 1957. 180pp.

187 Larsell, Olof. The Doctor in Oregon; A Medical His-
      tory. Portland, OR: Binfords & Mort, 1947. 671pp.

188 Lavender, David. Land of Giants; The Drive to the
      Pacific Northwest, 1750-1950. Garden City, NY:
      Doubleday, 1958. 468pp.

189  LaViolette, Forrest E.  Struggle for Survival; Indian
     Cultures and the Protestant Ethic in British Colum-
     bia.  Toronto: University of Toronto, 1961.  201pp.

190  Lazell, J. Arthur.  Alaskan Apostle; The Life Story of
     Sheldon Jackson.  New York: Harper, 1960.  218pp.

191  LeWarne, Charles P.  Utopias on Puget Sound, 1885-
     1915.  Seattle: University of Washington, 1975.
     325pp.

192  Livingston-Little, D. E.  An Economic History of North
     Idaho, 1800-1900.  Los Angeles: Journal of the West,
     1965.  133pp.

193  Loewenberg, Robert J.  Equality on the Oregon Fron-
     tier; Jason Lee and the Methodist Mission, 1834-43.
     Seattle: University of Washington, 1976.  287pp.

194  Lomax, Alfred L.  Pioneer Woolen Mills in Oregon.
     Portland, OR: Binfords & Mort, 1941.  312pp.

195  Lucia, Ellis.  The Big Woods; Logging and Lumber-
     ing ... in the Pacific Northwest.  Garden City, NY:
     Doubleday, 1975.  222pp.

196  _____.  Klondike Kate; The Life and Legend of Kit-
     ty Rockwell.  New York: Hastings House, 1962.
     305pp.

197  _____.  The Saga of Ben Holladay; Giant of the Old
     West.  New York: Hastings House, 1959.  374pp.

198  Lyman, William Denison.  The Columbia River; Its
     History, Its Myths, Its Scenery, Its Commerce, 4th
     ed.  Portland, OR: Binfords & Mort, 1963.  367pp.

199  _____.  Illustrated History of Walla Walla County,
     State of Washington.  W. H. Lever Publishing Co.,
     1901.  510pp.

200  McClelland, John M.  Longview; The Remarkable Be-
     ginnings of a Modern Western City.  Portland, OR:
     Binfords & Mort, 1949.  158pp.

201  McCornack, Ellen Condon.  Thomas Condon; Pioneer
     Geologist of Oregon.  Eugene: University of Oregon,
     1928.  355pp.

202  McDonald, Lucile.  Coast Country; A History of South-
     west Washington.  Portland, OR:  Binfords & Mort,
     1966.  184pp.

203  _____.  Where the Washingtonians Lived.  Seattle:
     Superior Publishing Co. , 1969.  224pp.

204  McKeever, Harry P.  British Columbia.  San Fran-
     cisco:  Chronicle Books, 1977.  192pp.

205  McKenna, Marian C.  Borah.  Ann Arbor:  University
     of Michigan, 1961.  450pp.

206  McKinley, Charles.  Uncle Sam in the Pacific North-
     west; Federal Management of Natural Resources in
     the Columbia River Valley.  Berkeley:  University
     of California, 1952.  673pp.

207  Macnab, Gordon.  A Century of News and People in the
     "East Oregonian," 1875-1975.  Pendleton, OR:  East
     Oregonian Publishing Co. , 1975.  397pp.

208  McNamee, Mary Dominica.  Willamette Interlude.  Pa-
     lo Alto, CA:  Pacific Books, 1959.  302pp.

209  McNelis, Sarah.  Copper King at War; The Biography
     of F. Augustus Heinze.  Missoula:  University of
     Montana, 1968.  230pp.

210  Maddux, Percy.  City on the Willamette; The Story of
     Portland, Oregon.  Portland, OR:  Binfords & Mort,
     1952.  229pp.

211  Madsen, Brigham D.  The Bannock of Idaho.  Caldwell,
     ID:  Caxton, 1958.  382pp.

212  Magnuson, Richard G.  Coeur d'Alene Diary; The First
     Ten Years of Hardrock Mining in North Idaho.  Port-
     land, OR:  Metropolitan Press, 1968.  319pp.

213  Malone, Michael P.  C. Ben Ross and the New Deal
     in Idaho.  Seattle:  University of Washington, 1970.
     191pp.

214  _____, and Richard B. Roeder.  Montana; A His-
     tory of Two Centuries.  Seattle:  University of Wash-
     ington, 1976.  352pp.

215 _____, and _____, eds. The Montana Past; An Anthology. Missoula: University of Montana, 1969. 376pp.

216 Marcosson, Isaac F. Anaconda. New York: Dodd, Mead, 1957. 370pp.

Marley, Bert W. SEE Etulain, Richard

217 Marple, Elliot. National Bank of Commerce of Seattle, 1889-1969. Palo Alto, CA: Pacific Books, 1972. 277pp.

218 Martin, Albro. James J. Hill and the Opening of the Northwest. New York: Oxford University, 1976. 676pp.

219 Martin, Boyd A. The Direct Primary in Idaho. Stanford, CA: Stanford University, 1947. 149pp.

220 Meany, Edmond S. History of the State of Washington. New York: Macmillan, 1910. 406pp.

221 Merk, Frederick. The Oregon Question; Essays in Anglo-American Diplomacy and Politics. Cambridge, MA: Harvard University, 1967. 427pp.

222 Miles, Charles, and O. B. Sperlin, eds. Building a State; Washington, 1889-1939. Tacoma: Washington State Historical Society, 1940. 607pp.

223 Miller, Donald C. Ghost Towns of Idaho. Boulder, CO: Pruett Publishing Co. , 1976. 102pp.

224 _____. Ghost Towns of Montana. Boulder, CO: Pruett Publishing Co. , 1974. 177pp.

225 _____. Ghost Towns of Washington and Oregon. Boulder, CO: Pruett Publishing Co. , 1977. 127pp.

226 Miller, Orlando W. The Frontier in Alaska and the Matanuska Colony. New Haven, CT: Yale University, 1975. 329pp.

227 Mills, Edward Laird. Plains, Peaks, and Pioneers; Eighty Years of Methodism in Montana. Portland, OR: Binfords & Mort, 1947. 244pp.

228  Mills, Randall V.  Railroads Down the Valley; Some
     Short Lines of the Oregon Country.  Palo Alto, CA:
     Pacific Books, 1950.  151pp.

229  _____.  Stern-Wheelers up Columbia; A Century of
     Steamboating in the Oregon Country.  Palo Alto, CA:
     Pacific Books, 1947.  212pp.

230  Minter, Harold A.  Umpqua Valley, Oregon and Its
     Pioneers.  Portland, OR:  Binfords & Mort, 1967.
     290pp.

231  Mohler, Samuel R.  The First Seventy-Five Years; A
     History of Central Washington State College, 1891-
     1966.  Ellensburg:  Central Washington State College,
     1967.  374pp.

232  Moore, Lucia W.  The Story of Eugene.  New York:
     Stafford House, 1949.  271pp.

233  Moore, Terris.  Mt. McKinley; The Pioneer Climbs.
     College:  University of Alaska, 1967.  202pp.

234  Morgan, Murray.  Skid Road; An Informal Portrait of
     Seattle.  New York:  Viking, 1951.  280pp.

235  Morice, Adrien G.  The History of the Northern In-
     terior of British Columbia, 3rd ed.  Toronto:  W.
     Briggs, 1905.  368pp.

236  Morley, Alan.  Vancouver; From Milltown to Metropo-
     lis.  Vancouver, BC:  Mitchell Press, 1961.  234pp.

237  Morris, Faye.  They Claimed a Desert [a history of
     Quincey, Washington].  Fairfield, WA:  Ye Galleon,
     1976.  383pp.

238  Morton, James W.  In the Sea of Sterile Mountains;
     The Chinese in British Columbia.  Vancouver, BC:
     J. J. Douglas, 1974.  280pp.

239  Mount Hood; A Guide.  (Federal Writers Project.
     American Guide Series. )  New York:  Duell, Sloan
     and Pearce, 1940.  132pp.

240  Nance, Ellwood C.  The Daniel V. McEachern Story;
     Saga of a Seattle Scot.  College Place, WA:  College
     Press, 1958.  246pp.

241  Naske, Clause M.  An Interpretive History of Alaskan
     Statehood.  Anchorage:  Alaska Northwest Publishing
     Co. , 1973.  192pp.

242  Neils, Selma M.  So This Is Klickitat.  Portland, OR:
     Metropolitan Press, 1967.  176pp.

     Nelson, Herbert B.  SEE  Hilleary, William M.

243  Nesbit, Robert C.  He Built Seattle; A Biography of
     Judge Thomas Burke.  Seattle:  University of Wash-
     ington, 1961.  455pp.

244  Neuberger, Richard L.  Our Promised Land.  New
     York:  Macmillan, 1938.  398pp.

245  Newell, Gordon.  Rogues, Buffoons, and Statesmen.
     Seattle, WA:  Superior Publishing Co. , 1975.  506pp.

246  _____ .  Ships of the Inland Sea; The Story of the
     Puget Sound Steamboats.  Portland, OR:  Binfords
     & Mort, 1951.  241pp.

247  Not in Precious Metals Alone; A Manuscript History of
     Montana.  Helena:  Montana Historical Society, 1976.
     296pp.

248  Ogden, Daniel M. , and Hugh A. Bone.  Washington
     Politics.  New York:  New York University, 1960.
     77pp.

249  O'Hara, Edwin V.  Pioneer Catholic History of Oregon.
     Portland, OR:  1911.  236pp.

250  Oliphant, J. Orin.  On the Cattle Ranges of the Oregon
     Country.  Seattle:  University of Washington, 1968.
     372pp.

251  Oliver, Herman.  Gold and Cattle Country.  Portland,
     OR:  Binfords & Mort, 1961.  312pp.

252  Olson, Joan.  Washington Times and Trails.  Grants
     Pass, OR:  Windyridge Press, 1970.  312pp.

     Onstad, Preston E.  SEE  Hilleary, William M.

253  Ormsby, Margaret.  British Columbia;  A History.
     New York:  Macmillan, 1958.  558pp.

_____ SEE  Allison, Susan

254  Palladino, L. B.  Indian and White in the Northwest; A
     History of Catholicity in Montana, 1831-1891, 2nd
     ed. Lancaster, PA: Wickersham Publishing Co. ,
     1922.  512pp.

255  Paterson, T. W.  Ghost Towns of the Yukon.  Langley,
     BC: Stagecoach Publications, 1977.  148pp.

256  Peltier, Jerome, Ed.  The Banditti of the Rocky Moun-
     tains and Vigilance Committee in Idaho.  Minneapolis:
     Ross & Haines, 1964.  190pp.

257  Penrose, Stephen B.  Whitman; An Unfinished Story.
     Walla Walla, WA: Whitman Publishing Co. , 1935.
     256pp.

258  Peterson, Emil R. , and Alfred Powers.  A Century of
     Coos and Curry; History of Southwest Oregon.  Portland,
     OR: Binfords & Mort, 1952.  599pp.

259  Peterson, F. Ross.  Idaho; A Bicentennial History.
     New York: Norton, 1976.  203pp.

260  Pethick, Derek.  Men of British Columbia.  Saanich-
     ton, BC: Hancock House, 1975.  223pp.

     Phillips, Paul C.  SEE  Stuart, Granville

261  Pomeroy, Earl.  The Pacific Slope; A History of Cal-
     ifornia, Oregon, Washington, Idaho, Utah, and Neva-
     da.  New York: Knopf, 1966.  403pp.

262  Potter, Jean.  Alaska Under Arms.  New York: Mac-
     millan, 1942.  200pp.

263  _____ .  The Flying North.  New York: Macmillan,
     1947.  261pp.

264  Potter, Miles F.  Oregon's Golden Years.  Caldwell,
     ID: Caxton, 1976.  181pp.

     Powers, Alfred  SEE  Peterson, Emil

265  Prochnau, William W.  A Certain Democrat; Senator
     Henry M. Jackson: A Political Biography.  Engle-
     wood Cliffs, NJ: Prentice-Hall, 1972.  360pp.

266   Prosser, Willaim F.   A History of the Puget Sound
      Country: Its Resources, Its Commerce, and Its Peo-
      ple.  New York:  Lewis Publishers, 1903.  2 vols.
      1188pp.

267   Ramsey, Guy Reed.   Postmarked Washington; Okanogan
      County.  Fairfield, WA:  Ye Galleon Press, 1977.
      60pp.

268   Robertson, Frank C.   Soapy Smith; King of the Fron-
      tier Con Men.  New York:  Hastings House, 1961.
      244pp.

      Roeder, Richard B.   SEE   Malone, Michael

269   Rogers, George W.   Alaska in Transition; The South-
      east Region.  Baltimore:  Johns Hopkins, 1960.
      384pp.

270   _____.   Change in Alaska; People, Petroleum, and
      Politics.  College:  University of Alaska, 1970.  213pp.

271   _____.   The Future of Alaska; Economic Consequen-
      ces of Statehood.  Baltimore:  Johns Hopkins, 1962.
      311pp.

272   Ruby, Robert H. , and John A. Brown.   Chinook In-
      dians; Traders of the Lower Columbia River.   Nor-
      man:  University of Oklahoma, 1976.   349pp.

273   _____.   Myron Eells and the Puget Sound Indians.
      Seattle:  Superior Publishing Co. , 1976.   122pp.

274   Ruhlman, John J.   A History of Northwest Regular
      Baptists.  Schaumburg, IL:  Regular Baptist Press,
      1976.  334pp.

275   Rushton, Gerald A.   Whistle up the Inlet; The Union
      Steamship Story.  Vancouver, BC:  J. J. Douglas,
      1974.   236pp.

276   Sale, Roger.   Seattle; Past to Present.  Seattle:  Uni-
      versity of Washington, 1976.   273pp.

277   Schmid, Calvin F.   Social Trends in Seattle.   Seattle:
      University of Washington, 1944.   336pp.

278   Schuddakopf, Jean, Ed.   Women of Washington; Wo-

men's Involvement in Community Concern--A Washington State History, comp. by the American Association of University Women, Washington State Division. Gig Harbor, WA: AAUW, 1976. 24pp.

279 Sheller, Roscoe. Courage and Water; A Story of Yakima Valley's Sunnyside. Portland, OR: Binfords & Mort, 1952. 263pp.

280 Sherfey, Florence E. This Was Their Time ... Pomeroy, Washington. Fairfield, WA: Ye Galleon Press, 1975. 188pp.

281 Sherwood, Morgan B. Alaska and Its History. Seattle: University of Washington, 1967. 475pp.

282 Slauson, Morda C. Renton; From Coal to Jets. Renton, WA: Renton Historical Society, 1976. 183pp.

283 Smurr, J. W., and K. Ross Toole, eds. Historical Essays on Montana and the Northwest. Helena, MT: Western Press, 1957. 304pp.

284 Snyder, Eugene E. Early Portland; Stump-town Triumphant. Portland, OR: Binfords & Mort, 1970. 182pp.

285 _____. Skidmore's Portland; His Fountain and Its Sculptor. Portland, OR: Binfords & Mort, 1973. 152pp.

286 Spence, Clark C. Territorial Politics and Government in Montana, 1864-89. Urbana: University of Illinois, 1975. 327pp.

287 Spencer, Omar C. The Story of Sauvies Island. Portland, OR: Binfords & Mort, 1950. 134pp.

288 Spokane and the Spokane Country; Pictorial and Biographical. DeLuxe Supplement. Vol. 1. Spokane, WA: S.J. Clarke, 1912.

289 _____. Volume 2.

290 Stefansson, Evelyn. Here Is Alaska, rev. ed. New York: Scribner's, 1959. 178pp.

Stewart, Edgar I. SEE Cox, Ross

291 Strong, Emory. Stone Age on the Columbia River.
Portland, OR: Binfords & Mort, 1960. 254pp.

292 Stuart, Granville. Pioneering in Montana; The Making
of a State, 1864-1887, ed. by Paul C. Phillips. Lincoln: University of Nebraska, 1977. 265pp.

293 Sundborg, George. Hail Columbia; The Thirty Year
Struggle for Grand Coulee Dam. New York: Macmillan, 1954. 467pp.

Tarshis, Rebecca. SEE Blair, Harry C.

294 Taylor, G. W. Timber; History of the Forest Industry
in British Columbia. Vancouver, BC: J. J. Douglas,
1975. 209pp.

295 Tetlow, Roger T. The Astorian; The Personal History
of DeWitt Clinton Ireland ... . Portland, OR: Binfords & Mort, 1975. 178pp.

296 Thompson, Erwin N. Shallow Grave at Waiilatpu; The
Sager's West, rev. ed. Portland: Oregon Historical
Society, 1973. 178pp.

297 Throckmorton, Arthur L. Oregon Argonauts; Merchant
Adventurers on the Western Frontier. Portland:
Oregon Historical Society, 1961. 372pp.

Tillamook History SEE Boge, Lila

Tiller, Lowell. SEE Clark, Keith

298 Toole, K. Ross. Montana; An Uncommon Land. Norman: University of Oklahoma, 1959. 278pp.

299 _____. Twentieth Century Montana; A State of Ex-
tremes. Norman: University of Oklahoma, 1972.
307pp.

_____. SEE Smurr, J. W.

300 Turnbull, George S. History of Oregon Newspapers.
Portland, OR: Binfords & Mort, 1939. 560pp.

301 Uncommon Controversy; Fishing Rights of the Muckle-
shoot, Puyallup, and Nisqually Indians. Seattle: University of Washington, 1970. 232pp.

302  Vaughan, Thomas, Ed.  The Western Shore; Oregon
     Country Essays Honoring the American Revolution.
     Portland, OR:  Oregon Historical Society, 1975.
     367pp.

303  Wardin, Albert W.  Baptists in Oregon.  Portland,
     OR:  Judson Baptist College, 1969.  635pp.

304  Warren, Sidney.  Farthest Frontier; The Pacific North-
     west.  New York:  Macmillan, 1949.  375pp.

305  Washington; A Guide to the Evergreen State.  (Federal
     Writer's Project.  American Guide Series. )  Port-
     land, OR:  Binfords & Mort, 1941.  687pp.

306  Watt, Roberta Frye.  The Story of Seattle.  Seattle:
     Lowman & Hanford, 1932.  387pp.

307  Webber, Bert.  Swivel-Chair Logger; The Life and
     Work of Anton A. "Tony" Lausmann.  Fairfield,
     WA:  Ye Galleon Press, 1976.  254pp.

308  Weis, Norman D.  Ghost Towns of the Northwest.
     Caldwell, ID:  Caxton, 1972.  319pp.

309  Wharton, David.  The Alaska Gold Rush.  Blooming-
     ton:  Indiana University, 1972.  302pp.

310  Wheeler, Keith.  The Alaskans.  (Old West Series. )
     Alexandria, VA:  Time-Life Books, 1977.  240pp.

311  Wickersham, James.  Old Yukon; Tales, Trails, and
     Trials.  Washington, DC:  Washington Law Book Co. ,
     1938.  514pp.

312  Willard, John.  Adventure Trails in Montana.  Helena:
     John Willard and the Montana Historical Society, 1964.
     243pp.

313  Williams, Richard L.  Northwest Coast.  New York:
     Time-Life Books, 1973.  184pp.

314  Willis, Margaret, Ed.  Chechacos All; The Pioneering
     of Skagit.  Mt. Vernon, WA:  Skagit County Histor-
     ical Society, 1973.  212pp.

315  _____ .  Skagit Settlers; Trials and Triumphs, 1890-

1920. Mt. Vernon, WA: Skagit County Historical
Society, 1975. 228pp.

316   Wilson, James Wood.  People in the Way; The Human
Aspects of the Columbia River Project.  Toronto:
University of Toronto, 1973. 200pp.

317   Winther, Oscar O.  The Great Northwest; A History,
2nd ed. New York:  Knopf, 1950. 491pp.

318   Wojcik, Donna M.  The Brazen Overlanders of 1845.
Portland, OR: Donna M. Wojcik, 1976. 566pp.

319   Wolle, Muriel Sibell.  Montana Pay Dirt; A Guide to
the Mining Camps of the Treasure State.  Denver:
Sage, 1963. 436pp.

320   Wood, Charles.  Spokane, Portland and Seattle Railway; The Northwest's Own Railway.  Seattle: Superior
Publishing Co. , 1974. 159pp.

Writer's Program of the Works Progress Administration  SEE  67, 164, 239, 305

# THE INDEX
## TO PEOPLE AND PLACES*

Abbett, Earl R.   2:12
Abbey, Henry J.   199:4
Abbotsford, BC   204:2
Abbott, Emma   104:6
Abbott, George   97:2
Abbott, H. B.   236:3
Abbott, John F.   199:2
Abbott, Leith   152:1   200:4
Abbott, M. D.   266:2
Abbott, M. H.   119:3   300:
   10
Abbott, Milt   295:6
Abbott, Twyman O.   119:1
Abdill, George B.   230:3
Abel, Anthony M.   266:1
Abel, William H.   203:1
Abercrombie, William Ralph
   63:8   288:4
Aberdeen, ID   23:1   24:3
Aberdeen, WA   14:1   16:6
   38:2   41:2   142:5   152:5
   180:4   195:10   222:4
   305:12
Abernethy, Alexander S.
   119:3   245:4
Abernethy, George   4:3
   44:12   73:6   84:3   119:9
   150:1   153:1   177:5   179:
   1   193:11   198:3   257:3
   284:5   297:52
Abernethy, Robert   294:4
Abrams, Lewis   68:5
Abrams, Will H.   232:5

Absolom, Charles Albert
   108:3
Accolti, Michael   208:20
   254:4
Achermann, Charles   199:1
Ackerson, J. W.   243:1
Ackles, George   150:1
Acme, WA   225:2
Acuff, William Henry   288:3
Adair, Bethenia Owens   302:
   1   SEE ALSO Owens-
   Adair, B
Adair, ID   98:2
Adams, A. J.   130:2
Adams, Alfred   21:9   140:1
Adams, Brock   265:5
Adams, C. W.   309:3
Adams, Charles M.   266:2
Adams, E. M.   266:3
Adams, Frank D.   266:1
Adams, Fred A.   293:35
Adams, Fred F.   119:1
Adams, George   245:5
Adams, George R.   161:2
Adams, J. L.   97:2
Adams, James W.   191:6
Adams, John F.   119:1
   150:1
Adams, Paul M.   227:6
Adams, Steve   99:3
Adams, Thomas   292:15
Adams, W. F.   304:2
Adams, W. L.   295:1

---

*See "How to Use This Index" on pages xi-xii.

Adams, W. Claude   2:9
Adams, W. Lloyd   59:9
  213:3
Adams, Waldo J.   2:4
Adams, William J.   73:14
Adams, William L.   150:6
  266:5   300:5   304:3
Adams, OR   207:3
Adams Camp, ID   102:5
Addis, Henry   191:3
Addy, WA   225:2   305:1
Adler, David   52:2
Adney, Tappan   161:1
Adobetown, MT   319:3
Adolf (Chief)   133:3   155:6
Adrian, WA   293:8   305:1
Aeneas, WA   267:1
Afognak, AK   19:6   63:1
  146:3
Agen, John B.   41:2
Agness, OR   41:1   258:6
Agnew, James D.   87:6
Agnew, Lee   96:2
Ah Fong   203:1
Ahgupuk, George   159:1
Ahtanum, WA   305:1
Aiken, Glen   97:2
Ailshe, James   102:4
Ainsley, George   87:4   91:7
  95:4   118:1
Ainsworth, John C.   6:4
  68:3   73:20   119:3   172:
  18   179:1   197:16   198:
  3   229:20   252:2   264:4
  284:3   297:6
Ainsworth, BC   47:1
Airlie, OR   75:3
Aitken, J. S.   102:4
Aiyansh, BC   189:2
Akiak, AK   8:10
Alamo, OR   264:2
Alatna, AK   137:2
Albany, OR   30:1   41:3
  68:6   75:14   82:4   104:7
  110:1   172:1   180:2   187:
  9   228:10   229:6   295:3
  297:3   300:7   303:10

  317:5
Albee, H. R.   41:1   210:4
Alberni, BC   165:12   253:2
  SEE ALSO Port Alberni
Alberton, MT   112:3
Albion, BC   126:6   131:5
  204:2
Albion, ID   23:5   118:2
  164:1   180:1
Albrecht, C. Earl   148:2
Alder, WA   305:1
Alder Gulch, MT   1:3   25:30
  46:7   48:10   76:30   133:
  47   155:4   197:6   214:4
  215:14   247:6   298:4
  SEE ALSO Virginia City
Alderman, Albert L.   150:3
Aldermere, BC   186:2
Alderson, William W.   48:9
  133:6
Aldred, William C.   251:3
Aldrich, Edwin B.   207:45
  300:3
Aldrich, John F.   266:3
Aldrich, Milton   199:2
Aldrich, Newton   199:1
Aldridge, MT   308:7
Aldwell, Thomas T.   100:3
  266:1
Alert Bay, BC   165:6   189:
  11   275:13
Alexander (Chief)   133:3
Alexander, George L.   300:3
Alexander, Hubbard F.
  266:2
Alexander, John B.   232:3
Alexander, Moses   43:2   105:
  5   117:6   118:2   213:2
  259:6
Alexander, Richard Henry
  236:7   238:3   294:2
Alexandria (Fort), BC   235:
  7   253:2   SEE ALSO
  Fort Alexandria
Alfalfa, OR   56:1
Alger, Lewis B.   38:1
Alger, WA   315:2

Algoma, OR  152:1
Alkali, OR  119:1
Allaeys, Honore B.  112:5
Allan, Allan Alexander
  "Scotty"  55:2
Allard, Joseph  186:2
Allen, Albert  106:3
Allen, Charles  292:7
Allen, Edward Jay  50:4
Allen, Edwin M.  266:2
Allen, Eric W.  232:2
Allen, George H.  191:12
Allen, George Washington
  Lafayette  314:3
Allen, H. H.  203:1
Allen, Henry T.  311:5
Allen, John B.  150:1  176:
  1  220:3  243:6  245:4
Allen, Pliny  245:6
Allen, Raymond D.  70:25
Allen, Samuel  150:1
Allen, William B.  266:1
Allen, William E.  176:1
  178:2  252:6  276:3
Allen, William James  61:
  14
Allen, William McPherson
  41:1  58:7  265:5
Allentown, OR  225:4
Alling, Frank  266:4
Allison, C. Leon  212:11
  SEE ALSO Siringo,
  Charles
Allison, John Fall  5:50
Allison, William  319:3
Allman, John (Jack)  25:2
  226:9
Allmond, Douglass  266:2
Allyn, WA  305:1
Alma, WA  267:1
Almira, WA  293:26  305:1
Almota, WA  27:2  119:5
  198:1
Aloha, WA  305:1
Alokut (Chief)  172:4  SEE
  ALSO Ollicut
Alpin, J. G.  208:2

Alpowa, WA  198:2
Althouse, OR  225:2
Altoona, WA  225:2
Altshuler, Samuel  266:2
Altyn, MT  135:5  319:5
Alvensleben, Alvo von  294:2
Alvin, WA  98:6
Alvord, Benjamin  30:9
  147:4
Alvord, Dorothy  169:24
Alvord, Thomas M.  150:1
Alvord, William  297:4
Amador, MT  78:1
American Falls, ID  23:3
  45:6  118:3  180:2
Ames, Edgar  69:8  163:4
Ames, Edwin Gardner  203:1
  305:2
Ames, George H.  266:2
Amity, OR  194:3
Amundson, C. O.  279:3
Amy, John P.  266:3
Anaconda, MT  1:2  46:5
  60:18  112:2  133:7  155:
  4  156:4  180:7  181:5
  214:3  215:10  216:50
  247:7  299:20  319:5
Anacortes, WA  14:1  41:1
  89:1  176:1  191:3  203:4
  246:3  252:3  305:2  314:
  18  315:19
Anaktuvuk Pass, AK  54:7
  66:3
Anatone, WA  119:1  305:1
Anders, T. J.  119:6
Anderson, Alexander Caulfield
  5:6  20:24  253:4  260:6
Anderson, Alexander J.  38:4
  257:33
Anderson, Alfred H.  9:2
  176:1  203:1
Anderson, Andrew S.  59:5
Anderson, Charles John
  309:5
Anderson, E. C.  303:5
Anderson, Elam J.  174:9
  303:4

Anderson, Eli K.  150:1
Anderson, Emmett T.   41:2
   245:5
Anderson, Eva Greenslit
   116:3
Anderson, Guy  41:1
Anderson, I. M. C.   148:5
Anderson, Isaac W.   82:3
Anderson, James A.   288:2
Anderson, James G.   71:5
Anderson, James Pickens
   134:7
Anderson, Louis F.   257:14
Anderson, Mabel  231:2
   278:1
Anderson, Magnus  203:1
   314:3
Anderson, Peter H.   281:23
Anderson, Reece  292:20
Anderson, Rezin  292:14
Anderson, Robert  23:5
Anderson, William R.   150:1
Andrews, Aubrey  169:14
Andrews, C. L.  150:1
Andrews, Grover  36:2
Andrews, Jesse  200:11
Andrus, Cecil  136:3  259:2
Angel, A. E.   212:7
Angell, Homer D.   49:5
   128:3  130:1  293:2
Angle, Grant  176:2  245:2
Anglin, WA  267:1
Angoon, AK  8:3  130:4
   269:6
Aniak, AK  63:1  117:2
Ankeny, Alexander P.   104:5
   119:2  179:4  210:3  264:3
   285:2
Ankeny, Levi  23:7  58:1
   104:2  106:6  119:1  217:1
   243:4  245:4  257:8  264:1
Annahootz (Chief)  149:4
Annapolis, WA  305:1
Antelope, ID  223:1
Antelope, OR  42:16  225:1
   300:3  308:6
Antle, John  140:1  165:2

189:2  294:2
Antoine, WA  267:1
Antone, OR  225:2  251:2
Anvik, AK  63:1  125:2
   130:2  159:2
Anvil City, AK  161:1  SEE
   ALSO Nome
Anyox, BC  275:3
Apgar, MT  135:6
Applegate, Jesse  50:13
   51:20  84:1  118:3  145:4
   150:3  162:7  177:3
   188:18  193:3  198:3
   264:2  297:5  302:4
   304:13
Applegate, Lindsay  188:7
   264:2  302:2
Applegate, OR  225:3
Appleton, WA  242:4
Aram, John  118:1
Archabal, John  118:2
Archer, ID  59:4
Arco, ID  23:6  24:2  164:1
Arend, Albert K.   124:9
Argenta, MT  46:3  76:4
   78:4  214:2  215:3  224:2
   319:6
Arlee (Chief)  155:13  181:4
   214:2
Arlee, MT  34:2  181:5  312:2
Arlington, OR  82:3  150:2
   198:1  251:3  300:2
Arlington, WA  14:1  57:1
   305:1
Armstead, Harry H.   46:2
   319:1
Armstead, MT  46:3  319:3
Armstrong, Everhardt  234:1
Armstrong, F. P.   198:5
Armstrong, Francis  69:3
Armstrong, H. C.   70:8
Armstrong, James M.
   288:3
Armstrong, John Henry
   266:2
Armstrong, Noah  46:3
   319:5

Armstrong, Pleasant 84:4
Arnold, Green 150:2
Arnold, Lawrence M.
   217:2
Arnold, Morris A. 217:7
Arnold, Winton Cumberland
   128:6 129:5 148:6
   160:1 241:10
Aronson, J. Hugo 215:8
Arrigoni, S. N. 295:9
Arrowhead, BC 151:5
   316:3
Arthur, Joseph M. 202:4
Arthur, Mark 102:4
Arctic, WA 305:1
Ash, Harry 196:2
Ash, Samuel A. 199:1
Ashby, John 280:2
Ashcroft, BC 47:1 123:5
Ashford, WA 267:1 305:1
Ashland, OR 17:4 41:3
   75:4 104:10 180:3
   194:6 210:4 300:2
   303:3 317:4
Ashley, James M. 1:1
   48:9 133:8 214:4
   286:27 298:1
Ashley, W. G. 245:5
Ashlock, Joey & Family
   108:4
Ashton, James M. 266:4
Ashton, ID 23:5 164:1
   180:3
Ashwood, OR 42:9 225:2
   308:5
Asotin, WA 119:5 198:1
   280:2 305:1
Asp, Charles 5:4
Assu, Billy 189:2
Astor, John Jacob 4:7
   132:2 176:5 177:8
   198:7 261:5
Astoria, OR 4:5 9:4
   41:6 50:11 72:5 73:4
   75:11 82:11 84:4 86:8
   97:12 104:16 109:11
   118:3 120:12 152:4
   153:1 163:4 172:7 180:6

   187:9 194:4 198:25
   202:10 221:23 229:20
   246:5 249:4 261:7
   272:12 295:17 297:16
   300:10 302:4 303:8
   305:4 317:6 SEE ALSO
   Fort George
Athena, OR 36:1 303:2
Atherton, John 96:1
Atkins, H. A. 306:3
Atkinson, George A. 91:5
Atkinson, George E. 266:2
Atkinson, George Henry
   38:2 68:4 108:1 257:4
Atkinson, J. F. 300:5
Atkinson, Solomon 140:4
Atlanta, ID 23:3 118:2
   223:3
Atlin, AK 63:1
Attalia, WA 41:2 305:1
Atwater, Mary Moor 214:2
Atwood, Evangeline 130:1
Atwood, James P. 150:1
Atwood, Robert B. 54:9
   66:7 128:7 129:7 130:2
   136:35 241:8
Auburn, OR 147:4 225:4
   264:6 303:2
Auburn, WA 14:1 89:1
   305:2 306:2
Aulbach, Adam 108:1
   212:38
Auld, Joseph C. 283:6
Ault, E. B. "Harry" 113:16
   152:1 191:8 276:7
Ault, James B. 191:4
Aumsville, OR 147:1
Aurora, OR 36:6 41:2
   144:50 147:1 152:3
   153:1 225:2 304:4
Austin, Louville L. 266:1
Austin, Mark 59:7 279:4
Austin, Minot 264:2
Austin, William A. 266:2
Austin, OR 225:1 251:3
   264:3
Avery, John C. 80:2 145:4
   150:2

Avery, Joseph  68:3
Avery, ID  98:14  118:1
Avon, MT  319:2
Avon, WA  14:1  314:5
   315:7
Axtell, William Henry  266:2
Ayers, Roy E.  214:4  215:5
Azwell, WA  198:1


Babb, MT  135:7  319:3
Babcock, Alveris D.  30:1
   51:3
Babcock, Chester N.  119:1
Babcock, E. F.  199:1
Babcock, George W.  199:2
Babcock, Ira Leonard  17:2
   44:6  84:8  162:7  187:4
   193:11  198:1
Babcock, J. L.  119:5
Babcock, John Pease  50:2
Babcock, Ruth M.  169:29
Babcock, Tim  214:3  215:5
Babine (Fort), BC  235:8
   SEE ALSO Fort Babine
Bach, Thomas C.  286:4
Bachelder, Charles  152:1
Bachtold, Alfred  199:1
Bachtold, John  199:1
Backus, Manson  217:28
Bacon, Daniel  95:1
Bacon, James H.  185:3
Bacon, John M.  56:1
   150:1  318:6
Bacon, William W.  52:3
Baer, Harry F.  27:2
   39:14  188:3
Baerlocher, B. A.  102:7
Baggs, Charles S.  133:3
   155:1
Baggs, Frank  319:3
Bagley, Clarence B.  7:4
   222:4  245:14  276:4
   277:7  306:7
Bagley, Daniel  31:10
   38:10  64:7  245:4
   276:4  282:4  306:13

Bagley, George  37:1
Bagley, H. B.  243:4
Bagwany, George  189:2
Bahr, Andrew  161:2
Bailey, Charles P.  303:14
Bailey, Edward F.  49:5
Bailey, I. J.  157:3
Bailey, Mark  232:4  302:2
Bailey, O. E.  88:3
Bailey, Philip  97:3
Bailey, Stephen S.  196:2
Bailey, W. E.  100:3
Bailey, William J.  84:3
   119:8  162:8  188:6
Bailey, William T.  86:2
Bailor, Ford L.  124:6
Baird, Charles S.  30:10
Baird, Ed D.  53:8
Baird, Ezra  95:1
Bajema, John  274:7
Bakeoven, OR  225:2  264:1
Baker, Alton  232:3
Baker, Bush T.  245:3
Baker, Charles  82:3
Baker, Cordell  274:10
Baker, Dorsey Syng  16:2
   41:2  92:2  108:1  119:19
   151:2  152:6  198:3  199:3
   203:2  222:6  228:23
   243:1  252:6  257:14
   305:5
Baker, Edward Dickenson
   35:233  145:4  153:2
   154:3
Baker, F. C. "Ed"  175:38
Baker, Frank R.  266:4
Baker, Fred  57:5
Baker, George Luis  41:1
   104:17  200:3  210:14
Baker, I. G.  214:3
Baker, John C.  303:11
Baker, John Sherman
   266:3
Baker, M.  150:1
Baker, Miner H.  276:2
Baker, Nathan  150:2
Baker, Ruth  144:33
Baker, Thomas,  150:1

Baker, W. William  152:1
  252:1
Baker, William L.  128:6
  241:2
Baker, OR  4:1  12:6  75:7
  87:4  104:6  114:6  152:4
  180:2  187:3  251:8  264:13
  303:5
Baker, WA  315:4
Balagno, Charles P.  185:2
Balch, Albert  203:2
Balch, .E. T.  157:2
Balch, Frederic Homer
  153:1
Balch, James A.  147:6
Baldridge, H. C.  213:5
Baldwin, H. H.  258:4
Baldwin, J. M.  199:1
Baldwin, AK  161:1
Balfour, BC  204:2
Balkwill, Samuel Rowtcliff
  266:2
Ball, H. M.  20:4
Ball, Jesse B.  150:1
Ball, John  38:2  153:1
Ball, Mottram D.  130:7
  149:5
Ball, Robert W.  12:4
Ball, W. A.  119:5
Ballard, David W.  43:1
  87:20  118:3  164:1
  179:2  211:12
Ballard, Levi W.  150:2  305:1
Ballard, William R.  243:2
  246:1
Ballard, WA  14:1  163:5
  178:5  203:1  243:2  276:6
Ballinger, Richard A.  261:5
Ballou, Robert  97:1
Baltes, Frank  295:12
Baltimore, John L.  300:4
Baltimore Colony, OR  258:7
Baltzo, C. Howard  128:2
  130:2
Bamfield, BC  123:3  165:4
  204:4
Bancroft, ID  23:3
Bancroft, WA  315:3

Bandini, Joseph  254:8
Bandmann, Daniel  181:2
Bandon, OR  195:3  258:14
Banfield, William E.  294:2
Banker, E. F.  293:20
Banks, Archie M.  266:1
Banks, Florence Aiken
  153:1
Banks, Frank  293:19
Banks, John  119:3
Banks, Llewellyn A.  302:3
Banks, Louis Albert  153:1
Bannack, MT  1:2  25:21
  26:3  46:10  48:25  76:37
  78:26  133:58  155:8
  156:5  181:4  211:2
  214:7  215:17  216:4
  227:7  247:12  256:30
  283:4  292:12  308:1
  312:5  319:37
Banner City, ID  223:1
Bannister, Frederick  200:6
Bannister, Henry Martyn
  168:200
Bannock City, ID  33:3
  118:1  308:1  SEE ALSO
  Idaho City
Bannock Jim (Chief)  211:4
  SEE ALSO Pagwhite
Bar, Lawrence  266:2
Baranov, Alexander A.
  18:2  28:10  77:13  140:5
  143:20  146:22  159:45
  161:8  272:4  281:20
Barber, James  205:3
Barber, S. J.  2:11
Barbor, B. C.  23:5
Barbour, Clitus  87:7
Barcelo, Peter  34:7  254:3
Barclay, Forbes  177:3
  187:16
Barden, Richard P.  60:5
Bardsley, William C.  266:2
Bargamin, Vic  103:4
Barge, Benjamin Franklin
  38:1  231:9
Baring, WA  305:1
Barker, Burt Brown  232:1

Barker, John  12:12
Barker, Nora  278:2
Barker, William  3:3  260:4
Barker, MT  319:8
Barkerville, BC  3:10  20:6
    47:2  123:5  204:2  235:2
    238:5  253:6
Barlow, Byron  266:3
Barlow, Calvin S.  266:2
Barlow, Samuel Kimbrough
    4:1  41:1  56:2  150:6  179:1
    198:1  239:4  252:2
    264:1  318:23
Barlow, William  150:1
Barnard, Charles F.  64:4
Barnard, Francis Jones
    5:6  138:2  260:6  266:2
Barnard, G. Harry  126:7
Barnes, Frank  200:6
Barnes, George A.  245:16
Barnes, Jane  72:4  121:2
    176:4  196:6  272:2
Barnes, William H. T.
    266:2
Barnes, William T.  119:4
Barnett, Carrick H.  199:2
Barnett, Eugene L.  150:1
Barnett, George E.  199:1
Barnette, Elbridge T.
    159:3  309:11  310:4
    311:3
Barnhart, William H.  297:5
Barnsley, John  275:11
Barnum, Eli M.  179:2
Barnum, William L.  2:7
Barnwell, Middleton S.
    53:29
Barrett, Charles A.  150:1
Barrett, David  140:1
Barrett, James S.  199:1
Barrett, William E.  307:15
Barrette, Louis A.  112:9
    319:3
Barrett's Station, MT  46:3
Barrow, AK  52:12  54:8
    63:1  66:4  130:7  137:15
    148:4  263:35  SEE AL-
    SO  Point Barrow

Barrows, John R.  156:2
Barry, Charles A.  124:7
Barry, J. Neilson  162:15
Bartholet, Matthew  150:1
Bartlett, Chester H.  266:2
Bartlett, Edward Lewis
    "Bob"  28:1  54:3  128:20
    129:27  130:29  160:3
    161:4  226:3  241:38
    262:2  271:6
Barto, Harold "Pete"  231:6
Bartruff, David E.  266:3
Basin, MT  209:3  224:2
    319:4
Bassett. G. W.  39:2
Bassett, Herman S.  27:6
Bassett, Jule  95:7
Bassett, Thomas E.  59:6
Bassett, Wilbur Fiske  27:10
    39:4  118:4  119:3  198:1
Batcheller, Willis T.  293:35
Bates, Charles O.  266:2
Bates, Ernest S.  152:1
Bates, F. M.  104:7
Bates, Kate Stevens  152:2
    222:8
Bates, OR  251:3  264:1
Battle Ground, WA  305:1
Bauer, Robert E.  199:1
Baumeister, Max  199:2  203:1
Baxter, John  134:6
Baxter, Seth  100:5
Bay Center, WA  14:1
    202:2  203:1  305:1
Bay City, OR  97:2  300:2
Bay City, WA  305:1
Bay View, WA  14:1  86:6
    315:4
Bayhorse, ID  164:1  223:2
    308:6
Bayley, J. R.  150:2
Bayne, Perry  276:4
Bayocean, OR  37:3  307:3
Beach, Abijah Ives  282:5
Beach, E. R.  257:3
Beachy, Hill  43:2  118:5
    132:2  134:4
Beall, Wellwood  178:2

Bean, Charles W.  38:3
Bean, James M.  311:1
Bean, Margaret  96:5
Bean, Robert  309:4
Bean, Robert S.  232:3
Beard, Charlie  61:5
Beard, John A.  199:1
Beard, William G.  266:4
Beardslee, L. A.  90:2
Beardsley, Ross  150:1
Bearmouth, MT  181:5
　224:4  319:5
Beartown, MT  76:8  78:8
　319:5
Beaton, Frank  40:12
Beatty, James H.  95:6
　106:9  205:7  209:3
Beaux Arts Village, WA
　305:1
Beaven, Robert  238:22
Beaver, Herbert  4:6  101:4
　177:4
Beaver, ID  97:1
Beaver, WA  305:1
Beaver Cove, BC  165:6
Beaverton, OR  75:7
Beavis, L. R. W.  161:3
Beazley, Ernest H.  275:23
Beck, David  41:8  70:10
　176:2  178:15  234:33
　244:25  245:2  248:2
　261:2  276:16
Beck, George C.  289:2
Beck, George F.  198:1
　231:7  305:1
Beck, Lester F.  232:2
Beck, William  191:4  210:4
Beck, WA  267:1
Becker, Oswald  199:1
Becker, Philip A.  199:2
Becker, W. S.  133:4
Beckett, Hugh N.  41:1
Bedard, Theodore  112:11
Beddoe, Darrell  274:7
Bede, Elbert  152:9  300:4
Bedford, Amy Aldrich  207:5
Bedford, Charles  266:3
Bedford, MT  46:4

Bedle, Ira W.  217:3
Beebe, MT  156:1
Beekman, C. C.  264:2
Beem, Martin  183:4
Beers, Alanson  44:5  68:2
　84:3  119:5  153:1  193:8
　198:1
Beezley, Joseph  150:2
Begbie, Matthew Baillie
　3:25  5:9  20:21  126:9
　138:4  238:17  253:20
　260:13
Begich, Nick  136:2  226:1
Behme, Antone  266:2
Beidler, John Xavier  25:9
　76:7  133:6  247:3
Beirnes, Helen  123:2
Belanger, Alexis  235:7
Belasco, David  104:9
Belding, George A.  197:1
Belfast, WA  191:2
Belknap, MT  319:4
Bell, Frank T.  41:1  293:16
Bell, George W.  266:2
Bell, J. A. "Joe"  37:2
Bell, James Francis  187:6
Bell, John Colgate  30:1
　150:1
Bell, John M.  266:2
Bell, Walter P.  203:1
　266:2
Bell, William N.  7:8  31:8
　80:12  276:8  306:11
Bella Bella, BC  275:4
Bella Coola, BC  3:6  204:6
　275:17
Belleville, WA  315:2
Bellevue, ID  23:5  118:2
Bellevue, WA  176:8  178:4
　276:2  305:1
Bellfair, WA  305:1
Bellinger, Charles B.  300:5
Bellingham, WA  16:8  31:4
　38:10  41:8  89:1  121:4
　152:3  178:4  180:8  191:11
　222:10  234:1  246:18
　252:6  276:3  293:13
　305:15  317:4  SEE ALSO

Whatcom
Bellique, Pierre  162:6
Belt, Horatio N.  288:2
Belt, MT  156:1  299:2
Belton, MT  135:10
Beltz, William E.  130:1
Bemis, Charles A.  102:5
  103:5
Bend, OR  17:3  41:2  42:25
  56:2  75:9  82:6  151:3
  152:3  180:3  187:2  196:30
  300:6  303:2
Benham, W. L.  107:6
Benjamin, Richard Manning
  39:11  108:4
Benn, Samuel  152:1  195:2
Bennett, A. A.  137:3  263:9
Bennett, Charles  119:5
  179:3
Bennett, Columbus  308:1
Bennett, George  258:5
Bennett, J. W. "Joe"  258:5
Bennett, James Abner  150:1
Bennett, John  305:1
Bennett, Nelson  150:3  203:2
  305:1
Bennett, Richard B.  238:3
Bennett, Thomas W.  43:2
  87:6  118:1  211:4
Bennett, William Andrew
  Cecil  126:3  165:2  253:3
  260:5  316:5
Bennett, YT  63:1  196:3
  255:1  309:6
Bensell, Royal A.  30:224
Bensin, Basil M.  148:3
Benson, Benny  28:1
Benson, Bertil William  266:2
Benson, Edwin F.  266:3
Benson, Frank W.  153:1
Benson, R. L.  187:7
Benson, Simon  9:7  195:3
Benton (Fort), MT  227:11
  292:25  SEE ALSO  Fort
  Benton
Benton, Sidney  150:1
Benton City, WA  305:1

Bequette, Neva LeBlond
  169:14
Bergan, Clarence O.  96:5
Berglund, A. J.  242:10
Bernard, B. F.  11:13
Bernard, Henry  212:2
Bernard, Joe  161:4
Bernard, R. F.  118:3
Berne, WA  305:2
Berney, Ulysses H.  199:2
Berriway, Jim  264:1
Berry, Clarence  311:2
Berry, Fred M.  116:2
Berry, George M.  119:3
Berry, John C.  118:2
Berry, John W.  266:2
Berry, M. P.  211:4
Berry, Warren A.  319:3
Berry, AK  63:1
Berryman, J. E.  199:2
Berryman, Richard J.  199:1
Bertanolli, Frank  175:11
Beswick, Norton  98:5
Bethany, OR  114:3
Bethel, AK  8:13  63:1
  115:3  125:2  130:4  159:2
  171:2
Bethel, WA  14:1
Bettinger, Lee  128:4
Bettis, Francis Allison
  196:4
Bettles, Girdon C.  311:3
Bettles, AK  137:3
Bettman, Monte M.  2:5
Bevan, Arthur Dean  187:6
Beverly, WA  305:1
Bewley, Crocket  177:8  296:4
Bice, Gerald Roy  203:1
Bickford, Walter M.  133:6
Bieker, Frank M.  23:4
  102:10
Bielenberg, John  155:2
Bienz, Thomas H.  70:7
Big Delta, AK  159:2  271:2
Big Head (Chief)  93:6
  108:6
Big Horn, MT  215:3

Big Lake, WA  315:7
Big Timber, MT  319:4
Big Star (Chief)  108:2
Bigelow, Daniel Richardson
    38:2  203:3  220:3
Bigelow, Harry A.  266:2
Bigelow, R. M.  306:3
Bigfoot (Indian)  11:4
Biggers, George W.  187:6
Biggs, OR  42:2  151:2
Bigham, Lester Allen  157:3
Bignold, Lewis E.  203:1
Bihler, Charles S.  266:3
Bill, Patrick (Chief)  32:10
Billings, Frederick  108:1
Billings, Joseph  161:9
Billings, William  150:1
    245:6
Billings, MT  1:1  48:5
    60:5  133:5  156:2  183:4
    214:4  215:11  247:13
    298:4  299:6  319:4
Billings, WA  108:1  SEE
    ALSO Cheney
Billingsley, Kirby  116:3
Bills, H. B.  157:2
Bilyeu, Lark  232:3
Binder, Anthony  230:2
Bingen, WA  305:1
Bingham, Charles E.  266:2
Bingham, Edward W.  302:3
Bingham, John E.  199:1
Binkley, J. W.  288:2
Binns, Archie  152:1  283:7
Birch, Arthur Nonus  3:5
    253:6
Birch, Stephen  311:1
Birch Creek, ID  223:1
Bird, John T.  96:5  150:1
Bird, Mathew  157:2
Birdsview, WA  305:1  315:4
Birge, George E.  266:2
Birmingham, William  266:2
Birnie, James  4:1  44:6
    150:1  179:1  203:2  208:4
    272:7
Bishop, Albert  32:2

Bishop, E. K.  217:2
Bishop, Ned  195:1
Bissel (Judge)  76:4
Bissell, G. G.  25:2  133:2
Bisson, Emile  112:7
Bisson, Francois  112:5
Bisson, Pete  112:13
Bjorklund, Vic  293:9
Black, Arthur Walter Shaw
    5:5
Black, Frank  234:2
Black, George  236:3
Black, George Harold  38:2
    231:25
Black, William L.  119:3
Black, William W.  266:3
Black Cloud, ID  212:1
Black Diamond, WA  225:3
    305:1
Black Pine, MT  319:5
Black Rock, OR  75:4
Blackbird, ID  308:2  SEE
    ALSO  Cobalt
Blackburn, Alexander  303:4
Blackburn, John B.  256:4
Blackfoot, ID  23:16  24:3
    45:4  118:2  180:2  211:2
Blackfoot City, MT  76:3
    78:9  319:6
Blackjack, Ada  161:2
Blackman, Alanson  150:1
Blackman, Arthur M.  150:2
Blackman, Henry  150:1
Blackwell, Cy W.  9:5
Blackwell, F. A.  99:2
Blackwell, George R.  319:3
Blain, Wilson  119:2  153:1
Blaine, Art  175:22
Blaine, David E.  31:3  179:1
    305:1  306:6
Blaine, E. F.  293:14
Blaine, J. P.  308:1
Blaine, James G.  95:4
    286:2
Blaine, WA  14:1  89:1
    222:4  305:1
Blair, "Doc"  279:5

Blair, George W.  157:3
Blair, Prior  232:4
Blake, Almon Clyde  266:2
Blake, Edward  238:12
Blake, H. L.  281:16
Blake, Henry N.  25:6  133:11
   286:5
Blake, Richard B.  288:3
Blakely, James M.  42:4
Blakely, William  150:1
Blalock, John  303:4
Blalock, Nelson G.  119:4
   150:2  198:1  199:3  207:1
   257:4
Blalock, Reuben Y.  303:18
Blalock, Y. C.  199:1
Blanchard, Dean  150:2
Blanchard, Elizabeth J.
   199:2
Blanchard, Richard  140:2
Blanchard, WA  191:3  315:4
Blanchet, Augustine Magloire
   Alexandre  34:4  93:4
   119:3  177:2  179:1  198:1
   208:6  249:5
Blanchet, Francois Norbert
   16:4  34:9  39:4  84:3
   93:20  119:12  132:1
   150:2  153:2  177:21
   179:1  193:10  198:3
   208:60  235:5  249:15
   272:2  305:6
Blanchet, Joseph  150:2
Blandford, Henry S.  199:1
Blankenship, J. W.  156:1
Blankenship, Robert  245:3
Blankenship, Russell  152:1
Blankenship, William F.
   157:3
Blanshard, Richard  3:10
   20:18  120:7  253:12
   260:4
Blanton, Joseph P.  117:11
Blattner, Frank S.  266:2
Blazer, Clarence  274:8
Blethen, Alden J.  41:4
   178:3  243:4  245:4

   276:10  305:1
Blethen, Clarence  176:1
Blethen, Joseph  69:3
Blew, W. W.  173:8
Blewett, Arthur R.  289:2
Blewett, WA  308:3
Blinkensdoerfer, Mr.  95:4
Blinn, Marshall  73:3  119:3
   203:2  245:3
Blinn, Samuel P.  73:2
Bliss, ID  23:3  164:1
Blitzen, OR  114:4
Bloch, Ernest  114:5
Bloedel, J. H.  122:3  176:2
   203:1  294:2
Blom, Jan  47:1
Blomgren, Darwin W.  274:5
Blomquist, John A.  266:2
Bloom, Samuel M.  150:1
Bloomer, Lillian  231:1
Blue Creek, WA  305:1
Bluestem, WA  152:1
Blumberg, Fred L.  266:2
Bly, WA  152:1
Blyn, WA  305:1
Blythe, Thomas S.  237:4
Boardman, Ella Helm  69:9
Boardman, Samuel Herbert
   111:4  162:4
Boardman, OR  198:1  207:2
   300:2
Boarman, Glenn R.  71:5
Boden, John  275:15
Bodie, WA  225:3  267:1
   308:7
Boeckman, Henry  103:4
Boeing, William Edward
   16:10  41:2  58:2  178:6
   217:6  245:2  252:3  276:2
Boettiger, John  41:1
   244:10
Bogard, Ben M.  303:7
Bogardus, E. M. M.  86:7
Bogle, Richard A.  199:2
Bohman, Ole  24:5
Boice, Dave  200:7
Boire, Leo M.  2:5

Boise, Reuben P.   51:35
  145:2   154:2   194:4
Boise, ID  SEE  Fort
  Boise
Bolan, Andrew J.   119:3
  220:4
Boldoc, John Baptist   208:11
Boles, ID  102:2
Boling, Vanaver   175:10
Bollong, John G.   266:2
Bolon, Andrew J.   58:3
  179:3   222:3
Bolster, WA  225:1  267:1
  308:4
Bolte, P. J.   155:2
Bolton, OR  75:2
Bomford, George C.   179:4
Bompas, William Carpen-
  ter   255:7   309:4
Bonanza, OR  225:2
Bonanza City, ID  118:1
  164:2   223:3   308:6
Bonaparte, WA  267:1
Bonar, James C.   157:6
Bond, R. G.   232:1
Bone, Homer T.   83:3
  88:3  206:4  244:7  245:6
  293:22   305:3
Bone, Scott C.   130:4
  159:3   241:2
Boner, William H.   266:2
Bong, Lawrence   274:5
Bonner, E. L.   181:4
Bonner, MT  181:8
Bonners Ferry, ID  23:3
  39:3   76:2   96:3   118:2
  151:3   164:1   180:2   182:10
  192:2   198:1   319:8
Bonneville, Benjamin Louis
  Eulalie de   4:9   33:5
  43:6   45:20   132:1   153:1
  198:7   305:6   317:5
Bonney, W. P.   222:6
Bonska, WA  267:1
Boomer, Alexander H.   87:3
Boone, George   114:4
Boone, William Judson   33:5

Booneville, OR  68:4
Boonville, ID  118:2  134:5
  147:1  SEE ALSO Dewey
Boose, Oscar L.   279:12
Booth, R. A.   200:4
Booth, Robert   30:1
Booth, Luke J.   150:1
Boothe, William R.   150:1
Boothroyd, William H.
  266:2
Borah, William Edgar   36:3
  83:5   88:11   105:25
  117:4   118:4   127:25
  130:3   164:2   170:511
  205:450   213:33   219:12
  244:20   259:20   261:7
  293:2
Borax, MT  98:3
Borbridge, John   54:2  66:3
Bordeaux, Thomas   266:4
Borden, Robert   238:7
Boren, Carson D.   7:4
  31:11   80:15   172:4
  178:5   222:3   276:7
  306:10
Boring, OR  75:2
Borland, Earl   137:2   161:1
  263:5
Borleske, Raymond Vincent
  "Nig"   88:1   257:2
Borst, Jeremiah W.   80:4
  150:1
Borst, Joseph   203:2
Bossburg, WA  225:1  305:1
Bosse, Bernard   102:3
Bostock, Hewitt   253:3
Boston, Alvin   199:1
Boston, ID  223:1
Boston Bar, BC  3:5  253:3
Boston Harbor, WA  152:7
Boswell, L. H.   303:7
Bothell, David C.   266:2
Bothell, WA  14:1  305:2
Botkin, Alexander   60:6
  286:2
Bott, Dean   274:5
Bottolfsen, C. A.   53:5

213:8 219:2
Bouchard, Joseph 112:5
Boucher, Emily 52:3
Boucher, Jean Baptiste SEE
  Waccan
Bouck, William 261:1
Bouillon, Victor J. 231:3
Boulder, MT 46:3 60:6
  247:5 319:5
Boulet, John Baptiste 179:1
Boultbee, John 236:3
Bourgeois, Eugene 199:2
Bourne, Jonathan 49:6
  205:4 244:7 261:7 264:1
  302:2
Bourne, OR 152:3 225:2
  264:4
Bourquin, George M.
  214:2 299:7
Bovard, C. L. 227:5
Bovey, Charles 308:2
  319:5
Bovill, ID 23:3 152:1
Bow, WA 191:2 315:4
Bowden, Francis C. 130:1
Bowen, John 173:7
Bowen, John C. 293:2
Bowerman, Jay 49:3 153:1
Bowers, C. J. 199:2
Bowlby, Wilson 150:1
Bowles, Jesse T. 179:1
Bowman, Amos 314:4
Bowman, Henry 150:1
  207:3
Bowmer, Angus L. 41:1
Bowmer, Harry L. 300:3
Bowser, William John
  236:2 238:4 253:25
Boyakin, A. 95:1
Boyce, John H. 150:2
Boyco, Edgar 66:2
Boyd, Helen 278:1
Boyd, Homer 217:9
Boyd, William P. 150:1
Boyd, OR 308:3
Boyds, WA 305:1
Boyer, C. Valentine 232:2

Boyer, Eugene H. 199:1
Boyer, John E. 199:2
Boyer, John F. 119:9
  199:4 252:1 257:9
Boyle, Charlie 67:4
Boyle, John L. 266:3
Boyle, Joseph J. 71:8
Boyle, Robert 203:1
Boylen, E. N. 207:2
Boyles, Elmore F. 289:3
Bozeman, John Merin 1:2
  13:3 25:3 46:3 133:11
  139:1 214:4
Bozeman, MT 1:2 46:3
  48:17 60:14 133:17
  156:3 181:4 183:9
  214:3 215:6 227:10
  247:7 292:12 319:11
Brabrook, E. D. 245:6
Brackett, George 150:1
  266:2 305:1
Bradbury, Clement Adams
  150:2
Bradbury, George W. 199:3
Bradford, Daniel F. 119:2
  229:13 297:4
Bradford, ID 223:1
Bradley, Frederick W.
  106:12 118:2
Bradley, Luther P. 266:4
Bradley, William Rush
  266:3
Bradner, Mike 136:6
Bradner, BC 47:1
Bradshaw, Charles Miner
  29:3 150:2
Brady, James H. 43:3
  205:4 219:6
Brady, John Green 55:3
  63:2 130:17 146:3
  149:12 159:8 160:4
  190:11 241:1 281:7
  290:3
Brainerd, Erastus 41:2
  163:1 178:2 234:9
  240:2 245:2 276:2
  281:6

Braley, Berton  67:7
Bramblet, Everett  274:20
Bramblet, Lyle  274:25
Branin, Alvertis  266:3
Brannan, Joseph  150:1
Brannin, Parker  207:3
Brannon, Melvin Amos
   117:15
Branstetter, Joseph  33:3
Brantley, Theodore  133:4
Bratton, Walter A.  199:1
   257:11
Brautigam, Phil  266:1
Brawley, Dewitt C.  266:2
Bray, Absalom F.  60:6
Brayman, Mason  43:2
   87:5  110:1  118:2  211:3
Brear, Samuel Davis  266:3
Brearly, John  23:5
Brechtel, Oswald  119:1
Breckner, Elmer L.  245:3
Breen, James  107:5
Breen, P. J. "Jack"  97:3
Breen, Peter  60:8  106:2
   127:5  212:13
Brelsford, Allan C.  179:1
Bremerton, WA  14:1  41:2
   169:4  246:11  293:4  305:7
Bremner, John  311:2
Brennan, Jim  67:8
Brents, Thomas Hurley
   29:4  36:3  74:1  119:7
   199:3  243:5
Bresee, Darius  266:3
Bretherton, B. J.  100:7
Brew, Chartres  3:8
   126:3  253:7
Brewer, B. F.  199:1
Brewer, Frank P.  266:2
Brewer, Henry Bridgman
   44:7  193:4  318:6
Brewer, John F.  199:2
Brewer, John W.  199:1
Brewer, Max  66:2
Brewer, Merton E.  199:1
Brewster, David  276:4
Brewster, Harlan Carey

253:7
Brewster, Horace  61:17
Brewster, WA  152:1  198:1
   267:1  293:6  305:1
Bridgeport, WA  198:1
   293:3  305:1
Bridgeport Bar, WA  152:4
Bridger, Mary Ann  177:24
   296:5
Bridger, MT  312:1
Bridges, Alfred Renton
   "Harry"  234:5
Bridges, J. C.  84:3
Bridges, Jesse B.  266:2
Bridges, Robert  113:3
Bridgford, Wayne  245:8
Bridgman, William B.
   279:10
Bridwell, J. F.  102;2
Brier, Howard  152:1
Briggs, Albert  150:2
Briggs, Frank A.  266:2
Briggs, O. W.  258:4
Brighouse, Samuel  236:8
   260:6
Briley, E. E.  102:2
Brilliant, BC  151:5  152:1
Brisco, BC  151:2
Briscoe, John  202:3
Bristow, Elijah  232:3
   318:5
Bristow, W. W.  51:40
Britt, Peter  264:1
Britton, George C.  266:3
Broadwater, Charles A.
   46:4  133:5  214:6  218:7
   286:15  319:5
Brocke, Frank O.  24:17
Brode, H. S.  257:3
Brodeck, Albert A.  57:14
   266:2
Broderick, Henry  176:2
   178:5
Brokus, WA  267:1
Bromily, Frank W.  157:2
Brondel, John B.  34:4
   254:3

Bronson, Adolph  282:6
Brook, Henry  150:1
Brookdale, WA  305:1
Brooke, George S.  150:1
Brooke, Lloyd  119:8  179:3
Brookes, A. M.  150:2
Brookfield, WA  198:1
Brookings, OR  258:4
Brooklyn, MT  78:1
Brooks, Alfred H.  130:7
   161:1  263:2  311:2
Brooks, Henry  155:3
   181:6
Brooks, James E.  231:6
Brooks, John E.  150:2
Brooks, Virginia  152:1
Brooks, AK  137:2  SEE
   ALSO Livengood
Brooks, MT  319:5
Brothers, OR  42:2
Brougher, J. Whitcomb
   303:29
Broughton, C. J.  203:1
Broughton, William R.
   41:1  287:6
Brouillet, John Baptiste A.
   4:2  118:2  119:4  177:13
   208:3  296:4
Brower, Charles D.  161:1
   263:6  290:2
Brower, Tom  290:2
Brown, Alonzo F.  102:11
   103:11
Brown, Alvah  199:2
Brown, Arthur H.  266:3
Brown, Benjamin H.  88:2
   150:2  257:5
Brown, Beriah  163:3
Brown, Carl  118:3
Brown, Cecil C.  303:8
Brown, Charles  203:1
Brown, Edwin J.  293:1
Brown, Elmer A.  237:4
Brown, Frank  102:4
Brown, Frederick Rufus
   266:2
Brown, Harold  275:25

Brown, Harvey K.  127:3
Brown, Horace O.  96:3
Brown, Horace T.  96:14
Brown, Hugh L.  35:1
   150:1
Brown, J. G.  57:7
Brown, Joel L.  202:4
Brown, John (Captain)
   172:10
Brown, John George "Koo-
   tenai"  135:7
Brown, L. P.  11:1  102:20
   103:10  192:2
Brown, Louis  112:12
Brown, Neil  266:2
Brown, Noah N.  157:3
Brown, Reuben Austin  157:2
Brown, Sam H.  49:5
Brown, Tabitha  41:1  172:14
Brown, William Walter
   42:7  110:1
Browne, Frank J.  38:5
Browne, George  266:3
Browne, Guy C.  157:3
Browne, H. E.  300:5
Browne, James J.  27:5
   39:1  91:2  96:6  108:4
   150:2  203:1  243:2
Browne, John J.  107:4
Brownell, D. C.  207:3
Brownell, Francis H.
   106:2  266:2
Brownell, George W.  86:3
Brownfield, Daniel F.
   220:2
Browning, Arthur  3:7
Browning, MT  135:9
Brownlow, W. H.  157:3
Brownson, Truman G.
   174:3  303:15
Brownsville, OR  75:5
   187:3  194:3  300:2
   303:3
Browntown, OR  225:2
Bruce, James W.  150:2
   199:2
Bruce, John P.  133:3

Bruce, Miner W.   130:1
Bruce, Robert   150:1
Bruce, Samuel M.   266:3
Bruce, William Perry
   119:5   203:1
Bruceport, WA   89:1   202:6
Bruegeman, Henry   102:8
   103:3
Brumbach, Virgil J.   97:3
Bruneau, ID   23:4   118:3
   164:1
Bruner, Ellwood   130:3
Bruney, E. H.   97:2
Bruntch, Emil   293:4
Brunton, William H.   119:2
Brush, William O.   266:2
Bryan, Enoch A.   38:19
   184:35
Bryan, J. W.   234:1
Bryan, Milton E.   199:1
Bryan, Robert Bruce   38:5
   266:3
Bryant, Cornelius   189:2
Bryant, Hilda   178:3
Bryant, William P.   145:5
Brynteson, John   281:15
Bryon, William   87:4
Bryson, John Bates   138:2
Brzezowsky, Frank   199:1
Buchanan, James D.   289:2
Buchanan, Jesse Everett
   117:58
Buchanan, Julien E.   94:5
Buchtel, Joseph   150:4
Buck, Norman K.   29:3
   88:2   95:2   96:2   172:2
   212:3
Buckhead, OR   152:1   SEE
   ALSO Sweet Home
Buckland, AK   8:7   161:1
Buckley, James L.   71:6
Buckley, James M.   107:6
Buckley, Spencer   318:9
Buckley, WA   14:1   191:2
   305:1
Bucoda, WA   14:1   89:1
   152:2   225:1   305:1

Budd, Edward R.   109:5
Buell, Edward D.   203:1
Buell's Mill, OR   30:3
Buena, WA   305:2
Buena Vista, ID   118:2
Buena Vista, OR   68:8
Buffalo Horn (Chief)   11:5
   111:3   118:3   134:8
Buffalo Hump, ID   102:2
   223:1
Buffam, William G.   318:6
Bugtown, ID   33:1
Buhl, ID   23:10   24:3   164:1
Buie, Thomas Russell   5:2
Bulkley, Charles S.   161:4
Bulkley, BC   186:10
Bull, Munson   207:4
Bull, Mathew Patrick
   207:15
Bull, Walter A.   150:1
Bullard, Catherine   231:4
Bullion, ID   223:1
Bumford, George C.   119:5
Bunce, Louis   41:2
Bunn, William   43:1   87:5
   95:11   261:1
Bunnell, Charles Ernest
   129:6   130:3   148:4
   159:5   262:9   290:1
Bunster, Arthur   238:45
Bunting, Charles   23:8
Bunton, William   256:7
Burbank, A. R.   150:2
Burbank, Andrew S.   157:2
Burbank, WA   305:1
Burbee, Jonathan   200:3
Burbidge, Fred   106:7
Burch, Albert   106:3
Burch, Benjamin F.   51:15
   150:2   179:1
Burch, E. C.   157:2
Burchett, G. J.   174:4
   303:11
Burden, Job   30:1
Burdick, Henry Peleg   266:2
Burdon, William Henry
   266:2

Burgdorf, ID 102:3 103:5
223:2
Burge, Andy 252:3
Burgess, David 191:7
Burk, P. J. 176:2
Burke, Eugene P. 71:10
Burke, George B. 266:1
Burke, John M. 95:3
106:11 192:2 212:2
Burke, Thomas 31:10
163:11 176:2 178:13
218:5 234:7 243:455
257:5 276:18
Burke, ID 23:1 34:3
39:1 108:3 118:6
127:2 152:1 164:1
212:10 223:4
Burkhart, Henry W. 266:4
Burksville, WA 119:1
Burley, ID 23:7 24:2
164:1 180:3
Burley, WA 152:4 191:45
220:2
Burlington, MT 78:1
Burlington, OR 75:2
Burlington, WA 305:1
314:6 315:13
Burmester, Theodore 87:3
Burnaby, Robert 236:3
Burnett, Horace 232:2
Burnett, James D. 150:1
Burnett, John 150:2
Burnett, Peter H. 119:4
284:3
Burnett, WA 225:1 305:1
Burnham, John B. 161:5
Burns, A. M. 295:6
Burns, Cyrus R. 106:4
107:4
Burns, E. B. 86:15
Burns, Gladys Carlson
278:1
Burns, Hugh 68:7 84:4
284:2
Burns, Robert 86:6 199:2
Burns, OR 41:2 42:4
75:2 110:10 114:12

172:3 251:5 300:3
Buroker, J. 199:1
Buroker, William H. 199:2
Burr, Daniel 199:1
Burr, Dixie 155:4
Burr, Frederick H. 155:2
283:4 292:20
Burrell, Lyman S. 157:2
Burroughs, Frank R. 203:1
Burrows, Charles E. 199:1
Burt, Andrew 181:3
Burton, BC 316:4
Burton, ID 59:7
Burton, WA 14:1 305:1
Burwash Landing, YT
255:1
Burwell, Austin P. 266:2
Busby, John 99:2
Bush, Asahel 35:2 51:10
85:2 145:40 150:2
162:3 179:1 300:19
304:6
Bush, George Washington
32:3 38:1 50:4 58:6
172:12 195:4 245:4
252:4 302:1 305:1
Bush, Harry 308:1
Bush, John 199:2
Bush, John S. 203:2
Bush, Newton W. 266:2
Bush, Richard 161:1
Bush, William Owen 203:2
Bushby, Arthur Thomas
5:8
Busia, John 115:2
Butchart, Robert 126:2
165:3
Butler, Edward Everett
266:2
Butler, Hillory 150:2
306:8
Butler, John S. 293:37
Butler, Thomas J. 87:2
Butler, William 265:7
Butler, William C. 57:18
266:2
Butrovich, John 128:3

130:1    241:2
Butteville, OR  68:10
  114:4  162:12  225:1
Button, Dorothy  278:2
Byam, Don L.  25:4  133:4
  155:1
Byars, W. H.  300:4
Bybee, James F.  287:3
Byers, W. S.  207:7
Byles, Charles N.  150:1
  203:1
Byrd, Julian  41:1  110:1
Byrne, Cornelius E.  39:6
Byrom, John  11:1


Cabbage, A. L.  280:4
Cable, MT  78:3  308:5
  319:7
Cache Creek, BC  204:3
Cadwell, Edward P.  150:1
Cady, Calvin Brainerd
  69:36
Cady, Melvin  276:3
Cady, Thomas  232:5
Cain, Andrew J.  118:2
  119:10  179:1
Cain, George W.  266:2
Cain, Harry P.  245:5
  261:2  265:10
Cain, James  266:2
Cain, Oscar  199:1
Calder, Frank  140:4
  189:2
Calderhead, J. H.  60:6
Calderhead, Samuel C.
  266:2
Caldwell, Hugh M.  113:2
Caldwell, Richard S.  179:3
Caldwell, ID  4:1  23:13
  24:7  33:38  117:3  118:11
  134:6  164:1  180:2  205:6
Cale, Thomas  159:2  241:4
Calentine, George C.  293:4
Calhoun, George V.  150:2
Calhoun, Samuel  314:4
Calkins, D. D.  266:3

Callaghan, J. J.  67:4
Callahan, Donald A.  213:3
  219:4
Callahan, Helen  309:3
Callahan, Kenneth  41:1
Callahan, William  199:2
Callaway, Edward C.  303:6
Callaway, James E.  133:7
  286:18
Callbreath, John C.  149:3
Callender, Frank R.  23:6
Callvert, Stephen A.  266:2
Calvin, James M.  283:5
Camas, WA  229:4  305:1
Cambie, Henry J.  238:3
Cambridge, ID  23:6
Cameahwait (Chief)  46:4
  259:3
Cameron, Alex  199:1
Cameron, David  3:7  253:7
Cameron, Duncan E.  20:6
  235:5
Cameron, James O.  294:3
Cameron, John A.  199:2
Cameron, John A. "Cariboo"
  3:3  253:3
Cameron, Salton  319:4
Camerontown, BC  3:3
  253:2
Camp Abbot, OR  42:2
Camp Cooke, MT  133:4
  139:2
Camp Denali, AK  52:3
  SEE ALSO Denali
Camp Howard, ID  102:2
Camp Lyon, OR  134:9
  139:4
Camp Polk, OR  42:8
Camp Sherman, OR  42:2
Campbell, A. J.  133:7
Campbell, Alexander Colin
  150:2
Campbell, Amasa B.  106:19
  203:1  288:2
Campbell, Charles A.  103:2
  118:2
Campbell, F. C.  150:2
Campbell, Fremont  266:2

Campbell, Hector  51:17
Campbell, Horace  266:2
Campbell, Ira  232:3
Campbell, James M.  179:1
Campbell, John  232:3
Campbell, Johnston B.  96:5
Campbell, Louis D.  266:3
Campbell, Prince L.  232:7
Campbell, Richard P.  266:2
Campbell, Robert  255:17
  309:3  311:1
Campbell, Thomas  302:1
Campbell, Will  215:4
  299:22
Campbell River BC  122:4
  165:19  204:5  275:10
Canal Flats, BC  50:8
  151:7  198:4
Candle, AK  63:1  137:5
  161:1  310:2
Canemah, OR  68:14  228:3
  229:8
Canestrelli, Philip  34:3
Canfield, Eugene  243:6
Canfield, W. D.  177:13
Canfield, ID  102:3
Cann, Thomas H.  163:2
Cannon, Anthony M.  27:11
  39:9  91:4  96:14  107:3
  108:9  150:1  305:2
Cannon, Charles W.  319:5
Cannon, Edward James
  288:3
Cannon, Richard D.  300:5
Cannon, T. J.  157:3
Cannon, William  84:4
Cantonwine, W. J.  119:1
Cantwell, Robert  152:1
Cantwell, AK  63:1  137:3
Canwell, Albert F.  70:20
  245:4  261:2  265:2
Canyon City, OR  36:2
  104:3  110:6  114:6
  147:8  187:3  225:4
  228:3  251:11  264:11
  300:3  303:2
Canyon City, YT  255:3

309:3
Canyon Creek, ID  59:5
Canyon Ferry, MT  319:6
Caplan, David  191:3
Carbonado, WA  305:1
Carcross, YT  63:1  255:1
Cardwell, Edward C.  46:3
Cardwell, Hugh  280:2
Cardwell, James R.  2:13
Cardwell, William B.  187:6
Cardwell, MT  46:3  319:3
Carey, Charles H.  150:1
Carey, ID  23:4  24:3
Caribel, ID  102:3
Caribou City, ID  223:1
Caris, Matthias A.  199:2
Carlisle, WA  50:1  305:1
Carlson, Edward P.  178:9
Carlson, Gustav A.  195:1
Carlson, Joseph E.  41:1
Carlson, Maxwell  217: 11
Carlson, William H.  169:7
Carlson, WA  305:1
Carlstrom, Fred  175:10
Carlton, OR  75:3  300:2
Carlton, WA  267:1  305:1
Carlyle, William Levi  117:7
Carlyon, P. H.  245:16
Carmack, George Washing-
  ton  28:2  130:1  149:2
  159:3  196:7  255:9
  281:1  309:9  311:4
Carman, Joseph Lincoln
  266:2
Carmical, Philip G.  42:1
Carmical, OR  42:1
Carmichael, Herbert  294:3
Carmichael, Russell  175:44
Carnation, WA  305:1
Carnes, William H.  199:2
Carney, Byron F.  49:4
Carpenter, B. Platt  286:12
Carpenter, Charles  150:1
Carpenter, Eli  47:1
Carpenter, Horace  30:2
  187:17
Carr, Edmund  306:5

Carr, Jesse L.   136:35
Carr, Job   203:1   305:4
Carrall, Robert William
   Weir   238:8   253:6
Carrick, Bruce   169:5
Carrighar, Sally   130:1
Carroll, Charles O.   70:9
Carroll, John F.   300:4
Carroll, John P.   214:2
   254:3
Carroll, Matthew   46:2
Carroll, P. P.   245:4
Carroll, MT   156:1
Carry, E. F.   113:3
Carson, John   150:2
Carson, Joseph K.   49:3
Carson, Luella Clay   232:4
Carson, M. C.   264:1
Carson, Robert Henry
   138:6
Cartee, L. F.   87:8
Carter, F. M.   97:2
Carter, Joseph L.   150:1
Carter, Sprague   207:2
Carter, Thomas H.   60:18
   133:4   155:6   156:2
   214:6   215:12   254:6
   286:5   319:5
Carter, William   284:4
Carter, MT   78:1   SEE
   ALSO Keystone
Carter-Cotton, Francis
   236:4
Caruana, Joseph   34:8
Carver, John A.   213:2
Carver, Parker   213:3
Carver, Stephen   75:3
Cary, C. B.   150:1
Cary, George Hunter   3:5
   126:3
Cascade, ID   23:6   24:2
   164:1
Cascade Locks, OR   151:3
   153:1   198:7   229:9
   264:2
Case, C. R.   74:3
Case, Frank D.   116:2

Case, Ira H.   266:3
Case, Otto A.   245:9
Case, Robert O.   152:2
Case, Samuel   150:2
Casey, George B.   185:3
Cashmere, WA   157:6
   203:2   305:2
Cashup, WA   305:1
Casino (Chief)   272:6   287:3
Cassiar, BC   161:1
Castle, MT   78:7   214:2
   224:2   319:11
Castle Rock, WA   14:1
   152:1   305:3
Castleford, ID   23:2
Castlegar, BC   151:6   316:3
Castleman, Nelson   199:3
Castleman, Philip F.   150:4
Cataldo, Joseph M.   27:3
   34:24   39:6   93:11   96:1
   103:9   108:9   118:2   192:2
   254:6   305:2
Cataldo, ID   39:3   118:5
   164:2   SEE ALSO Sacred
   Heart Mission
Cates, Lew A.   300:5
Cathcart, Isaac   57:1   150:1
Cathlamet, WA   203:1   252:3
   272:3   284:1   305:2
Cation, James   199:2
Catlin, John   150:2
Catlin, Seth   200:4
Catlow, John   87:6   110:3
   134:2
Caton, Nathan T.   119:15
Caughlan, John   70:25
Cauvel, Austin Lynn   199:2
Cavanaugh, James Michael
   286:9
Cavanaugh, Thomas H.
   245:4
Cavanaugh, William T.
   266:2
Caven, Frank   76:4
Cavender, Charles A.
   266:2
Cavetown, MT   78:2

Caviness, John L.  150:1
Cawston, Richard Lowe  5:8
Cawston, BC  5:2
Cayton, Horace R.  58:9
  252:1
Cayuse, MT  78:1
Cazadero, OR  75:8  228:3
Cazeno, OR  68:2
Cedar Junction, MT  319:3
Cedarville, WA  305:1
Celilo, WA  229:23  242:3
Cement City, WA 315:3
  SEE ALSO Knappton
Cementville, WA  202:1
  SEE ALSO Knappton
Centerville, ID  33:2  87:1
  223:2
Centerville (Butte), MT
  67:15  167:5  319:6
Centerville, OR  119:2
Central, OR  75:5
Central City, MT  319:3
Central Ferry, WA  280:1
Centralia, WA  14:1  32:4
  57:2  58:3  82:6  92:4
  152:2  176:2  180:2
  195:2  222:6  252:5
  305:6
Chadwick, H. A.  276:2
Chadwick, Stephen Fowler
  51:30  150:2  153:1
  245:3  261:1  293:2
Chadwick, William F.  286:3
Chaffee, Eugene B.  53:60
Chaffee, Stephen E.  279:6
Challis, ID  23:5  164:1
Chaloner, Samuel Bucknam
  266:1
Chamberlain, George Earle
  49:15  86:6  130:3
  153:1  261:1
Chamberlain, P. B.  119:2
  199:2  257:2
Chamberlin, George Harris
  199:2
Chamberlin, Martin L.  150:1
Chambers, Andsworth H.
  150:2  245:5

Chambers, James W.  266:2
Champagne, YT  255:2
Champion, Charles  136:15
Champion, Joseph C.  37:5
Champion, MT  319:2
Champoeg, OR  4:1  44:4
  50:3  68:18  84:6  114:6
  153:3  162:404  172:2
  177:3  193:15  198:10
  229:9  249:2  297:6
  317:7
Chance, Arthur W.  2:10
Chandalar, AK  63:1
Chandler, George C.  174:6
  303:6
Chandler, William M.  150:1
Chapaka, WA  267:1
Chapin, Alfred C.  107:5
Chapin, Chester W.  107:4
Chapin, Herman  243:2
Chapleau, Joseph A.  238:7
Chaplin, Daniel  150:1
Chaplin, John R.  266:3
Chapman, Ad  103:5
Chapman, Adam M.  266:2
Chapman, Benjamin M.
  157:3
Chapman, C. C.  49:6
Chapman, Charles H.  232:4
  302:2
Chapman, John W.  106:4
Chapman, W. Orr  213:11
Chapman, William  150:3
Chapman, William H.  150:1
Chapman, William O.
  266:2
Chapman, William W.  150:16
  179:1  210:8  284:4
Charles, William  5:10
Charlot (Chief)  34:3  48:3
  133:8  155:31  181:11
  214:2  254:4  292:6
Chase, Clifford E.  116:2
Chase, E. S.  95:3
Chase, Elmore Yocum  30:6
Chase, Henry Martyn  119:20
  150:2  179:3
Chase, James Harvey  116:2

Chase, Marvin  157:3
  293:14
Chase, Mary  97:3  203:1
Chase, Will  263:1
Chase, William H.  130:1
Chase, BC  47:2
Chatanika, AK  63:1  281:6
Chattaroy, WA  27:2  305:1
Chausse, F. W.  86:3
Cheadle, Walter B.  238:6
Chealander, Godfrey  178:3
Cheenik, AK  281:21
Chehalis, WA  14:1  89:1
  152:3  203:2  222:9
  252:3  305:3
Chelan, WA  157:17  198:5
  293:5  305:2
Chemainus, BC  122:5
  165:5
Chemaway, OR  93:7
Chemeketa (Salem), OR
  4:1  44:11  93:2  193:6
  198:5
Chena, AK  281:11  309:3
  311:2
Chena Hot Springs, AK
  63:1  137:4
Chenamus (Chief)  272:12
Cheney, B. G.  94:1
Cheney, WA  15:2  16:2
  27:10  38:12  39:3
  41:2  94:10  96:7  108:11
  220:5  305:3  SEE ALSO
  Billings, WA and Depot
  Springs
Chenoweth, Hardin  229:2
Chenowith, F. A.  245:5
Cherbourg, WA  100:7
  SEE ALSO Port Angeles
Chesaw, WA  203:2  225:4
  267:1  305:1  308:6
Chesebro, J. G.  102:4
Chessman, Merle R.  207:7
  300:4
Chetco, OR  258:3
Chetwynd, BC  204:3
Chewelah, WA  16:2  39:7

  203:1  305:2
Chicaloon, AK  130:1
Chicken, AK  63:2  263:1
Chico, MT  319:4
Chico, WA  305:1
Chilberg, J. E.  178:5
Chilcotin (Fort), BC  123:9
  204:10  235:2  SEE AL-
  SO Fort Chilcotin
Childs, Thomas Bromley
  203:1  266:2
Chilkat, AK  18:1  255:2
Chilkoot Barracks, AK
  63:1  130:3  161:1  SEE
  ALSO Fort Seward
Chillawack, BC  204:2
Chinlac, BC  235:4
Chinn, Mark A.  119:4
  179:15
Chinook, MT  319:3
Chinook, WA  14:1  109:3
  202:14  272:12  305:1
Chinookville, WA  202:4
Chipman, Lloyd L.  200:4
Chirouse, Eugene Casimir
  179:1
Chitina, AK  63:1  130:3
Chittenden, J. R.  43:1
Chittick, Victor  152:1
Chopaka, WA  267:1
Chouteau, Pierre  48:9
  133:13  214:5  215:6
Choteau, MT  156:1  312:2
Christensen, Carl  157:3
Christenson, Christian
  57:7
Christie, Alexander  71:18
Christie, J. H.  41:1
Church, Campbell  232:1
Church, Frank F.  12:14
  105:3  129:2  241:1
  259:10  261:1
Cincinnati, OR  68:4  SEE
  ALSO Eola
Cinnabar, MT  78:4
  319:5
Circle, AK  63:2  66:2

81:8   149:2   159:8   190:10
196:2   255:2   281:2
309:30   311:10
Circle Hot Springs, AK
  63:1   137:3
Clackamas, OR   68:5
Claessens, William   93:5
Claggett, William H.   29:4
  95:11   133:4   259:2   286:7
Clallam Bay, WA   100:13
Clancey, MT   78:2
Clancy, John   268:1
Clancy, R. G.   199:2
Clancy, William   67:6   156:4
  167:2   209:18   214:2
  216:10   299:3   319:3
Clapp, Cyrus F.   100:3
  150:2
Clapp, Rufus   199:1
Clapp, William M.   41:1
  58:3   83:1   172:15   244:3
  252:5   293:99
Claquato, WA   203:1   305:3
Clark, Adelbert B.   266:3
Clark, Albert   266:2
Clark, Barzilla   213:14
Clark, Charles W.   133:6
  155:7
Clark, Chase A.   213:4
Clark, D. Worth   105:10
  213:15   259:3   261:1
Clark, F. Lewis   106:40
Clark, Frank   245:7
Clark, Harvey   4:2   84:3
Clark, Hiram   297:6
Clark, I. A.   202:5
Clark, James   288:2
Clark, John Judson   57:1
  266:2
Clark, John S.   150:1
Clark, Newton   239:3
Clark, Patrick   203:1   212:13
Clark, Ransom   119:2   203:1
  257:2
Clark, Ray   293:12
Clark, T. J. V.   150:2
Clark, W. A.   133:7

Clark, W. T.   116:3   157:3
Clark, Walter E.   130:15
  159:3
Clark, William A.   199:2
  203:1
Clark, William Andrews
  1:5   60:31   67:25   133:24
  155:47   156:16   167:17
  188:7   209:30   214:30
  215:30   216:18   247:8
  286:14   298:15   299:9
  319:24
Clark, MT   308:5   SEE AL-
  SO Kirkville
Clark Fork, ID   23:1   164:1
Clarke, Arthur E.   23:11
Clarke, James A.   303:4
Clarke, John   132:3
Clarke, John L.   59:7
Clarke, Patsy   95:2
Clarke, Samuel A.   300:7
Clarke, William D.   266:2
Clarkia, ID   118:3
Clarkson, Robert   156:4
Clarkson, William   5:3
Clarkston, WA   198:2   305:1
Clarksville, OR   147:3
  264:1
Clarno, Andrew   42:4
Clarno, OR   42:1
Clatskanie, OR   152:2
Clatsop Village, OR   44:8
  272:5   297:3
Clausen, C. W.   245:6
Claypool, Charles E.   311:2
Clayson, Fred H.   255:3
Clayton, Albert P.   157:2
Clayton, Ashford   230:3
Clayton, George   264:1
Clayton, ID   164:3
Clayton, WA   305:1
Cle Elum WA   36:1   163:3
  305:1
Clear Lake, WA   315:5
Clearwater, ID   102:4   223:1
Cleary, Frank   311:1
Cleary, AK   63:1   281:3   309:3

Cleaveland, Elisha B.   266:2
Cleek, OR   42:1
Clegg, C. H.   311:1
Cleland, Lucille Horr   278:1
Clem, Richard H.   88:2
Clemen, Rudolf A.   257:4
Clemens, Moses   112:10
Clement, Victor M.   106:7
  192:6   212:9
Clendening, Bruce   106:10
Cleveland, WA   88:3
Cliff, Harry R.   187:7
Cliff, ID   223:1
Clifford, Cecil L.   227:4
Clifford, Miles L.   266:2
Cline, William H.   279:14
Cline Falls, OR   42:4
Clinton, BC   123:3   309:3
Clinton, MT   319:2
Clinton, WA   119:1   305:1
Clise, James W.   203:1
Clothier, Harrison   150:2
  266:2   314:4
Cloud, W. B.   279:8
Clough, David M.   57:64
Clover, WA   267:1
Clute, John Stilwell   5:2
Clymer, Christian   282:6
Clymer, John   96:1
Coady, Michael S.   266:1
Coalman, Elijah   239:4
Coalmont, BC   47:1
Coalpo (Chief)   272:5
Coates, David C.   108:4
Coats, A. S.   303:5
Cobalt, ID   223:2   308:1
  SEE ALSO Blackbird
Cobb, Calvin   23:3   95:3
  127:4   170:3   205:6
Cobban, Roy M.   247:4
Cobleigh, N. F.   257:4
Coboway (Chief)   272:7
Coburg, OR   75:5
Coburn, Catharine A. S.
  152:1
Coburn, John   286:4
Coburn, Robert   61:50   214:3

Coburn, Walt   61:50
Coburn, Will   61:26
Cocalalla, ID   39:1
Coccola (Father)   41:1
Cochran, George M.   266:2
Cochran, J. W.   232:2
Cochran, James E.   266:1
Cochran, James W.   119:2
Cochran, John G.   199:2
Cochran, M. Fidd   237:6
Cochran, Silas D.   118:1
Cochrane, William   163:4
Coe, Earl   70:4   245:6
Coe, Lawrence W.   119:3
  172:4   198:2   229:6
Coeur d' Alene, ID   23:8
  27:2   39:9   96:5   97:9
  99:14   106:40   107:5
  108:2   118:6   127:25
  164:1   180:6   181:3
  192:10   198:1   212:7
  215:4   317:5
Coffee, John M.   245:5
Coffey, Robert Calvin
  187:9
Coffin, Alma   247:4
Coffin, Delos H.   199:1
Coffin, Everett D.   246:2
Coffin, Frank R.   95:2
Coffin, Stephen   179:1
  210:4   284:8
Coffin, Thomas C.   213:7
Coffman, Noah B.   203:1
  217:1   222:9   266:2
Cogswell, John   232:2
Cohen, D. Solis   150:1
Cokedale, WA   315:6
Colbert, Fred   202:3
Colbert, WA   305:1
Colby, WA   14:1
Cold Bay, AK   263:5
Coldfoot, AK   159:1   309:2
Coldwell, E. L. "Jerry"
  300:5
Coldwell, Henry   47:1
Cole, Cash   148:2
Cole, Charlie   234:1

Cole, Ira 283:5
Cole, Merwin L. 70:8
Cole, Thomas F. 209:4
Cole, William 245:7
Coleman, John T. 266:2
Coley, Ward 70:6
Colfax, Schuyler 295:2
Colfax, WA 16:5 27:10
 39:7 41:1 91:2 96:4
 108:5 119:11 150:1
 163:2 305:1
College, AK 63:1 241:3
 290:7
Collender, ID 223:1
Collins, Dean 152:3
Collins, Dennis 258:5
Collins, E. B. 148:2
Collins, George W. 30:4
Collins, John 243:4
Collins, Lillian E. 169:12
Collins, Luther M. 80:5
 234:3 306:13
Collins, Timothy E. 60:4
 133:10
Collins, Ulric L. 266:2
Collison, William H. 10:6
 140:5 186:2
Colman, James M. 178:5
 234:3 243:3 246:1 276:6
 306:3
Coloma, MT 78:2 224:2
 319:2
Colton, WA 152:1 305:1
Columbia Center, WA 280:3
Columbia City, WA 284:1
 SEE ALSO Vancouver, WA
Columbia Falls, MT 135:5
 215:2 216:17 299:3
Columbus, WA 198:1
Colville, WA 16:7 27:11
 34:10 39:5 41:1 96:5
 97:3 107:8 108:8 112:5
 119:6 198:6 SEE ALSO
 Fort Colville
Colwood, BC 165:2
Coman, Edward Truman
 184:31 288:2

Combination, MT 319:4
Combs, Alex 115:6
Combs, R. P 200:4
Comcomly (Chief) 39:5
 196:2 198:2 202:6
 272:30 287:4
Comeford, James Purcell
 150:2 266:1
Comegys, George 119:2
Comer, R. H. J. 264:2
Comet, MT 224:5
Comfort, George 227:4
Commander, Kingsmill
 152:1 191:4
Comox, BC 3:4 165:9
Compo, Charles 4:3 84:1
 177:6
Compton, Ivan J. 116:2
Comstock, James M. 288:5
Comstock, Ralph J. 23:4
Comstock, Ross J. 23:4
 24:4
Concomly (Chief) SEE
 Comcomly
Conconully, WA 225:4
 267:1 305:3
Concord, ID 102:5 223:1
Concrete, WA 305:2 315:11
Conda, ID 164:1 216:3
Condon, James B. 30:7
Condon, John T. 38:5
Condon, Thomas W. 42:5
 144:1 153:1 198:1
 201:355 232:5 302:50
Condon, OR 82:4 300:2
Condon, WA 267:1
Condon Ferry, WA 267:1
Cone, Charles E. 293:4
Cone, G. A. 68:2
Cone, Harry W. 102:6
Conger, George C. 245:3
Congle, J. B. 150:1
Conklin, George H. 282:6
Conklin, Mary Ann 31:7
Conklin, Robert 175:23
Conley, Frank 299:2
Conmey, Thomas S. 266:2

Connel, Robert  38:2
Connell, WA  293:6  305:2
Connella, James  57:1
Conner, James J.  314:3
Conner, W. C.  300:6
Connett, J. E.  149:2
Connolly, Christopher P.
  205:5
Connolly, William  235:7
Connolly (Fort), BC  235:2
Connor, Samuel P.  266:3
Conover, Charles T.  217:1
Conrad, Charles  314:3
Conrad, Chesley T.  266:3
Conrad, John H.  215:3
Conrad, W. G.  133:6
Conroy, John  114:3
Conser, George  152:2
Considine, John  104:10
  196:3  234:29
Considine, Tom  234:8
Constantine, Charles
  255:19
Conway, WA  315:6
Cook, Amos  84:2
Cook, Ebenezer  69:5
Cook, Francis H.  27:13
  41:2  96:5  108:2  150:2
Cook, Howard  319:11
Cook, John  9:8
Cook, Ralph  266:3
Cook, W. T.  150:1
Cook, OR  75:3
Cooke, Charles P.  150:2
Cooke, Edwin N.  150:2
Cooke City, MT  78:4  215:3
  312:2  319:8
Coombs, Jacob L.  30:1
Coombs, Samuel F.  7:2
  234:1  266:2
Coon, Charles E.  245:4
  266:3
Cooney, Edward H.  155:2
Cooney, Frank H.  214:2
Cooper, Enos  31:5
Cooper, James  20:11
Cooper, James T.  230:7

Cooper, John T.  118:2
  172:7  212:3  259:2
Cooper, Walter  133:5
Coos Bay, OR  9:5  41:2
  73:15  75:3  82:5  97:4
  104:8  152:3  201:4
  249:2  258:3  303:5
  317:3  SEE ALSO Marsh-
  field
Coover, Thomas  133:5
Cope, Fred  131:2
Copeland, Thomas  199:2
Copeland, Wallace R.  199:1
Copeland, William E.  191:9
Copenspire, Frederick H.
  266:2
Copley, George  256:3
Copper Center, AK  63:1
  130:2
Copperfield, OR  12:12
  114:5  152:10  153:1
  225:2
Copperopolis, MT  78:3
  319:3
Coquille, OR  258:15  300:3
Corbaley, Gordon C.  96:5
Corbaley, Richard  150:1
Corbett, Don Carlos  243:2
  305:1
Corbett, Frank E.  133:4
Corbett, Henry W.  91:4
  110:2  150:3  261:2
  297:50  300:4
Corbin, Austin  107:9
  203:2
Corbin, Daniel Chase  39:4
  96:2  97:1  99:3  107:270
  108:1  188:3  192:5  203:2
  212:4
Corbin, MT  319:3
Corcoran, Paul  118:1
  127:7  205:4  259:1
Cordiner, Ralph  176:4
Cordon, Guy  49:5  128:4
  130:7  241:4
Cordova, AK  28:1  63:1
  128:3  130:19  143:3

148:4   159:6   160:4   161:2
263:5   281:3   310:3
Cordray, John F.   41:1
104:14
Corey, Merton H.   266:2
Corkrum, Francis M.   199:2
Corliss, Charles W.   234:1
Corman, Clyde   175:35
Cormier, Frederic   112:9
Cornelius, Thomas R.   119:5
150:8   179:17   220:3
264:2   318:9
Cornish, Nellie Centennial
69:283   104:2   276:9
278:2
Cornoyer, Narcisse A.
119:113   150:1   179:9
207:5
Cornucopia, OR   114:7
225:3   264:3
Cornwall, Clement F.
238:5
Cornwall, Neil   9:4
Cornwell, James M.   119:3
Cornwell, Orville   308:1
Corpron, Douglas   88:9
Corriery, Pauline   114:3
Cort, John   104:14   234:4
305:3
Corvallis, OR   30:3   41:4
68:17   75:13   104:7
147:2   187:4   210:9
228:28   229:17   297:9
300:9   303:7   317:6
Corwin, F. E.   308:1
Corwin, MT   308:2
Cosgriff, J. E.   23:6
Cosgrove, Hugh   208:27
Cosgrove, Humboldt Jack
246:1
Cosgrove, Samuel G.   203:1
245:4   305:1
Coshaw, Oliver P.   150:2
194:3
Cosley, Joe   135:6
Cosmopolis, WA   14:1   41:1
73:5   305:1
Costa, Jack   311:1

Costigan, Howard   58:2
70:26   176:1   234:2
244:2   261:1
Cottage Crove, OR   75:3
97:2   187:2   228:18
300:4
Cotter, William D.   266:2
Cotterill, George F.   41:1
57:3   58:11   234:10
243:2   245:9   276:19
Cottonwood, ID   11:4   23:5
26:4   27:3   102:20   103:6
118:3
Cottonwood, MT   133:7
292:4   SEE ALSO Deer
Lodge
Couch, John M.   44:1
150:2   152:2   198:1
210:8   284:10   297:14
Cougar, WA   152:1
Coulee City, WA   36:2
293:36   305:2
Coulee Dam, WA   267:1
Coulson, MT   78:6
Coulter, Robert   213:12
219:2
Coulter, Wayne   175:13
Council, Mary Lee   241:4
Council, ID   23:3
Council City, AK   63:1
130:1   159:2   281:26
Coupe, Nellie Moore   278:1
Coupe, Thomas   203:3
Coupeville, WA   14:1   89:1
203:9   305:2
Courson, Kenneth   231:3
Courtenay, BC   165:3   204:2
Courtney, W. F.   150:1
Courtway, Anthony B.
157:2
Cover, Thomas   25:3
Covington, Richard   203:1
305:3
Cowan, David   25:4
Cowan, George F.   27:10
Cowden, Harrison   266:2
Cowen, David   245:5
Cowen, E. D.   96:2

Cowgill, Robert P.  305:1
Cowichan, BC  165:6
Cowles, Alfred  96:30
Cowles, Cheney  96:8
Cowles, Samuel D.  150:2
Cowles, William H.  41:2
    83:2  96:120
Cowley, Henry T.  27:9
    39:7  41:1  91:206  96:4
    108:13
Cowley, Michael M.  27:4
    39:5  288:2
Cowlitz, WA  14:1  194:10
Cox (Judge)  235:3
Cox, Anderson  119:15
    150:1  199:2
Cox, Fred O.  199:2
Cox, George  274:11
Cox, Harvey R.  266:3
Cox, Isham  258:3
Cox, Joe B.  195:8
Cox, L. B.  207:7
Cox, Norris R.  2:7
Cox, Ray  117:1
Cox, Ross  27:3  39:8
    108:20  272:3
Cox, Rowland J.  52:2
Cox, William  266:2
Cox, William Columbus
    266:4
Cox, William George  253:7
Craddock, Chet  251:4
Craig, Adna C.  150:2
Craig, David Watson  300:8
Craig, George H.  94:4
Craig, John Templeton  42:3
Craig, Morte H.  185:1
Craig, William  43:1  93:5
    103:6  119:9  132:1  177:6
    179:2  188:4
Craig, AK  63:1  269:6
Craighead, Edwin Boone
    299:4
Craigmont, ID  23:8  24:3
Craigue, Nelson  57:3
Cranbrook, BC  107:3  122:3
    204:4

Crandall, Sidney G.  266:2
Crane, OR  114:3
Craven, R. M.  227:4
Crawford, Hank  155:4
Crawford, Jim  176:2
Crawford, Medorem  119:6
    177:2  249:1
Crawford, Ronald C.  266:3
Crawford, Samuel L.  41:1
    217:1
Crawford, Willard  95:3
Crawford, William J.  303:5
Crawford, ID  23:2
Creamer, Charles  148:1
    262:1
Crease, Henry Pering Pel-
    lew  5:4  126:3  238:17
    253:15
Creighton, Frank  242:4
Creighton, John  25:3
Crellin, John  202:5
Crenshaw, Henry  37:4
Crescent Bay, WA  100:11
Cressman, L. S.  291:7
Creston, WA  151:3  152:4
    305:1
Crickmer, William Burton
    5:3
Criderman, William  173:7
Cridge, Edward  3:6  5:3
    10:3  126:4  165:3  253:3
    260:9
Cripe, Calvin  137:7
Crocker, Benjamin D.  199:1
Crocker, D. B.  106:3
Crockett, Walter  150:1
Croft, Chancy  136:6
Croft, Fred F.  194:3
Crofton, BC  165:4
Croke, James  249:4
Crollard, Fred M.  116:2
Cromie, Robert J.  236:3
Crompton, Harold N.  275:6
Cromwell, John B.  266:4
Cronemiller, Fred P.  300:4
Croner, C. C.  232:5
Cronin, Dan  234:3

Cropp, James F.   203:1
Croquet, Adrian J.   30:1
  249:2
Crosby, Alfred   284:1
Crosby, Clanrick   50:2
  150:2   203:1   245:5
  284:2
Crosby, Frank L.   266:4
Crosby, H. R.   234:1
Crosby, John   Schuyler
  286:25
Crosby, Nathaniel   73:12
  264:2   284:15   302:2
Crosby, Thomas   140:3
  189:3
Cross Hollows, OR   308:1
  SEE ALSO Shaniko
Crossen, James B.   150:1
Crosson, Joe   137:7   233:4
  262:4   263:35
Croup, Eli W.   199:1
Crow, David   152:1
Crow, James J.   150:2
Crow, John   114:4
Crowe, George R.   199:2
Crowell, Henry A.   199:2
Crum, Charles   299:2
Crumback, John Henry
  100:7
Cruse, Thomas   214:2
  319:6
Cruse, W. J.   23:4
Cudihee, Edward   234:1
  266:2
Cuess, WA   267:1
Culbertson, Alexander
  48:16   133:11   141:4
  247:4
Culbertson, Frank   106:15
  212:5
Culbertson, MT   215:3
  299:2   312:1
Culdesac, ID   23:5   24:2
Cullen, John W.   147:5
Cullen, William E.   286:3
  289:4
Culligan, James A.   71:11

Culver, OR   42:6
Cumberland, BC   165:5
Cumming, W. A.   2:11
Cummings, Amos   199:2
Cummings, Charles F.
  199:2
Cummins, J. M.   300:5
Cummins, James   199:1
Cummins, Jesse   199:1
Cummins, Woodson   199:1
Cumyow, Wan A. (William)
  238:6
Cundiff, Jerry L.   88:2
Cunha, Joseph   207:3
Cunningham, Charles   207:6
Cunningham, Imogen   278:1
Cunningham, James Calvin
  289:3
Cunningham, John G.   288:2
Cunningham, Richard A.
  212:12
Cunningham, Robert   186:2
Cunningham, WA   293:4
Cuprum, ID   164:1   223:1
Curl, James   179:3
Currey, George B.   147:9
Currey, George Huntington
  300:6
Curry, George Law   51:4
  68:3   119:8   145:13
  153:2   179:15   188:4
  198:2   300:10   304:3
Curry, Harvey "Kid"   61:45
  319:2
Curry, AK   63:1   137:3
Curtis, Edward J.   43:1
  87:17   95:1   118:1   212:12
Curtis, Melville   266:2
Curtis, Ned   95:3
Cusack, Harry L.   245:4
Cushman, F. W.   245:6
Cushman, I. B.   73:5
Cushman, Orrington   141:4
Cusick, WA   305:1
Custer, Charles Sumner
  282:4
Custer, ID   118:1   164:1

223:4   308:5
Cut Bank, MT  1:2  135:4
Cutler, Lyman A.   20:2
  32:1   252:1
Cutter, Kirtland K.   39:2
  83:2   96:1   203:7
Cyphers, Levi H.   150:1
Cyr, John R.   112:4
Cyr, Philip   112:6
Czizek, ID   102:2


Dacres, George   199:4
Dadisman, Martin V.   191:9
Daggett, H. M.   185:3
Daggett, J. M.   212:1
Dagon, Theophilus   144:3
  296:11
Dahl, Claus John H.   266:2
Dahler, Charles L.   212:1
Daisy, WA   305:1
Dakin, Paul Worth   266:2
Dalby, Ezra Christensen
  59:5
Dale, Harrison C.   117:40
Dale, William   266:2
Dalgleish, David   194:2
Dalgleish, John W.   266:2
Dall, William Healy   8:6
  149:5   159:7   161:8   168:2
  311:2
Dallam, Frank M.   96:13
  108:2   157:2
Dallas, A. G.   3:5
Dallas, G. M.   212:10
Dallas, OR   30:1   75:10
  114:7   187:4   300:5
Dalles (The), OR   4:16
  36:3   50:6   84:3   90:6
  93:13   97:5   108:3   110:3
  151:6   182:11   198:42
  229:7   252:4   257:8   264:7
  SEE ALSO Fort Dalles;
  North Dalles; and The
  Dalles
Dalles Mission, OR   44:11
  119:9   153:1   SEE ALSO

Waskopum Mission
Dalton, Jack   134:2   255:4
Dalton Post, YT   255:3
Daly, Ida F.   278:1
Daly, Marcus   1:2   46:6
  60:29   67:33   106:2
  133:30   155:36   156:15
  167:18   181:5   188:9
  203:1   209:31   214:27
  215:24   216:80   218:3
  247:11   286:7   298:20
  299:10   319:25
Dammarell, Frank K.   23:4
Dammon, J. D.   150:1
Dana, Marshall N.   293:4
Dance, Walter B.   25:3
  133:6   292:6
Daniel, James R.   150:2
Daniels, George W.   191:7
Daniels, J. W.   33:2
Daniels, John H.   199:1
Daniels, W. Byron   203:1
Daniels, William B.   43:2
  87:4   118:2
Danielson, Arthur   152:2
Danielsville, MT   319:2
Danilson, W. H.   211:19
Danson, Robert John
  288:2
Danville, WA   225:1   305:1
D'Arcy, P. H.   162:13
Darling, Charles A.   266:2
Darling, Henry   275:13
Darling, James Masten
  266:2
Darling, Scott   308:1
Dart, Anson   27:1   188:2
  202:1   211:2   272:10
Dartford, WA   305:1
D'Aste, Jerome   254:6
Daulton, John W.   199:1
Davenport, Homer   153:1
  300:4
Davenport, John C.   27:2
  305:1
Davenport, Louis M.   41:1
  96:7   108:1
Davenport, T. W.   35:6

Davenport, ID SEE Gem, ID
Davenport, WA 92:1 108:1
   203:1 293:3 305:1
David, Lester W. 294:4
Davidson, Alpheus 266:2
Davie, Alexander E. B.
   238:13
Davie, Allen Jones 84:2
Davie, Theodore 126:4
   238:16 253:3
Davies, Joshua 107:2
Davies, Juanita 231:5
Davies, Mary Carolyn
   152:2
Davies, T. A. 41:1
Davies, William W. 36:14
   41:1 119:3
Davin, Hippolyte 199:2
Davis, Andrew J. 133:5
   155:3
Davis, Arthur W. 184:25
Davis, B. L. N. 314:5
Davis, Clark 266:3
Davis, George A. 150:2
Davis, George L. 266:2
Davis, Henry C. 266:5
Davis, Jack 43:1
Davis, James H. "Cash-
   up" 27:3 108:3 266:1
   305:1
Davis, James S. 150:1
Davis, John A. 199:1
Davis, John W. 145:3
   153:1
Davis, Lewis H. 203:1
Davis, Lorenzo A. 199:1
Davis, Minot 175:7
Davis, Rowland E. 266:3
Davis, Rufus J. 266:2
Davis, S. P. 303:7
Davis, Samuel D. 95:2
Davis, Thomas J. 33:3
Davis, W. F. 118:2 127:4
Davis, William H. 266:2
Davis, William R. 88:2
Dawne, E. J. 130:1
Dawson, F. G. 185:3

Dawson, George 255:4
Dawson City, YT 28:5
   63:1 81:13 115:7 130:3
   143:3 146:21 159:12
   161:5 190:6 195:1
   196:50 255:45 281:4
   309:26 311:3
Dawson Creek, BC 40:21
   204:3
Day, Albert M. 12:3
Day, Benjamin B. 280:3
Day, Cassius M. 103:4
Day, Edwin Mahlon 266:4
Day, Eph 87:4
Day, Henry Loren 106:6
   118:1 212:4
Day, J. H. 119:2
Day, Jesse N. 119:10
Day, John 198:3
Day, W. W. 119:2
Day, William T. 288:2
Dayton, OR 30:6 68:7
   75:3 114:3 147:1 229:8
   300:2
Dayton, WA 38:1 82:2
   96:2 119:25 198:1
   203:4 280:8 303:7
   305:1
Deadwood City, ID 223:1
Deady, Matthew P. 51:90
   144:2 145:25 150:2
   154:3 187:7 232:7 300:5
   302:3 304:10
Deal, Richard W. 150:2
Dean, Dorothy 231:3
Dean, Edwin 274:10
Deans, James 20:5
DeArmond, Jerome C.
   191:8
Dears, Thomas 235:3
Deary, William 118:1
Deary, ID 23:3 118:1
Dease, John Warren 39:3
Dease, Peter Warren
   235:3
Dease Lake, BC 204:3
DeBeck, E. K. 189:4

Deborgia, MT  98:9
DeBruler, Ellis  266:3
Debus, Harry  199:2
DeCicco, Mike M.  49:5
Decker, Horace Percival
  266:2
Declo, ID  23:1
DeCosmos, Amor  126:8
  238:42  253:26  260:9
DeCuis, A. P.  30:1
Deer Lodge, MT  1:1  25:6
  26:6  48:11  60:4  76:6
  133:23  155:4  181:7
  183:6  215:7  216:6  227:7
  247:10  256:3  292:11
  312:1  319:32  SEE ALSO
  Cottonwood, MT
Deer Park, WA  96:1  305:1
Deering, Ivah  278:1
Deering, AK  28:2  63:1
  125:4  137:3
Defenbach, Byron  213:9
Deggaller, Edward  266:1
DeGroff, Edward  149:6
Dehning, A. A. "Bert"
  175:6
Deighton, John "Gassy
  Jack"  158:6  236:11
DeLacy, Hugh  70:50  176:1
  261:1
DeLacy, W. W.  133:7
Delamar, Joseph R.  95:3
  106:4  134:1
DeLamar, ID  134:10  164:1
  223:3
Delaney, George  199:3
DeLashmutt, Van B.  23:3
  102:3  106:4  150:2  192:2
  210:5  212:5
Delaunay, John B.  71:13
DeLin, Nicholas  41:1  305:3
Dellinger, John S.  300:5
DeLore, Mathilde Grenier
  114:5
Delorme, B.  249:2
Delta, ID  23:2  212:4
Dement, Frank S.  199:2

Demerais, Louis  140:2
Demers, Modeste  4:2  6:2
  7:7  34:8  93:9  119:6
  177:12  198:2  208:14
  235:9  249:9  252:3
  272:3  305:3
Demers, Telesphore Jacques
  112:13
Demersville, MT  78:5
  112:1  319:4
Deming, WA  305:1
De Moss, James M.  150:1
Dempsey, Christopher C.
  289:2
Dempsey, Robert  46:4
  292:13
Denali (Camp), AK  115:12
  SEE ALSO Camp Denali
Denison, James S.  119:4
Denney, John C.  266:3
Denney, Nathaniel B.  199:3
Dennis, Bruce  300:6
Dennis, Graham Barclay
  288:4
Dennison, Ammi Prince
  179:1
Denny, Arthur Armstrong
  7:20  16:5  31:36  38:5
  58:3  73:5  80:8  119:7
  141:5  150:4  163:3
  172:2  176:4  178:20
  220:11  222:8  234:6
  243:9  245:9  266:13
  276:25  305:3  306:60
  317:4
Denny, David Thomas  7:11
  31:15  80:5  150:1  172:2
  176:2  178:5  243:3
  276:16  305:2  306:20
Denny, O. O.  246:2
Dent, Frederick T.  87:2
Denton, Marion G.  266:2
Denver, ID  23:2  102:10
Depot Springs, WA  108:1
  SEE ALSO Cheney, WA
Derby, BC  3:3  20:2  47:1
  253:4  SEE ALSO

Fort Langley
Derbyshire, Glenn B. 289:3
De Rouge, Etienne 97:1
Derry, Norman E. 157:3
DeSaule, James SEE
Saule, James D.
Deschamps, Alfred E.
112:9
Deschamps, Romulus 112:8
Deschutes, OR 42:1
Desert, OR 42:2
Deshaw, William 7:7
DeSmet, Pierre Jean 1:6
4:2 6:4 34:54 39:9
43:2 45:7 46:5 48:14
93:21 99:5 118:4 119:4
132:2 133:8 155:14
177:5 181:6 198:3
208:10 249:8 305:4
DeSmet, ID 164:2
Des Moines, WA 14:1
DeSoto, Alexander 266:2
DeSpain, Jeremiah B.
150:2 207:5
Detwiler, Lewis 157:4
Devin, Bill 176:1
Devin, Henry L. 266:2
Devine, Fred 252:1
Devine, John S. 110:10
134:5 172:4 250:4
DeVoe, Emma Smith 58:3
108:5 278:1
Devore, John F. 150:5
DeVos, Peter 34:10 93:2
208:8 249:3
Dewar, James M. 119:1
199:3
Dewdney, Edgar 3:3 5:50
20:2 235:2 238:10
253:3 260:6
Dewey, Delbert M. 289:2
Dewey, Henry Bingham
38:5
Dewey, William H. 33:2
36:13 118:6 127:3 164:1
Dewey, ID 118:1 134:2
164:1 223:3 SEE ALSO

Booneville, ID
Dewey, MT 319:4
Dewey, WA 315:3
DeWindt, Harry 161:10
Dexter, John A. 281:3
Diamond, C. L. 308:2
Diamond, John 232:3
Diamond City, MT 46:6
48:6 76:5 78:7 133:8
215:7 319:8
Diamond City, WA 202:4
Dibble, Carmi 266:3
Dick, Franklin T. 150:1
Dick, Harry A. 240:3
Dickerson, William Wiley
266:1
Dickey, W. A. 115:2
Dickey, ID 164:1
Dickinson, A. S. 199:1
Dickinson, Abraham C,
119:1
Dickinson, Harvey L.
266:2
Dickinson, Merville C.
266:2
Dickinson, W. H. H. 181:8
Dickson, A. E. 275:13
Diefendorf, Ben 23:4
Dietz, George W. 294:3
Dill, Clarence Cleveland
16:3 36:1 41:1 58:2
83:276 92:2 96:7 172:2
222:5 245:9 261:3
293:5
Dillehunt, R. B. 187:6
Dilling, George W. 41:1
234:3
Dillingham, AK 63:1 271:2
Dillon, William H. 150:1
Dillon, MT 46:5 48:2
215:4 319:9
Dimmick, George W. 230:3
Dimmick, Thomas M. 258:3
Dimmick, Zeba 230:4
Dimond, Anthony J. 28:3
128:6 129:19 130:38
148:2 226:14 241:13 262:9

Dimsdale, Thomas J.   1:2
 25:25  46:3  48:8  133:9
 155:1  214:5  256:4
 286:2  292:8  298:3
 319:5
Dinges, Solomon  199:1
Dingwall, Daniel  314:4
Dingwall, Ewen C.   178:4
Diomedi, Alexander  34:4
Dirk, Limey  32:5
Disautel, WA  267:1  308:5
Dishman, WA  305:1
Disinger, William  232:1
Disque, Bryce P.   195:3
Disston, OR  75:2  228:8
Divide, MT  319:5
Divilbiss, James W.   203:1
Dix, George E.   258:3
Dixie, ID  33:8  102:11
 103:3  118:3  223:1
Dixie, WA  119:1  305:1
Dixie Town, OR  264:1
Dixon, Charles Leonard
 282:6
Dixon, James  87:4
Dixon, Joseph M.   133:3
 155:4  156:4  181:5
 214:11  215:10  283:18
 298:6  299:35
Dixon, William W.   60:4
 133:8
Doane, Nehemiah  30:1
Dobbins, William K.   70:22
Dobell, Larry  299:2
Dobson, John  266:3
Dobson, Thomas  282:9
Dockrill, Frank  186:4
Dockton, WA  305:2
Dodd, Elmer P.   207:5
 300:5
Dodd, (Mrs.) J. Bruce
 96:3
Dodds, George W.   96:3
Dodge, James Rufus  230:1
Dodge, Orvil  258:12
Dodge, Solomon  30:5
Dodge, William Sumner

 130:2  149:8  161:1
Dodge (Junction), WA  305:1
Dodson, MT  61:2
Doescher, John F.   191:3
Dog Town, MT  292:12
Dogfish Village, AK  63:1
Dohm, Edward C.   245:6
Dolbeer, Jack  176:1
Dollar, William  99:5
Dolphe, Joseph N.   29:6
 303:5
Donahoe, Francis  266:3
Donahue, Thomas  294:1
Donald, George  203:1
Donald, James T.   88:4
Donaldson, Paul D.   172:4
 293:8
Donaugh, Carl C.   49:5
Doncaster, Hiram  150:2
Doneen, John W.   157:2
Doniphan, ID  223:1
Donlan, Edward  112:5
Donnell, Robert W.   155:3
 319:3
Donnelly, ID  23:2
Donohoe, Ed  265:3
Donohue, Dan J.   183:5
Donovan, John Joseph
 266:4
Doolan, R. A.   10:2
Dooley, John  199:2
Dorbandt, Frank  263:8
Dore, John F.   41:1  176:2
 178:2  234:7  244:15
 261:1
Dorena, OR  228:4
Dorion, Pierre  33:12
 39:4  72:2  198:2
Dornan, George  242:3
Dorr, Charles W.   130:6
Dorris, Edgar A.   199:2
Dorris, George B.   232:5
Dorval, Gertrude  112:1
Dosewallips, WA  152:2
Doty, James  141:10  179:2
Doughty, William M.   84:2
Douglas, Arthur  176:2

Douglas, Sir James 3:50
5:20 10:5 20:100 120:30
126:32 131:14 138:7
140:7 189:10 235:22
238:12 253:100 294:6
Douglas, James 4:7 101:4
177:8 198:2
Douglas, AK 14:1 63:1
130:9
Douglas, WA 305:1
Dovell, John 150:1
Dovenspeck, N. J. 292:5
Dover, ID 164:1
Dow, W. O. 116:2
Dowell, Benjamin F. 150:3
179:4
Downey, William R. 150:1
Downey, ID 23:5
Downing, Ben 311:3
Downing, J. J. 27:11 39:12
41:1
Downs, Horace P. 150:1
Doyle, Charles W. 113:4
Doyle, Thomas 212:4
Draham, George 245:5
Draham, Mark H. 266:3
Drake, Alexander M. 42:6
Drake, Lee D. 207:11
Drake, Montague W. T.
238:5
Drennan, G. I. 82:4
Drew, Edwin P. 30:2
Drew, Joseph W. 30:2
179:1
Drewry, David T. 266:2
Drewsey, OR 56:3 225:3
SEE ALSO Gouge Eye
Dreyer, Frank 266:2
Driggs, John 190:6
Driggs, ID 23:9
Driscoll, John Lynn 23:6
24:5 53:16
Drissler, John H. 266:2
Drittenbas, Harry 293:3
Driver, W. C. 303:5
Drum, Henry 150:3 266:4
Drumheller, Daniel M. 3:2

39:3 83:2 108:1 250:3
Drumheller, Jerome 27:1
Drumheller, Jesse 119:2
199:1
Drumheller, Joseph 70:6
184:1 245:2
Drummond, ID 23:2
Drummond, MT 319:3
Dryden, ID 102:3
Dryden, WA 157:4 305:1
Dryer, Thomas Jefferson
35:5 41:2 51:110 145:5
179:1 210:2 239:1
284:9 300:12 304:3
Dubois, Frederick T. 29:18
59:3 95:11 105:8 118:5
170:15 205:9 211:3
213:3 219:2 259:12
261:1
Dubois, Jesse K. 95:8
Dubois, ID 23:3 95:1
164:1
Dubreuil, Adolph 112:4
Ducharme, Baptiste 112:7
Ducheney, Rocque 202:3
Duckabush, WA 152:2
Duddenhausen, August
203:1
Dudoward, Alfred 186:3
Dueber, Peter 150:1
Duff, Walter 303:8
Dufresne, Julian 112:5
Dufresne, William 112:13
Dugan, Frank P. 119:7
Duggan, Larry 67:4
Dullahant, Clarence 282:4
Dumon, John H. 266:2
Dunbar, Cyrus Vader 266:2
Dunbar, John H. 245:8
Dunbar, Oscar W. 300:7
Dunbar, Ralph O. 150:2
266:4
Dunbar, Robert W. 145:4
Dunbar, William Rice
150:2
Duncan, A. L. 86:20
Duncan, Hazel B. 169:21

63                                    DUNCAN

Duncan, Hugh  227:9
Duncan, James A. "Jimmy"
    113:30  234:2  276:3
Duncan, John W.  96:1
Duncan, Lewis J.  51:7
    67:4  167:2
Duncan, Mel G.  279:5
Duncan, Robert H.  194:6
Duncan, William  3:7
    10:395  18:5  20:2  28:1
    55:3  90:7  130:2  140:14
    146:10  149:6  186:7
    189:22  269:5
Duncan, BC  47:1  123:3
    165:9  204:2
Dundee, OR  75:4
Dundore, Mary Margaret
    71:7
Dungeness, WA  14:1  89:1
    100:18  273:11  305:1
Duniway, Abigail Scott
    85:5  108:1  172:18
    197:1  245:3  252:1
    295:2  302:9  304:9
Duniway, Benjamin C.  172:3
Dunlap, Alexander I.  266:1
Dunlap, Isaac  266:1
Dunlap, John K.  199:1
Dunlevy, Peter  47:1
Dunn, Adam Duncan  184:30
Dunn, Alfred J.  212:22
Dunn, F. B.  232:7
Dunn, Reubin  95:3
Dunne, Joe E.  49:4
Dunne, William F.  299:6
Dunsmuir, James  165:7
    238:15  253:16
Dunsmuir, Robert  3:2
    126:7  131:3  165:7
    238:16  260:6  294:2
Dunvegan, BC  40:5
Dupont, WA  305:1
Dupuis, Edward  68:2
Dupuyer, MT  312:1
Du Rell, B. M.  23:12
Durham, N. W.  27:24  293:4
Durie, David  243:7

Durkan, Martin J.  245:3
Durkin, Jimmie  96:4
    108:1  305:2
Durnell, Thomas C.  266:2
Durrent, James Arthur
    266:2
Dussault, Arthur  112:6
Dutch Harbor, AK  28:3
    63:1  146:3  161:6  262:8
    290:4
Dutton, MT  299:2
Dwight, Daniel H.  288:4
Dworshak, Henry C.  105:3
    118:1  259:2
Dye, Eva Emery  153:1
    304:5
Dyea, AK  28:2  63:1  81:4
    130:3  159:6  161:1  166:1
    190:4  255:7  281:3  309:5
    310:4
Dyer, R. B.  73:4
Dysart, George  266:2
Dysart, James S.  150:1


Eades, Moses  30:1
Eades, Solomon  30:1
Eagle, AK  63:2  130:9
    137:2  143:2  146:3
    241:2  309:14  310:5
    311:12
Eagle City, ID  23:7  99:3
    106:5  108:4  118:3  212:4
Eagle Cliff, WA  152:1
    305:1
Eagle Rock, ID  23:6
Eagleson, Ern G.  33:4
Eakin, S. B.  232:3
Earhart, Rockey P.  150:2
Earles, Michael  100:9
    266:2
Earlington, WA  282:4
Early, Michael J.  71:13
Easterbrook, George T.
    202:3
Easton, John Louden  266:1

Easton, WA 305:1
Eastport, ID 164:1
Eastvold, Don 245:4
Eaton, Abel E. 150:2
Eaton, Cora Smith 58:2
Eaton, Frank Blaney 187:5
Eaton, James Francis
257:23
Eaton, O. M. 80:4 306:4
Eaton, William Burton 266:2
Eaton, AK 125:2
Eatonville, WA 203:1 305:1
Ebbert, George Wood 84:3
150:2 162:8
Eberlin, Laura 169:20
Eberman, N. A. 150:1
Eberschweiler, Frederick
34:7
Ebey, Isaac N. 16:3 20:3
92:2 100:2 121:3 131:3
220:7 222:5 234:1 245:4
305:3
Eccles, Marriner S. 23:5
Echo City, OR 119:1
Eckerson, Theodore John
150:2 179:2
Eckert, J. L. 103:6
Eckstein, Nathan 293:2
Ecton, Zales N. 214:2
215:4
Eddy, R. A. 181:6
Eden, ID 23:2
Edens, John James 266:4
Edgar, Henry 133:6
Edgerley, Eldon 199:2
Edgerton, Sidney 1:3 25:14
43:1 46:2 48:16 87:3
133:21 155:4 156:2
188:3 214:7 215:3 247:5
283:2 286:30 319:6
Edgewood, BC 316:10
Edison, WA 152:2 191:15
314:5 315:14
Ediz Hook, WA 100:10
Edmiston, J. E. 119:4
Edmonds, WA 41:2 305:3
Edwards, Caldwell 60:8

Edwards, David Bartlett
266:1
Edwards, Frank 234:1
Edwards, John Griffith
42:2
Edwards, Norman 274:5
Edwards, Philip Leget
44:7 93:5 114:3 162:3
188:4 193:5
Eells, Cushing 4:14 16:9
17:3 27:7 36:2 39:3
50:10 91:8 93:14 96:5
108:18 119:13 150:2
177:32 188:3 198:3
222:26 252:9 257:30
305:7
Eells, Edwin 222:3 257:6
273:3
Eells, Myron F. 119:1
177:1 220:3 257:9
273:122 305:2
Egan (Chief) 11:13 134:6
172:3 207:3 259:2
Egan, D. Daun 266:2
Egan, William A. 28:2
128:15 129:8 130:8
136:16 160:2 271:17
Egavik, AK 161:2
Ehrlich, WA 315:5
Eichelberger, Frank E.
23:4
Eichler, Charles H. 199:2
Eielson, Carl Ben 63:4
137:16 161:2 262:2
263:45 311:1
Eisenbeis, Charles 150:1
203:1
Eisenhart, Albert 274:14
Eisentrager, Harley 274:8
Ekalaka, MT 156:1 312:1
Eklutna, AK 8:10 63:1
281:3 290:1
Elba, ID 23:1
Elbe, WA 305:1
Elder, James 266:2
Eldorado, OR 225:2
El Dorado City, MT 76:3

Eldridge, Edward  150:2
Eldridge, Harlan D.  199:2
Eldridge, Hugh  266:2
Eldridge, Jay Glover  117:18
Electric, MT  308:9
Electron, WA  305:1
Elfers, Henry  103:3
Elgin, OR  300:2
Elicker, Charles  265:8
Elim, AK  8:6
Eliot, Thomas Lamb  302:40
    304:2
Elk City, ID  23:2  102:20
    103:4  105:2  118:6  192:7
    223:1  256:6
Elk City, MT  133:4  247:4
Elkhorn, MT  46:2  214:2
    224:7  319:6
Elkhorn, OR  97:1
Elkins, Luther  51:28
Elkton, OR  230:10
Ellamar, AK  63:1  146:4
Ellensburg, OR  86:8  258:4
Ellensburg, WA  17:5  36:1
    38:7  121:4  198:1  220:4
    222:10  231:7  293:7
    305:4  317:3
Elling, Henry  319:3
Ellingsworth, William  199:3
Elliot, Edward Charles
    299:15
Elliot, Henry Wood  149:6
    161:4
Elliot, Jacob S.  37:2
Elliott, Andrew Charles
    138:4  238:3  253:3
Elliott, Elijah  56:5
Elliott, Henry S.  266:2
Elliott, Howard  279:3
Elliott, John S.  150:1
Elliott, John T.  127:5
Elliott, Marion L. "Mike"
    49:2
Elliott, Otis J.  264:1
Elliott, P. C.  203:1
Elliott, William  150:2
Ellis (Chief)  4:3

Ellis, Arthur B.  191:9
Ellis, James  276:11
Ellis, John F.  275:5
Ellis, Robert E.  130:2
Ellis, Thomas  5:8
Ellison, David  266:3
Ellison, Price  5:2  253:3
Ellisport, ID  39:2
Ellisport, WA  305:1
Ellsworth, Harris  49:5
Ellsworth, Stukely  150:1
Elma, WA  14:1  305:2
Elmer City, WA  267:1
Elsensohn, Alfreda  102:16
Elsensohn, Lewis  102:9
Elsie, OR  152:1
Elsner, Robert  161:1
Elstereit, August  266:1
Elston, John B.  203:1
Eltopia, WA  305:1
Elwahco (Chief)  272:6
Elwha, WA  273:8
Elwyn, Thomas  138:3
Ely, Arline  278:1
Ely, Philologus  150:1
Emerick, Solomon  150:2
Emerson, George Harvey
    150:1  266:3
Emerson, J. S.  294:2
Emery, Bradley  88:3
Emery, MT  78:2
Emmett, ID  17:2  23:8
    24:2  118:3  164:1
Emmitt, Kearney  230:3
Empire City, OR  9:4  30:2
    104:6  225:2  249:1
    258:19
Endicott, WA  119:3  280:1
Enger, Norval  172:3
Engle, Abraham Woolman
    266:2
Engle, Helen  278:1
Englestadt, Edwin  281:3
English, Dave  102:6
Enneking, Frank  103:4
Ennis, Christopher  199:2
Ennis, William H.  161:2

ENNIS                        66

Ennis, MT  319:3
Enterprise, OR  12:3  82:2
  300:4
Entiat, WA  157:13
Entrup, William  102:6
Enumclaw, WA  89:1  152:1
  305:2
Eola, OR  68:7  172:1
  SEE ALSO Cincinnati
Ephrata, WA  36:4  41:2
  151:2  172:13  198:1
  252:4  293:120  305:1
Epley, H. C.  2:4
Epley, WA  267:1
Epstein, Jesse  276:8
Equality, WA  57:2  152:4
  191:75  315:5
Era, ID  223:1
Erb, Donald Milton  232:6
Erholm, Charles  266:2
Ericksen, Gerh.  266:1
Erickson, August  41:1
  151:2  152:5  195:3
Erickson, John E.  156:1
  214:7  215:6
Erickson, K. O.  100:4
Ermatinger, Francis  39:6
  45:8  101:2  118:1  177:4
Erwin, Samuel H.  119:3
Eshelman, James F.  266:2
Esler, Anton M.  106:7
  107:6  212:19
Esmeralda, ID  23:3  223:1
Espy, R. H.  202:7  203:1
Esquimalt, BC  3:20  20:5
  120:50  126:6  165:14
  238:6  253:12
Estacada, OR  75:7  228:7
Ester, AK  281:2
Estes, George  152:8
Estes, Hugh P.  199:2
Estes, William B.  157:2
Eureka, MT  319:5
Eureka, OR  12:9
Evans, Andrew J.  199:1
Evans, Brock  12:15
Evans, Daniel J.  178:4

  245:10  265:6
Evans, Elwood  58:16
  141:3  245:17
Evans, Emmett  199:1
Evans, John  97:9  266:2
Evans, John M.  181:6
Evans, John Stark  232:2
Evans, Lewis Orvis  216:6
Evans, Mark A.  199:2
Evans, Milton  119:1  199:2
Evans, Morgan  155:4
Evans, Robley D.  161:4
Evaro, MT  112:3
Evenson, Ole J.  9:7
Everest, Wesley  32:4
  176:1  252:5
Everett, Amasa  314:7
Everett, Frank  266:2
Everett, John  100:5
Everett, WA  7:2  14:1
  16:6  32:8  41:8  57:267
  58:6  121:3  178:8  180:7
  191:6  195:5  234:2
  243:1  246:15  252:8
  265:11  276:9  293:6
  305:17
Everson, Ever  266:1
Everson, William G.  303:5
Evolution, ID  212:3

Fabrique, William Alexander
  230:3
Fackler, St. Michael  33:6
  150:2
Failing, Henry  119:2
  163:1  174:4  197:3
  210:7  285:10  297:41
  303:7
Failing, Josiah  150:2
  210:5  297:6
Fairfax, WA  305:1
Fairfield, ID  23:7
Fairfield, OR  68:7
Fairfield, WA  203:2
Fairhaven, WA  203:3

Fairview, BC  47:1
Fairview, ID  223:1
Fairweather, H. W.  150:1
Fairweather, William  25:12
133:6  319:6
Fairweather, William A.
266:2
Falcon, ID  98:6
Falconer, J. A.  245:4
Fales, Wesley  103:7
Falkenberg, Kristian  88:4
Fallon, Jake  156:5
Faloma, OR  152:1
Fanjoy, Joseph  80:4
306:4
Fanning, Katherine  136:4
Farewell, AK  263:3
Fargo, S. B.  119:4
Farley, Rod  175:21
Farlin, William L.  155:3
319:3
Farlin, MT  78:2  319:1
Farmington, WA  119:3
296:2
Farnham, Thomas J.  4:6
153:1  162:5  198:1
Farquharson, Mary Nichols
278:1
Farrar, William H.  51:100
119:2  145:5  179:5
Farrell, J. D.  234:2
Farrell, Thomas J.  26:3
Farrell, ID  23:2
Farron, BC  152:1
Farrow, E. S.  11:5
Farwell, George H.  157:2
Fassett, Charles M.  96:2
Fastabend, John A.  9:3
Faubert, Henry  266:2
Faucette, John  199:1
Faulkner, Herbert L.  130:1
241:1
Faulkner, L. B.  245:10
Fauquier, BC  316:6
Faussett, Robert J.  57:12
Faust, Leo H.  173:12
Favor, A. J.  119:2  280:4

Fay, James D.  163:2
Fay, John Edward  268:4
Fazzio, Tony  287:2
Featherstone, Henry  138:2
Featherville, ID  223:1
Fee, James A.  207:4
Fee, James H.  150:1
Fee, Mary  91:3
Fehl, Earl  302:3
Fejes, Claire  66:2
Fejes, Joe  66:5
Felida, WA  89:1
Felker, Leonard  234:4
Fell, James  238:7
Fell, Theron E.  150:2
Fellman, B. F.  303:5
Fenn, Frank A.  102:15
103:15
Fenn, S. S.  87:3  102:5
103:3
Ferdinand, ID  23:5  102:7
Fergus, James  1:1  48:7
133:9  156:2  214:3
247:4  286:2  292:5
319:3
Ferguson, Archie  137:1
263:29
Ferguson, Clark  150:1
Ferguson, David  266:4
Ferguson, Emory C.  57:5
58:10  150:1  266:4
Ferguson, Fidella  295:21
Ferguson, J. Edward  116:3
Ferguson, James W.  157:2
Ferguson, John R.  150:1
Ferguson, Walter S.  199:2
Ferndale, WA  14:1  41:4
203:2
Fernie, BC  204:2  253:6
Ferrel, Brewster  199:2
Ferrel, Joseph W.  199:2
Ferrel, O. R. "Ren"  279:4
Ferrel, Seth A.  199:1
Ferrel, Thomas J.  199:1
Ferrell, William "Dick"
99:5  118:2
Ferrell, ID  99:6

Ferris, Joel E.  96:3
Ferriss, Alvin T.   150:1
Ferry, Clinton Peyre
    150:2  266:6
Ferry, Elisha P.   29:5
    38:2  119:4  150:1  163:7
    176:2  222:12  243:10
    245:16
Ferson, E. E.   279:4
Feusi, Balthassar  34:3
Fickel, John  161:2
Fidalgo, WA  252:1  314:6
    315:3
Field, James  56:40  318:34
Field, M. E.   116:2
Fierens, J. T.   249:2
Fiester, Henry  202:3
Fife, William H.   150:2
Filer, ID  23:6  164:1
Finch, D. B.   246:4
Finch, John Aylard  95:2
    106:20  203:1  212:11
Finck, Conrad  152:1
Finck, Henry Theophilus
    50:4  144:7
Findlay, James  275:7
Fine, Joe  114:3
Finlay, Jacques Raphael
    27:9  39:19  192:2
Finlayson, Duncan  131:4
Finlayson, Roderick  3:11
    20:45  126:5  140:8
    253:7
Finlen, Miles  209:7
Finn, MT  319:3
Finney, Frank  99:1
Finucane, Francis J.   106:5
Fir, WA  315:5
Firth, ID  23:2
Fischer, Victor  241:9
Fisher, Alexander  235:7
Fisher, Charles  232:1
Fisher, Charles H.   38:1
    300:7
Fisher, Ezra T. T.   179:2
    303:20
Fisher, George C.   266:1

Fisher, Joseph  99:3
Fisher, Nile  274:6
Fisher, William F.   95:4
Fishtown, WA  315:2
Fisk, James L.   319:6
Fisk, Robert E.   247:5
    286:25
Fisk, Thomas P.   200:10
    266:3
Fiske, Eugene Rufus  187:12
    230:3
Fitch, George A.   39:5
Fitzgerald, C. B.   113:3
Fitzgerald, Joseph  54:6
Fitzgerald, Maurice  110:3
Fitzhugh, Edmund C.   222:3
Fitzpatrick, Louis J.   2:6
Five Crows (Chief)  4:3
    198:4
Fix, Andrew J.   119:2
    199:2
Fixott, Henry Cline  2:17
Flagg, E. H.   300:5
Flamm, Charles  59:1  95:1
Flamm, Henry  59:4
Flanagan, Patrick  258:7
Flanders, Alvin  119:8
    245:3
Flanders, George H.   210:4
Flat, AK  63:1  137:4
Flathead Post, MT  188:6
Flavel, George  295:13
Flavel, OR  75:2  82:3
Flavelle, Aird  294:2
Flegel, Austin F.   49:6
Fleming, A. G. "Arch"
    279:25
Fleming, John  196:2
Flemming, Thomas Chalmers
    266:3
Fletcher, Arthur  178:1
    252:1  265:1
Fletcher, Francis  150:2
Fletcher, Hooney  175:15
Flett, John  150:3
Flewelling, Albert Laurance
    288:2

Flint, ID  223:1
Flohr, Michael  199:1
Florence, ID  23:4  36:2
  43:1  76:8  87:5  102:32
  105:2  118:9  119:2  147:1
  164:2  192:5  223:5  251:4
  259:5
Florence, OR  73:6  300:2
Flynn, Elizabeth Gurley
  108:6
Fogg, James E.  59:5
Fohl, Theodore  152:1
Fohn-Hansen, Lydia  148:3
Folchi, Aloysius  34:6
Foley, Thomas S.  265:3
Follansbee, F. E.  245:4
Foote, A. D.  259:3
Forbes, Charles  25:2
Forbes, John B.  266:1
Forbes, Peter Dewar  150:2
Ford, David  150:1
Ford, James A.  96:6  293:26
Ford, Luther M.  100:2
Ford, Otis  264:1
Ford, Sam C.  156:1  214:8
  215:7  247:8
Ford, Sidney S.  141:3
Ford, WA  41:1
Forest, OR  42:1
Forest City, MT  78:4  319:3
Forest Grove, OR  41:1  75:7
  187:6  195:10  201:3  273:4
  296:2
Forest Queen, OR  308:2
Forks, WA  100:7  152:2
  305:1
Forney, James H.  102:1
  117:5
Forrest, Robert W.  203:1
Forrester, J. W. "Bud"
  207:16
Forrester, Michael A.  207:4
Forsmann, J. B.  102:8
Forster, George M.  288:2
Forsyth, John  274:8
Forsyth, MT  60:3
Fort Adamas, AK  311:1
Fort Alexander, AK  77:4

161:2
Fort Alexandria, BC  3:10
  253:7  SEE ALSO Alex-
  andria
Fort Assinniboine, MT  48:8
  139:2  247:7
Fort Astoria, OR  177:2
  272:7  SEE ALSO Astoria
  and Fort George
Fort Babine, BC  20:2
  186:2  SEE ALSO Babine
Fort Belknap, MT  48:13
  61:23
Fort Bellingham, WA  139:1
  305:1
Fort Benton, MT  1:6  25:14
  39:4  48:40  61:9  76:22
  112:7  133:85  139:7  141:6
  155:8  156:9  181:7  183:5
  214:6  215:24  247:22
  283:12  298:3  319:37
  SEE ALSO Benton
Fort Bidwell, OR  114:1
Fort Boise, ID  4:9  33:21
  43:1  45:9  56:15  84:1
  87:6  101:3  132:4  139:2
  177:9  198:2  211:9
  318:8
Fort C. F. Smith, MT  48:8
  133:10  139:2  183:3
  247:4
Fort Camosun, BC  20:22
  165:3
Fort Campbell, MT  48:5
Fort Canby, WA  202:14
  272:5  305:1
Fort Casey, WA  203:1
  220:2  305:1
Fort Cass, MT  48:4
Fort Chardon, MT  48:4
Fort Chilcotin, BC  47:1
Fort Clatsop, OR  41:1
  121:3  132:1  153:1
  198:3  215:5  272:7
  302:6
Fort Columbia, WA  109:3
  272:6  305:1
Fort Colville, WA  3:4  4:4

FORT CONNAH

27:15   48:6   101:2   108:8
133:8   155:4   177:4   192:4
198:3   203:1   252:3   253:6
257:4   305:5   317:7   SEE
ALSO Colville
Fort Connah, MT   48:6
214:3   215:5
Fort Constantine, YT   255:10
Fort Cudahy, AK   255:6
311:1
Fort Custer, MT   48:8   139:2
214:3   247:4
Fort Dalles, OR   42:9   139:3
153:1   179:2
Fort Davis, AK   130:2
Fort Egbert, AK   125:5
130:3   311:1
Fort Ellis, MT   26:4   46:5
48:19   133:16   139:3   183:4
214:4   247:6
Fort Fizzle, MT   26:8
Fort Flagler, WA   220:2
Fort Frances, YT   255:5
Fort George, BC   40:4   SEE
ALSO George and Prince
George
Fort George, OR   4:2   6:3
84:1   132:3   177:4   187:7
198:3   202:5   221:4   272:22
302:1   317:8   SEE ALSO
Astoria and Fort Astoria
Fort George Wright, WA
96:4   108:4   305:2
Fort Get There, AK   166:1
SEE ALSO Fort St. Michaels
Fort Gibbon, AK   125:5
130:2
Fort Gilliam, OR   84:1
Fort Grahame, BC   40:13
Fort Halkett, YT   255:2
Fort Hall, ID   4:17   43:7
45:466   48:4   56:5   87:9
93:6   95:9   101:4   118:20
132:2   133:13   134:5   164:7
177:12   198:3   211:50
257:3   259:11   264:4   317:9
318:25

Fort Harney, OR   110:8
134:3   139:2
Fort Harrison, MT   183:8
Fort Henrietta, OR   179:13
Fort Henry, ID   164:2
Fort Herchmer, YT   255:9
Fort Hope, BC   253:6   SEE
ALSO Hope, BC
Fort Hoskins, OR   30:19
SEE ALSO Hoskins (Fort)
Fort Kamloops, BC   20:22
253:7   317:4   SEE ALSO
Kamloops
Fort Kenai, AK   130:1
Fort Keogh, MT   26:4
48:9   139:4   172:2   214:5
Fort Klamath, OR   42:3
Fort Lafayette, OR   30:3
SEE ALSO Lafayette
Fort Lander, WA   SEE
Lander (Fort)
Fort Lane, OR   139:2
Fort Langley, BC   3:16
20:3   47:2   120:2   123:6
131:7   253:16   260:7
272:2   283:3   317:7   SEE
ALSO Derby, BC
Fort Lapwai, ID   139:4   SEE
ALSO Lapwai (Fort)
Fort Lawton, WA   305:2
Fort Lemhi, ID   43:3   76:4
105:9   132:1   211:13
259:4
Fort Lewis, MT   48:6
183:4
Fort Lewis, WA   41:2
305:3
Fort Liscum, AK   130:3
Fort Logan, MT   48:10
139:3
Fort McKenzie, MT   48:7
Fort McLeod, BC   40:8
317:6   SEE ALSO McLeod,
BC
Fort McLoughlin, BC   20:3
131:8
Fort McPherson, YT   255:5

Fort Maginnis, MT   48:6
  139:2   156:3   247:5
  319:5
Fort Manuel Lisa, MT   48:3
  215:7
Fort Misery, ID   102:3
Fort Missoula, MT   48:8
  181:18
Fort Nez Perce, WA   6:3
  132:2   172:3   198:1   305:1
  SEE ALSO Fort Walla
  Walla
Fort Nisqually, WA   7:12
  32:4   73:4   120:3   131:9
  203:2   222:9   260:3
  272:2   305:6   SEE ALSO
  Nisqually, WA
Fort Okanogan, WA   6:1
  16:3   198:3   253:8   272:2
  305:3   317:5
Fort Owen, MT   48:8   76:5
  112:4   133:22   155:13
  181:8   198:1   211:3
  247:7   256:3   283:3
Fort Peck, MT   214:3
Fort Piegan, MT   48:4
Fort Reliance, YT   63:1
  159:6   255:7   309:8
Fort Richardson, AK   130:3
  159:3   281:2
Fort Rock, OR   42:4
Fort Rodd Hill, BC   47:1
Fort Rupert, BC   3:12   10:2
  20:4   131:5   165:9
Fort St. James, BC   3:4
  20:2   40:8   123:7   253:5
  317:6   SEE ALSO St.
  James, BC
Fort St. John, BC   40:49
  123:3   159:6
Fort St. Michael, AK   81:12
  130:1   311:1   SEE ALSO
  St. Michael, AK
Fort Sarpy, MT   48:6
Fort Selkirk, BC   77:10
  81:3   159:4   255:14
  281:4   309:6   311:2

Fort Seward, AK   130:4
  SEE ALSO Chilkoot Bar-
  racks
Fort Shaw, MT   48:20
  133:11   139:3   214:3
Fort Sheppard, BC   3:3
  107:2
Fort Sherman, ID   27:8
  96:2   99:5   108:2   118:1
  139:2   192:3   212:6
Fort Simcoe, WA   139:5
  198:1   203:2   305:2
Fort Simpson, BC   3:14
  10:4   77:5   131:9   140:4
  159:4   189:8   255:9
  281:2   317:3   SEE ALSO
  Port Simpson
Fort Spokane, WA   16:3
  27:15   96:3   108:5   132:2
  139:2   272:3   305:6
Fort Stager, BC   161:1
Fort Starvation, WA   202:2
Fort Steele, BC   47:1
Fort Steilacoom, WA   58:5
  92:3   139:2   172:3   179:1
  203:2   305:6
Fort Stevens, OR   151:3
  272:4
Fort Stikine, BC   22:10
  140:2   159:4
Fort Tako, BC   20:5   131:5
Fort Taylor, WA   27:5
Fort Umpqua, OR   30:4
Fort Union, MT   48:30
  141:5   214:5   215:9
  247:10
Fort Vancouver, WA   4:27
  5:5   16:24   22:15   84:5
  93:25   101:8   118:9
  120:11   132:3   139:3
  162:13   172:26   177:57
  179:3   187:20   198:13
  202:4   208:5   221:4
  229:16   252:12   253:9
  260:7   272:20   284:4
  287:9   296:6   297:20
  302:3   305:9   317:20

Fort Victoria, BC  20:13
  120:9  123:7  131:5
  165:12  221:1  253:11
  260:9  284:1
Fort Walla Walla, WA  4:19
  16:6  17:10  27:23  45:8
  58:5  96:2  101:10  118:12
  133:15  139:4  177:53  179:5
  198:9  222:7  229:7  252:4
  257:4  296:16  305:4  317:9
Fort Ward, WA  220:2  305:2
Fort Ware, BC  40:9
Fort William, OR  22:15
  45:5  84:2  198:1  284:2
  287:10  SEE ALSO William
  (Fort)
Fort Worden, WA  220:2
  305:1
Fort Wrangell, AK  143:4
  146:8
Fort Yale, BC  20:6  172:2
  253:10  SEE ALSO Yale,
  BC
Fort Yamhill, OR  30:12
  139:1
Fort Yukon, AK  77:15
  130:2  137:1  159:11
  161:2  168:4  190:10
  255:12  271:3  281:4
  290:2  309:9  311:7
Fortes, Joe  236:4
Fortuna Ledge, AK  63:1
  SEE ALSO Marshall, AK
Forty Mile, YT  63:1  81:7
  159:6  160:2  161:1  255:15
  309:25  311:3
Foss, Louis  266:4
Fossil, OR  42:2
Foster, Addison, G.  106:5
Foster, Barney  176:2
Foster, Edward Walker
  266:3
Foster, Frank  199:2
Foster, George H.  275:7
Foster, John H.  199:2
Foster, Joseph L.  150:1
  306:4

Foster, Michael  152:1
Foster, William Trufant
  152:1  184:12
Foster Station, OR  119:2
Four Lakes, WA  27:3
  108:2  305:1
Fourtner, Samuel  266:2
Fowler, Charles E.  163:2
Fowler, Charles R.  266:2
Fowler, Enoch S.  150:2
Fowler, George W.  266:2
Fowler, J. B.  191:5
Fowler, W. G.  266:1
Fox, Amos T.  124:10
  203:1
Fox, Jay  41:1  58:1  152:2
  191:25
Fox, William  40:5
Fox, AK  281:1  309:3
Fozzard, Jim  130:1
Fralick, J. G.  23:6
Frame, John W.  57:13
France, George W.  261:1
  266:2
France, W. H.  195:2
France, Will  217:2
Frances, WA  225:2
Franchere, Gabriel  198:4
  272:7  291:3
Francis, Karl  115:5
Francis, Simeon  30:2
Francis, T. P.  266:2
Frank, Alberta  152:4
Frank, Emil  157:2
Frank, Irving  274:20
Franklin, George J.  203:1
Franklin, Howard  255:5
Franklin, John  161:5
Franklin, ID  11:1  23:2
  43:1  87:6  95:1  118:7
  132:1  164:2  259:4
  304:2
Franklin, WA  163:1
Frary, Thomas Corwin
  119:3  266:3  280:3
Frase, C. W.  74:2
Fraser, Angus  294:1

Fraser, Donald 3:9 126:4
Fraser, E. P. 187:6
Fraser, H. W. 238:5
Fraser, Paul 3:2 20:70
  40:4 235:10
Fraser, Simon 22:75 40:5
  235:15 253:6 260:5
  272:2
Frasier, Clark 94:6
Fratt, Charles D. 266:4
Frazer (Judge) 212:6
Frazer, Jacob 150:1 207:7
Frazier, Frank 207:4
Fredenburg, Charles H.
  303:9
Fredericks, John "Slim"
  173:6
Fredonia, WA 315:2
Freeding, Conrad 130:1
Freedom, ID 223:1
Freehafter, A. L. 219:3
Freeland, WA 191:25
  152:1 305:1
Freeman, Miller 176:2
  178:3
Freeman, Otis W. 94:5
Freeman, Yancy 279:4
Freer, Frank 203:1
Freewater, OR 114:3
  300:2 SEE ALSO Milton-
  Freewater
Freiday, Jacob A. 266:3
Fremont, OR 42:1
French, Burton L. 213:4
  219:7
French, Permeal Jane
  117:11
French, Peter 41:1 42:3
  110:167 114:15 134:12
  152:7 172:18 188:3
  250:4
Frenchglen, OR 110:2
Frenchtown, MT 34:2 48:2
  112:173 181:13 254:3
  319:5
Frenchtown, WA 198:1
Fretag, Louis E. 264:1

Frey, J. J. 161:1
Friday Harbor, WA 89:1
  305:1
Friendly, S. H. 232:12
Frisbee, Don C. 82:7
Fritz, Jacob 179:2
Frizzell, George 185:4
Frost, John H. 272:8
Frost, Joseph H. 44:8
  93:7 97:4 302:3
Frost, Robert 266:3
Fruitland, ID 23:4
Fruitland, WA 305:1
Frye, Charles 176:1
Frye, George F. 246:1 306:7
Fryxell, Roald 252:1
Fuchs, Matt 102:3
Fugitt, Cecil 175:16
Fuller, Ethel Romig 152:1
Fuller, Frank 311:1
Fuller, George W. 27:14
  243:1
Fuller, Hiram G. 219:2
Fuller, John H. 199:1
Fuller, Otis Byron 157:3
Fuller, Richard E. 176:1
  178:2 276:4
Fuller, Steward 106:3
Fullerton, Mark A. 266:2
Fultz, Hollis B. 245:5
Fulwiler, James 157:3
Funk, George H. 245:5
  266:2
Funkhouser, Frank 83:9
  293:7
Fuqua, Jordan 37:1
Furguson, James F. 264:1
Furness, John 266:2
Furnish, W. J. 207:7
Furth, Fred 150:2
Furth, Jacob 217:2 243:8
  266:3 276:5
Fyfer, Julius T. 150:1


Gabel, Joseph A. 266:2

Gagnier, John Baptiste 30:3
Gaines, John Pollard 145:13
   153:1 172:2 179:2 284:3
Gairdner, Meredith 187:17
Gaisford, George 275:5
Gakona, AK 311:1
Galata, MT 312:1
Gale, James Newton 300:5
Gale, John P. 266:5
Gale, Joseph 84:12 119:5
   188:2 198:3
Galen, Hugh 46:3
Galen, MT 46:2
Galena, AK 63:1
Galena, ID 223:1
Galena, OR 225:2 308:4
Galena, WA 225:2
Gallagher, Jack 25:5 133:7
   256:5 280:3
Gallagher, Peter 211:11
Gallagher, Sterling 136:8
Gallant, G. Edgar 130:1
Gallatin, MT 46:4 48:3
   78:3 292:7
Gambell, AK 8:6 52:1
   115:5 161:1 271:4
Gamwell, Roland Greene
   203:1
Ganahl, Frank 212:5
Gandy, Joseph Edward
   288:4
Gandy, Joseph P. 178:4
Gandy, Lloyd 27:2
Gannon, George H. 184:16
Garden, J. F. 236:2
Garden City, ID 23:1
Gardey, Jon 115:100
Gardiner, MT 319:4
Gardiner, OR 9:11 73:4
   229:3
Gardner, Johnson 221:6
Garfield, WA 119:1 305:1
Garfielde, Selucius 87:3
   119:8 176:1 243:1
   245:9 306:4
Garland, Jasper 157:2
Garneill, MT 156:2 319:2

Garner, Fay 274:6
Garner, John Earl 59:3
Garnet, MT 78:3 224:6
   319:4
Garnett, Frank 122:3
Garnett, Robert Seldon
   203:2
Garr, H. H. 133:4
Garrand, Victor 34:6
Garretson, Hiram F. 266:3
Garrett, Coydon "Nifty"
   245:4
Garrett, Frank D. 289:2
Garrison, Pliney 318:9
Garrison, MT 319:4
Garrison City, WA 152:2
Garry, Spokane 4:1 11:1
   16:4 27:22 93:7 108:30
   132:1 155:3 252:24
Garton, Art 293:4
Gary, George 93:4 153:1
   193:14 208:3 302:2
Gasser, George W. 148:11
Gaston, John 199:2
Gaston, Joseph 150:2
   188:4 197:27
Gastown (Vancouver), BC
   158:7 236:21
Gatch, Thomas M. 38:11
   153:1
Gates, Jasper 314:5
Gates, John 150:1
Gates, William 311:1
Gatzert, Bailey 234:2
   243:5
Gauglersville, MT 78:2
Gault, Franklin Benjamin
   117:27 124:9
Gavin, Michael J. 71:5
Gay, George Kirby 68:3
   84:5 150:2
Gearhart, OR 261:1
Geary, Edward Payson
   187:9
Geary, Edward R. 91:12
   176:1 194:4
Geddis, S. R. 150:1

Gee Hee 276:4
Geer, Herman J. 150:2
Geer, Theodore T. 86:2
153:1
Gehr, W. S. 157:2
Geiger, John 173:9
Geiger, William 4:3 177:6
187:6 296:5
Geiser, Albert 264:3
Geiser, OR 264:3
Geist, Otto W. 52:3 129:2
290:1
Gellatly, John A. 157:1
245:5 293:3
Gem, ID 127:4 212:5
Genesse, ID 23:10 24:7
118:3
Genevay, Lucien 199:1
George, Hugh N. 150:1
George, J. B. 279:10
George, Presley 150:1
George, Wyatt A. 119:7
George (Fort), BC 235:3
SEE ALSO Fort George
Georgeson, Charles Christian 226:5
Georgetown, MT 319:5
Georgetown, WA 234:2
Gerald, Clarence 234:5
Gerber, Joseph 114:3
Gerber, Mary 114:3
Gerding, Ben 102:4
Gerlinger, George T. 288:2
Gerlinger, OR 75:3
German, Mildred R. 278:1
German Gulch, MT 319:3
Gervais, Joseph 93:4 119:2
162:17 193:3 198:1
Gething, Neil 40:5
Getz, P. A. 38:1 231:11
Gholson, Charles E. 199:2
Gholson, Richard D. 141:3
234:1 245:4
Giaudrone, Angelo 279:3
Gibbon, John 36:3
Gibbonsville, ID 223:1
Gibbs, A. L. 200:6

Gibbs, Addison Crandall
147:4 153:2 197:3
Gibbs, George 179:1
Gibbs, Isaac L. 87:2
Gibbs, Mifflin Wistar 260:4
Gibbs, Sabin A. 266:2
Gibson, J. Gordon 122:9
Gibson, Paris 214:8 218:7
Gibson Jack (Chief) 211:10
Gibson's Landing, BC 204:4
275:6
Giesy, Andrew Jackson
187:6
Giesy, Christian 144:5
203:1
Giesy, John 144:5
Gifford, ID 23:3
Gifford, WA 305:1
Gig Harbor, WA 14:1
191:4 246:4 305:2
Gilbert, Elon 88:16
Gilbert, Helen S. 169:9
Gilbert, Horace M. 203:1
Gilbert, James H. 232:3
Gilbranson, J. N. 150:1
Gilchrist, Charles 203:1
Gilchrist, Colin 157:3
Gilchrist, OR 42:1
Gilday, Robert 266:2
Giles, Milton 245:4
Giles, Theodore 266:1
Gilfrey, John T. 232:4
Gilkerson, Charles 199:1
Gilkerson, Harry 199:1
Gilkerson, Thomas 199:2
Gill, Abe 61:15
Gill, Hiram C. 16:2 41:2
57:2 176:3 178:4
234:15 243:2 245:6
261:1 276:5 304:2
Gill, Roy R. 96:1 293:54
Gillam, Harold 263:33
Gilles, George 175:14
Gillespie, Jacob 232:3
Gillespie, James R. 266:2
Gillette, Ben 52:14
Gillette, Theodore W. 266:3

Gillham, Alonzo 199:2
Gilliam, Cornelius 119:4
  150:9 177:3 296:7
Gilliam, Washington Smith
  119:3 199:2
Gillihan, Martin 287:2
Gilliland, Isaac 177:4
Gillis, W. D. 213:3
Gilman, Daniel Hunt 178:5
  243:41 276:4
Gilman, James M. 150:1
Gilman, Samuel D. 127:6
Gilman, WA 163:2 243:2
  SEE ALSO Issaquah
Gilmore, William A.
  130:1
Gilmore, AK 281:2
Gilmore, ID 23:1 223:2
Gilpin, Jack F. 240:2
Gilstrap, William H. 222:3
  266:4
Gilt Edge, MT 78:4 156:2
  224:2 319:7
Gingrich, Christian O.
  266:2
Ginn, Richard 199:2
Giorda, Joseph 34:11
  254:8
Girard, Franklin 213:4
Givler, William 41:1
Glacier, BC 198:1
Gladstone, OR 228:3
Glasford, William 199:1
Glasgow, Joseph Mont-
  gomery 266:2
Glasgow, MT 156:4 183:2
  215:4 227:4 247:3
Glass, Henry 90:3
Glassey, H. F. 185:2
Glaude, Napolean 112:6
Gleason, A. B. 150:1
Glen, Robert A. 96:4
Glen, Robert J. 266:2
Glendale, MT 46:4 78:3
  224:4 319:11
Glendinning, Malcolm 96:8
Glendive, MT 1:1 133:6

277:4 247:8 298:3
  312:1
Glennie, Thomas 5:14
Glenn's Ferry, ID 4:1
  11:2 23:11
Glenwood, ID 102:5
Glenwood, WA 242:6
Glidden, Lewellin M. 266:2
Glidden, Stephen S. 107:6
  150:1 212:10
Glisan, Rodney 150:2
  187:14 210:4
Glover, James Nettle 27:26
  39:35 41:1 58:9 91:13
  92:3 96:6 106:6 107:3
  108:24 203:1 288:6
  305:1
Glover, ID 102:2
Goble, OR 75:4
Gochnour, George 279:5
Godsell, Philip H. 40:6
Goetz, Anthony 34:2
Goetz, Harry F. 27:5
  39:1
Goetz, Jacob "Dutch Jake"
  27:2 39:14 41:2 96:4
  108:14 172:3 212:2
  305:1
Goff, ID 102:2
Gohl, William 195:3
Gold Bar, WA 225:2 305:1
Gold Beach, OR 41:2 225:2
  258:9
Gold Butte, MT 78:2 224:1
Gold Coin, MT 319:3
Gold Creek, MT 78:13
  224:2 319:5
Gold Hill, OR 225:2
Gold River, BC 165:11
Golden, Charles 57:3
Golden, John 203:1
Golden, BC 151:6 198:4
  204:3
Golden, ID 102:3 223:1
Golden, OR 225:2 308:8
Golden, WA 267:1
Golden Age Camp, ID 308:4

Goldendale, WA  92:1  203:1
242:10  252:4  305:2
Goldsmith, Bernard  197:3
229:4
Goldsmith, Moses  234:2
Goller, Herman  34:2
Golovin, AK  137:1  161:2
Good, John B.  20:3
Goodall, James P.  150:2
Goodall, Oliver P.  150:1
Goodell, Melancthon Z.
150:2
Goodhue, James P.  199:2
Gooding, Frank R.  23:7
24:4  127:6  170:6  205:7
213:5  219:3
Gooding, ID  23:3  24:2
164:1  180:2
Goodloe, William  245:3
Goodman, William S.
199:2
Goodpasture, James P.
203:1
Goodsell, James  49:3
Goodwin, Frank M.  292:8
293:5
Goodwin, George W.  150:1
Goodwin, Moses E.  207:6
Goose Prairie, WA  88:12
Gordon, David W.  238:5
Gordon, Tom  161:1
Gordon, WA  267:1
Gormley, Matt H.  266:2
Gorton, Slade  245:3
Gose, Jack  176:1
Gose, Mack F.  257:3
280:4
Gosnell, Thomas  189:3
Goss, Albert S.  184:7
293:12
Gossett, Charles  213:4
Gottschalk, Max  161:11
Gouge Eye, OR  41:2  SEE
ALSO Drewsey, OR
Gould, George A.  258:7
Gould City, WA  280:2
Goulder, William A.  56:20

118:1  318:12
Govan, Charles L.  191:8
Gove, Herbert H.  266:3
Gove, Warren  150:2
Gower, George Lewis  203:1
Gowey, J. F.  245:4
Grabinski, Philip  9:2
Grace, ID  23:5
Graham, A. B.  229:3
Graham, Harriet Cowles H.
96:4
Graham, James  288:5
Graham, Orlando  314:4
Graham, ID  223:1
Grand Coulee, WA  41:2
172:14  180:4  244:7
293:11  305:1
Grand Forks, BC  47:3
152:1  204:3
Grand Forks, YT  255:5
311:2
Grandidier, Charles  5:2
Grandview, ID  23:5
Grandview, WA  305:1
Grandy, Benjamin W.  150:1
Grange City, WA  119:4
315:7
Granger, Walter N.  279:7
305:3
Granger, WA  305:1
Grangeville, ID  23:7  26:3
120:30  103:5  106:8
117:4  118:4  164:1
172:2
Granite, MT  60:4  78:6
214:4  224:8  308:6
319:13
Granite, OR  225:2  264:5
308:3
Granite City, ID  223:1
Granite Falls, WA  57:1
305:1
Granite Hill, OR  308:2
Grannis, John  25:5
Grant, James C.  292:7
Grant, John F.  46:3  133:5
155:3  292:22

Grant, John M.  191:4
Grant, Richard  45:12
  155:2  198:1  292:12
Grant, Roland D.  302:1
  303:7
Grant, W. Colquhoun  20:3
Grant, Walter C.  294:2
Grants Pass, OR  41:1  82:3
  152:1  300:6
Grantsville, ID  118:1
  308:2  SEE ALSO Lees-
  burg, ID
Granville, BC  158:8
  238:3
Grassi, Urban  34:13
  254:3
Gravel, Mike  54:2  265:2
Graves, E. O.  243:3
Graves, Franklin Pierrepont
  38:4
Graves, James R.  303:5
Graves, Jay P.  124:7
  203:1
Graves, Morris  41:1
Gray, George C.  150:1
Gray, John Hamilton D.
  238:5  295:12
Gray, Maxine Cushing
  278:1
Gray, Milton Clark  289:3
Gray, William Chandler
  108:13
Gray, William Henry  4:37
  33:4  93:17  101:6  119:25
  150:3  153:1  177:66
  187:15  188:12  194:1
  198:7  257:5  296:12
Grayland, WA  305:1
Grayling, AK  130:1
Grays Harbor, WA  9:8
  32:3  41:5  62:10  73:15
  92:5  100:18  121:6
  152:5  163:2  169:3
  180:7  195:40  252:3
  305:13  317:6
Great Falls, MT  1:2  46:2
  48:7  60:11  61:8  133:20

156:6  180:7  181:3
183:4  214:3  215:30
218:6  247:25  299:8
319:20
Greaves, Joseph Blackburn
  5:2
Greeley, William B.  195:15
Green, Alfred E. A.  189:5
Green, Edith Starrett  49:5
Green, George  266:2
Green, Harry  289:3
Green, John Henry Thomas
  87:7
Green, Jonathan  140:3
Green, Joshua  131:6  217:9
Green, Leon  113:13
Greenaway, A. H.  157:3
Greenaway, WA  267:1
Greenback, OR  308:6
Greenbank, WA  305:1
Greenberg, Henry W.  96:4
Greencreek, ID  102:12
Greene, Alexander  69:10
Greene, Charles Kennedy
  266:2
Greene, Richard A. C.
  252:2
Greene, Roger Sherman
  178:3  234:9  243:6
Greenhorn, OR  225:2
  264:7
Greenough, Thomas L.
  106:2
Greenwood, MT  319:5
Gregson, Virginia  278:1
Gresham, OR  75:3  228:5
Grew, David  305:1
Griffen, Burrell W.  150:2
Griffin, Clarence E.  266:2
Griffin, Fred L.  266:2
Griffin, Henry H.  264:3
Griffin, James W.  87:5
Griffin, John S.  84:4
  177:4
Griffith, Luther H.  266:2
Griffith, Robert M.  199:1
Griffith, S. D.  116:2

Griffiths, Austin E.   234:1
Griffitts, Thomas C.   163:2
  243:5
Griggs, Alexander   116:1
Griggs, Chancey W.   266:5
Griggs, Everett G.   195:5
Griggs, Herbert S.   266:2
Grigsby, George B.   130:3
Grim, Alta M.   169:11
Grimes, George   33:3
  132:1
Grimison, Anna   246:2
Grimm, S. Edwin   266:1
Grinnell, Fred B.   106:4
Grisdale, WA   152:3   195:2
Gross, A. L.   212:4
Gross, Avrum M.   136:10
Gross, Morris   266:2
Gross, William   252:1
Grotto, WA   305:1
Grouleaux, Charles   97:5
Grove, James T.   266:2
Grover, Lafayette   51:100
  87:3   145:15   150:3
  153:1   163:5   194:7
  197:1
Grubb, Stephen G.   94:7
Gruening, Ernest   52:1   54:2
  128:30   129:564   130:16
  136:9   137:1   148:5   157:7
  160:13   190:6   226:14
  241:35   262:20   269:24
  271:19   290:2
Grupe, Mary A.   231:9
  278:1
Guernsey, D. C.   119:7
Guheen, J. J.   95:1
Guichard, Ralph E.   119:11
  199:2
Guilbert, Frank W.   96:4
Guinean, Thomas   150:1
Guleke, Harry   103:14
Gulick, Fred E.   2:5
Gulley, Emmett   152:2
Gunanoot, Simon   186:3
Gunn, Arthur   116:2   157:3
Gunn, Elisha T.   245:4

Gunston, Malcolm E.   266:2
Gunther, Erna   278:1
Guthridge, Benjamin G.   199:2
Guyer, John A.   207:5


Haaga, Agnes   278:1
Haas, Saul   88:6
Hadley, Alonzo M.   266:2
Hadley, E. W.   228:5
Hadley, Hiram E.   266:2
Hadley, Lindley H.   130:3
  266:3
Hadlock, Samuel   150:2
Hadlock, WA   14:1   89:1
Haga, O. O.   53:22
Hagan, Albert   212:3
Hagelin, John L.   281:17
Hagerman, ID   4:1   23:5
  164:1
Hagerty, Cornelius   71:5
Haggart, William   316:5
Haggin, James B.   319:4
Haggist, Fred   199:2
Haggland, Paul   52:2
Haglund, Ivar   41:4
Hague, Isaac N.   266:2
Hagwilget, BC   161:1
Hahtalekin (Chief)   26:3
Haig-Brown, Roderick
  140:6
Hailey, John   29:8   87:9
  95:19   207:4   211:1
Hailey, Thomas G.   207:4
Hailey, ID   23:9   24:2
  118:5   211:2
Hailstone, William   236:5
  260:5
Haines, John Charles
  150:1   243:18   266:3
  276:8
Haines, John M.   43:1
Haines, AK   63:1   130:11
  143:1   148:2   159:4   161:1
  190:3   269:6
Haldane, Benjamin A.   10:5

Hale, Horatio 4:3
Hale, Julius F. 266:4
Halfway, OR 114:3 225:2
Hall, Alfred H. 189:3
Hall, Allan 140:2
Hall, Amos 25:2
Hall, Arnold Bennett 232:6
Hall, Charles H. 187:8
Hall, E. O. 4:4 177:4
Hall, George Washington
264:2 272:3
Hall, Jay H. 199:1
Hall, John H. 38:1
Hall, Laura E. 191:12
Hall, Oliver 288:2
Hall, Reason B. 30:1
68:2
Hall, Sylvester 202:2
Hall, Ves 299:6
Hall, Washington 202:6
Halladay, Henry Woods
191:8
Hallauer, Josephine Pardee
278:1
Haller, G. Morris 243:8
Haller, Granville Owen
118:2 119:4 150:6
179:5 203:1
Haller, Joseph 47:1 138:3
Hallgren, Harley K. 303:7
Halliday, William 140:7
189:7
Halloran, Patrick 150:1
Halsey, OR 187:3
Halterman, Carl 275:7
Hamaker, Gilbert 49:4
Hamber, Eric 294:2
Hamel, Edmond 112:9
Hamersley, A. St. George
275:10
Hamilton, Edward S. 266:4
Hamilton, Gavin 235:5
Hamilton, Hiram 33:5
Hamilton, James 86:10
Hamilton, William T.
181:5
Hamilton, MT 48:3 155:1

299:4 319:4
Hamilton, WA 225:2 305:1
315:11
Hamma Hamma, WA 152:2
Hammer, Emerson 266:2
Hammond, Andrew Benoni
75:4 181:10 215:4
228:5 247:3
Hammond, George 181:3
Hammond, Jay S. 115:2
136:50 160:3
Hammond, John Hays 95:1
192:4
Hampson, W. B. 293:6
Hampton, OR 42:2
Hanan, Archimedes 150:1
179:1
Hanbury, John 294:4
Hance, Tom 47:1
Hanceville, BC 47:1
Hanchett, William H. 30:1
Hancock, Samuel 56:30
305:1 318:16
Hand, James 103:4
Handley, T. B. 37:1
Handsaker, Lester S. 266:1
Haney, Bert E. 49:7
Haney, R. P. 279:4
Hanford, Cornelius H. 31:8
150:2 222:4 234:3
243:16 276:5 306:3
Hanford, Edward 306:5
Hanford, Thaddeus 41:1
Hanford, WA 16:3 41:2
62:3 82:5 151:5 176:2
198:3 293:4
Hankin, Philip James 3:6
Hankin, Thomas 186:3
Hanley, Kennedy J. 106:9
Hanley, William 110:3
134:7
Hanna, John 104:7
Hanna, Mark 60:7
Hannah, Adolphus Brice
150:3 179:1
Hannon, Champ 247:3
Hansell, Stafford 207:3

Hansen, Borghild 309:4
Hansen, Charles T.  288:2
Hansen, George  12:4
  259:3
Hansen, Julia Butler  203:1
  245:9
Hansen, Ole  289:2
Hansen, ID  23:3
Hanson, A. K.  191:5
Hanson, Charles  73:5
Hanson, Clarence  175:9
Hanson, Harold  176:1
Hanson, N. G.  52:2
Hanson, Ole  113:30  176:1
  178:10  234:9  245:5
  261:2  276:6  293:1
  305:2
Hanson, Walter  98:15
Hanson, William Lewis
  265:2
Happy, Cyrus  106:8
  288:3
Harber, W. K.  214:3
Harbert, Joseph W.  199:3
Harbour, Alvin  213:5
Hardin, MT  48:2
Harding, Elisha Jenkins
  179:1
Harding, Roderick R.  266:3
Hardman, David  111:2
Hardman, Solomon  199:2
Hardwick, Francis T.
  124:15
Hardy, Fred  311:3
Harer, John H.  199:2
Harford, John  150:2
Hargreaves, Richard T.
  38:1  94:3
Harkness, H. O.  23:4  95:8
Harkness, J. C.  212:2
Harlem, MT  247:3  319:5
Harlin, Charles A.  157:3
Harlow, M. H.  232:9
Harlow, Richard  46:2
Harlowtown, MT  299:2
  312:1  319:7
Harm, Frank D.  266:2

Harman, Urias S.  199:1
Harmen, Charles T.  199:1
Harmon, D. W.  235:9
Harmon, Ulysses Edgar
  266:2
Harmony, WA  191:4  315:3
Harney, Edward W.  209:7
  298:4
Harney, OR  97:2  134:2
Harnish, J. Lester  303:5
Harper, Al  63:8
Harper, Arthur  255:15
  309:13
Harper, Jerome  47:2
Harper, John Lawrence
  289:2
Harper, Joseph L.  199:2
Harper, Thaddeus  47:2
Harper, OR  56:2
Harpster, ID  102:6
Harrais, Margaret Keenan
  130:1
Harries, Thomas  282:7
Harriman, Edward H.
  161:2
Harrington, Frederick Well-
  ington  266:2
Harrington, J. J.  161:1
  311:1
Harrington, Mark W.  38:4
Harrington, WA  305:1
Harris, Charles A.  116:2
Harris, Charles W.  71:8
Harris, Clyde B.  207:3
Harris, George C.  30:1
Harris, George W.  150:1
  243:2
Harris, James McElroy
  266:2
Harris, John  102:4
Harris, Kenneth  140:4
Harris, Lawrence T.
  232:6
Harris, Mitchell  245:6
  266:2
Harris, Moses  230:4
Harris, Ned (Chief)  189:2

Harris, Richard 143:4
149:4
Harris, Thomas W. 181:5
232:6
Harris, William J. 288:5
Harrisburg, ID 102:4
Harrisburg, OR 68:4
229:8 300:2
Harrison, Carl M. 2:14
Harrison, M. V. 150:1
Harrison, Russell B. 286:7
Harrison, S. J. 279:24
Harrison, William H.
279:8
Harrison, ID 23:4 99:4
164:1 212:3
Harrison, MT 46:2
Harrison Hot Springs, BC
204:3
Harritt, Jesse 56:40
Harry, John Alva 258:2
Harstad, Bjug 266:2
Hart, Charles Calmer
83:5 96:2
Hart, Francis G. 199:1
Hart, John 253:14
Hart, John W. 59:5 170:4
Hart, Louis F. 58:3
184:16 200:3 245:22
Hart, Margaret Janet 123:3
Hart, Thomas D. S. 199:2
Hartley, Edward 57:3
Hartley, Roland H. 38:5
57:41 58:12 92:2
184:27 222:4 231:6
245:31 261:2 293:5
305:1
Hartline, WA 293:6 305:1
Hartman, Charles S. 60:22
133:6
Hartman, George A. 207:6
Hartman, John P. 222:6
Hartman, Sarah McAllister
32:16
Hartman, Washington 266:2
Hartness, Nellie 114:5
Hartness, Orlander W. 199:2

Hartson, Augustus 314:3
Hartson, George E. 150:1
Harvey, Amos 30:9
Harvey, Daniel 194:5
Harvey, Floyd 12:11
Harvey, J. T. 185:5
Harvey, Walter M. 266:2
Haskell, C. T. "Tom"
116:2
Haskell, Ella Knowles
60:14
Haskell, Forbes P. 266:2
Haskill, Edwin N. 266:2
Haskins, Harold 175:8
Haskins, William 212:7
Hasmark, MT 319:4
Hassan, WA 267:1
Hassel, MT 224:1 319:4
Hassell, R. B. 57:6
Hastie, Thomas Peers
266:4
Hastings, Henry W. 199:1
Hastings, L. B. 150:2
Hastings, Lansford W.
193:9
Hastings, BC 158:3
236:10 238:4
Hatch, George C. 266:1
Hatch, WA 267:1
Hatfield, Mark O. 12:7
49:3 261:3
Hathaway, John S. 203:2
Hathaway, M. R. 150:2
Hattrup, Hubert 102:3
Hauber, Martin H. 199:2
Hauerbach, Otto A. 157:6
Haugen Junction, MT 98:6
Hauser, Samuel T. 48:7
60:8 76:7 107:7 133:20
155:2 156:3 192:2
214:13 215:8 218:2
247:8 283:4 286:30
298:5
Hauswirth, Charles A.
156:1 167:2
Hautier, Alphonse 138:3
Hautier, Louis 138:3

Hauxhurst, Webley J.    37:6
   84:7   162:11   193:2
Havermale, Samuel G.
   27:6   39:2   91:2   108:3
   150:1   288:3   305:1
Havillah, WA   225:1   267:1
   308:3
Havre, MT   1:3   34:2   48:2
   156:5   214:2   215:5
   247:4   299:3   312:1
   319:4
Hawkins, Harry A.   266:1
Hawks, Archie McLean
   266:3
Hawley, James H.   23:6
   43:2   95:15   118:3
   127:25   170:7   205:12
   219:3   259:4
Hawley, Willis C.   162:3
   261:2
Hawthorne, B. J.   232:2
Hay, Ing   264:2
Hay, Marion E.   96:4
   203:1   245:16   293:3
Haycox, Ernest   152:2
Hayden, Benjamin   179:1
Hayden, Gay   150:3
Hayden, Obadiah B.   266:2
Hayden, William   157:2
Haydon, Walton   258:5
Hayes, Ernest   71:6
Haylmore, Maude   138:5
Hayne, Murray   255:10
Haynes, Hank   176:2
Haynes, John Carmichael
   5:9
Haynes, Myron W.   174:8
Haynes, Oscar   199:2
Hays, Gilmore   87:3
Hays, William H.   199:2
Hayton, Thomas   266:2
Hayward, C.   126:4
Hayward, William L.   232:2
Hazeltine, George I.   264:3
Hazelton, BC   10:1   63:1
   123:7   186:17   SEE ALSO
   New Hazelton

Hazelton, ID   23:4   24:2
Hazen, Oliver M.   282:6
Hazlitt, Henry   102:6
Hazlitt, Lewis Mackey
   296:5
Headlee, Thomas E.   57:1
Headquarters, ID   164:1
Healy, John Jerome   161:7
   255:7   309:3
Healy, AK   63:1
Heard, Walter A.   303:7
Heater, Jacob   212:2
Heath, Thomas   213:2
Hebberd, Charles   293:23
Hebeler, Amanda   231:8
   278:1
Heberden, William Henry
   266:1
Hebo, OR   37:1
Heckes, John   202:1
Heckman, Hazel   278:1
Heckman, J. R.   130:5
Hecla, MT   78:1
Hedden, John Nicholson
   230:4
Hedges, Absalom Fonts
   68:6   179:1
Hedges, Cornelius   48:7
   133:14   214:3   247:4
   283:4   286:6
Hedges, Samuel H.   293:4
Hedley, BC   47:2
Heffner, Charles X.   307:5
Heflron, John   279:7
Hegg, Fred A.   266:2
Hegg, O. H.   274:21
Hegg, Peter L.   266:2
Hegness, John   137:2
Heilig, Calvin   104:12
Heilner, Sigismund A.
   150:1
Heim, Joseph G.   266:3
Heinmiller, Carl W.   241:1
Heintzleman, B. Frank
   128:2   129:8   130:2
   148:7   160:1   241:4
   262:3

Heinze, Frederick Augustus
  60:14  67:17  107:18
  151:3  155:9  156:20
  167:12  188:5  209:230
  214:14  215:10  216:23
  247:4  298:10  299:12
  319:7
Heisler, OR  42:2
Heisterman, H.  126:4
Helena, ID  223:1
Helfrich, Prince  114:4
Helix, OR  207:1
Hell Gate, MT  25:3  48:5
  76:8  78:7  112:6  155:8
  181:17  215:7  247:3
  292:9  298:4  319:3
Hellenthal, J. A.  241:2
Hellmuth, Joseph  119:4
Helm, Boone  36:19  256:4
Helm, Herman  102:4
Helmcken, John Sebastian
  3:28  5:3  20:7  123:5
  126:7  238:17  253:30
  260:13  283:4
Helmericks, Harmon  66:3
Hembree, Absalom J.
  119:14  179:9
Hembree, Waman Clark
  179:3
Hemingway's Landing WA
  SEE Ilia, WA
Hemmer, Patrick  226:4
Hemmingsen, Matt  122:4
Hemphill, Wylie  217:3
Hemrich, Andrew  163:4
Henault, Pete  12:13
Henderer, Charles G.  230:2
Hendershott, James  150:1
Hendershott, S. B.  51:7
Henderson, Robert  255:6
  309:5
Hendrick, Archer Wilmot
  257:11
Hendricks, Anton  102:5
Hendricks, August  102:5
Hendricks, Gottfried  102:4
Hendricks, James Madi-

son  232:1
Hendricks, T. G.  232:12
Hendry, John  294:9
Hendryx, H. E.  264:1
Heney, Mike  161:1
Heney, Thomas  212:4
Henny, D. C.  293:11
Henry, Anson Gordon
  87:13
Henry, Francis  245:8
Henry, Horace C.  69:5
  217:2
Henry, J. H.  311:1
Henry, Thomas Newton
  266:3
Henry, William J.  266:2
Henryville, OR  225:2
Hensler, Gus  266:3
Hensley, Willie  54:3
  136:4
Heppner, Henry  111:14
  150:2
Heppner, OR  75:1  82:3
  119:2  150:2  152:9
  187:3  207:6  300:3
  303:4
Herbert, George A.  150:1
Herbert, George F.  150:1
Herbert, ID  59:3
Hermann, Binger  86:5
  258:5
Hermann, Henry  258:8
Hermann, Mildred R.
  241:5
Hermann, Otto  240:4
Hermiston, OR  207:3
Herrall, George  150:2
Herren, John  56:7  318:17
Herrick, Fred  99:4  118:3
Hershfield, Lewis H.  133:6
  286:2
Hertz, Wayne  231:6
Hess, Henry  49:3
Hess, Luther C.  137:3
  226:5
Hesseltine, Charles R.
  289:3

Heston, John W.   38:2
Heurlin, Rusty  130:1
  159:2
Hewitt, Christopher  306:6
Hewitt, Henry  57:15  150:2
  266:5
Hewitt, Ruth E.   169:11
Hewson, Robert  10:4
Heyburn, Weldon Brinton
  95:7  106:28  170:8
  205:9  212:8  219:7
  259:3
Heyburn, ID  23:4
Hibbard, ID  59:3
Hibben, Ethelbert C.
  145:17
Hibbs, Y. N.   95:4
Hickel, Walter J.   54:30
  129:6  130:4
Hickey, Michael  67:4
Hickman, Richard O.   286:3
Hicks, B. N.   245:4
Hicks, Urban East  38:1
  163:3  245:3  300:5
Hickson, WA  315:2
Hidden, Lowell Mason
  203:1
Higday, Hamilton  200:3
Higgins, Christopher Power
  133:8  155:24  181:30
  292:10
Higgins, David  41:1  126:6
Higgins, Frank  181:6
Higgins, W. B. S.   181:5
Higginson, Ella  153:1
  252:1  278:1
High, J. N.   211:7
Highland City, MT   78:2
  319:3
Highley, D. K.   199:2
Hildebrand, William H.
  266:2
Hilger, MT  319:4
Hill, Bradford L.   266:3
Hill, Charles E.   266:3
Hill, Claiborne M.   303:8
Hill, David  84:3  198:1

Hill, E. K.   38:2
Hill, Fleming R.   150:2
Hill, Frank D.   266:1
Hill, George W.   303:5
Hill, J. M.   199:2
Hill, John Lindsay  187:6
Hill, Knute  293:10
Hill, Reuben C.   187:6
  303:5
Hill, Robert C.   150:1
Hill, Sam B.   245:2  248:3
  293:27
Hill, Samuel  151:4  152:2
  203:3  222:4  243:9
  305:1
Hill, Tom (Nez Perce)
  132:1  177:9
Hill, Walter Hovey  102:44
Hill, William J.   87:5
  118:2
Hill, William Lair  150:3
Hilleary, William M.
  147:240
Hillis, William  173:6
  319:3
Hillman, C. D.   245:4
Hillman, John W.   42:2
  97:3
Hillman, OR  42:1
Hillman City, WA  14:1
Hills, George  5:33  126:5
Hills, George E.   185:3
Hillsboro, OR  38:1  75:10
  84:2  172:3  187:3  229:2
  300:2
Hillyard, WA  108:1
Hillyer, Alfred S.   279:9
Hilscher, Frank W.   289:4
Himes, George H.   84:1
  162:5  179:2  300:3
Hinch, Nicholas  231:1
Hinckley, Francis  191:4
Hinckley, Timothy Duane
  266:3
Hindley, W. J.   108:4
Hindley, W. W.   293:2
Hindman, Samuel M. W.   42:2

Hinds, Thomas R.   209:7
Hines, Gustavus  44:25
   50:7   84:5   93:6   119:7
   150:2   162:13   193:8
   198:1   220:3
Hines, Jack  161:1
Hinkle, J. Grant  245:4
Hinman, Alanson  4:2
   150:2   177:3   296:9
Hinman, W. E. "Ed"  157:3
Hinson, Walter B.   303:27
Hippler, Arthur  54:2
Hirsch, Edward  150:3
Hitchcock, Philip S.   49:2
Hitchcock, William  279:9
Hobart, C. W.   222:4
Hobbins, James R.
   216:10
Hobbs, Fern  152:10
Hobson, Dorothy Ann   195:6
Hobson, Eben   54:2
Hobson, J. B.   47:2
Hobson, John  150:2
Hobson, S. S.   133:5
Hobson, Silas  144:20
Hobson, MT  312:1
Hodde, Charles W.   245:10
Hodgis, John H.   199:1
Hoecken, Adrian  34:11
   93:4
Hoefer, John  162:5
Hoey, Richard  138:2
Hofercamp, Herman  266:1
Hoffman, A. J.   102:5
Hoffman, C. R.   173:12
Hoffmann, John  199:4
Hoffmeister, Bertram
   294:1
Hogan, Frank Vorhies
   203:1   266:2
Hogan, Thomas S.   60:5
Hogan, William  60:9
Hogg, Thomas Egerton
   42:2   75:3   152:1   228:22
Hoggatt, Wilford B.   55:1
   130:7   146:3   159:7   241:3
Hogue, Glenn  231:6

Hogue, Harvey A.   179:1
Hohl, George J.   266:2
Hoke, Mac  207:3   251:4
Holbrook, Amory  300:6
Holbrook, E. D.   87:7
Holbrook, Henry  5:3
Holbrook, Noyes B.   103:2
Holbrook, Stewart H.   41:2
   176:3   195:18
Holcomb, George  266:1
Holden, E. M.   213:2
Holden, Horace F.   37:1
Holden, J. Wesley  213:4
   219:2
Holder, William  300:5
Holes, Lucius T.   266:2
Holgate, John  234:2   306:6
Holladay, Ben  6:5   25:5
   31:5   41:3   46:3   75:9
   87:4   118:3   153:2   163:11
   188:9   197:374   198:1
   210:7   229:8   234:3
   285:5   297:9
Holland, Ernest O.   38:12
   117:2
Holland, John  176:1
Hollister, Madison E.   87:6
Hollister, ID  23:3
Holman, Frederick V.   162:6
Holman, James D.   202:13
Holman, Joseph  84:2
   150:2
Holman, Rufus  49:2   261:2
Holmes, Charles S.   73:5
   242:11
Holmes, Hal  293:5
Holmes, Harrison  242:6
Holmes, Robert D.   49:6
   261:1
Holmes, Roscius  242:6
Holmes, Sandy  255:4
Holmes, W. H.   150:2
Holohan, Peter J.   212:3
Holt, Charles L.   266:2
Holt, George  149:2
Holt, John M.   133:4
Holt, Ray  114:4

Holter, Anton M.   25:3
   319:5
Holy Cross, AK   63:1   149:2
Holyoke, Richard   217:2
Home, WA   41:4   57:1
   152:5   191:75   304:3
   305:2
Homedale, ID   23:1
Homer, Joseph A.   294:2
Homer, Joshua Attwood
   Reynolds   5:3
Homer, William H.   95:10
Homer, AK   63:1   115:3
   148:2
Homestead, OR   12:4   114:4
   225:2
Honcharenko, Agapius   149:3
Honeyman, Nan Wood   49:7
   244:2
Honner, Howard   157:3
Hood, Charles   266:3
Hood, Charles Edward
   199:2
Hood, John A.   199:1
Hood, John R.   199:3
Hood River, OR   75:3   82:5
   151:2   180:2   187:2   300:4
   317:4
Hoogdal, WA   315:3
Hooker, W. F.   150:1
Hoonah, AK   130:6
   269:3
Hooper Bay, AK   63:1
Hoople, Joseph A.   203:1
Hoover, R. K. "Herb"
   175:15
Hoover, W. H.   216:6
Hooyboer, John J.   71:11
Hope, AK   63:1
Hope, BC   3:20   5:20   20:7
   204:6   SEE ALSO Fort
   Hope, BC
Hope, ID   39:3   164:1
Hopkins, James F.   266:4
Hopson, Eben   136:4
Hoquiam, WA   14:1   16:5
   32:2   41:3   73:5   100:5

142:3   152:5   163:3
180:4   195:4   203:2
305:10
Horan, Michael   116:2
   157:3   203:1
Horan, Walt   206:3   293:5
Horde, Jane Hamilton
   278:1
Horen, Peter   256:5
Horetzky, Charles   40:6
Horgan, W. D.   167:2
Horn, Mildred Keith   169:18
Horne, J. W.   236:5
Horr, Alexander   191:15
Horr, Ralph A.   293:11
Horse Heaven, OR   308:7
Horseshoe Bend, ID   23:5
Horsfal, Edward   213:2
Horsfall, William   258:4
Horsley, Albert E.   SEE
   Orchard, Harry
Horton, Dexter   7:1   31:8
   80:3   176:3   178:4   243:2
   266:4   276:3   305:1   306:10
Horton, William N.   246:2
Hoskins, OR   75:2   147:5
   SEE ALSO Fort Hoskins
Hosmer, Hezekiah Lord
   25:5   133:14   247:3
   286:15
Hosmer, Paul   196:2
Hoss, Theodore   266:2
Hough, A. M.   25:6   227:8
Houghton, WA   14:1   79:4
Houle, Joseph   112:5
Hoult, Enoch   150:1
Housel, Charles   307:2
Houser, John   280:5
Houser, Max   280:3
Houser, William   280:4
Houston, John   107:2   186:2
Houston, Milton   179:3
Houston, William   181:4
Houston, ID   223:1
Hove, Charles   266:2
Hovenden, Alfred   150:2
Hovey, A. G.   150:1   232:6

Hovey, John Payne  266:2
Howard, Albert V.  319:5
Howard, B. F.  319:5
Howard, Edward D.  71:6
Howard, Harry M.  119:4
  289:3
Howard, John  84:1
Howard, Joseph Kinsey
  214:8  247:3  299:6
Howard, Joshua A.  199:1
Howard, Oliver O.  11:12
  36:10  43:3  132:3  139:6
  198:2
Howard, Roscoe  175:12
Howard, William W.  266:2
Howard, OR  42:1
Howarth, William  266:2
Howay, F. W.  3:3
Howe, Alvah B.  266:1
Howe, Frank  61:22
Howe, Herbert Crombie
  232:3
Howe, John P.  104:13
Howell, Benjamin  287:3
Howell, Ithamar M.  245:4
  266:3
Howell, S. P.  150:1
Howes, Henry E.  212:4
Howlett, S. R.  87:3
Howse, Albert E.  5:3
Hoxey, G. W.  157:3
Hoyne, Thomas  157:3
Hoyt, Bertha Wright  242:7
Hoyt, John P.  87:5  150:1
  220:2  243:3
Hoyt, Joseph  194:7
Hubbard, Thomas Jefferson
  84:5  162:7  287:3
Hubbard, William  242:8
Huberdault, G.  208:4
Huddleson, Cal  103:2
Huddleston, James  232:8
Hudson, Robert Gray  266:2
Hudson, WA  267:1
Hudson Hope, BC  40:35  204:5
Huelsdonk, John  100:8
Hufty, Baldwin  266:2

Huggins, Edward  150:2
Hughes, C. A.  41:1
Hughes, Glenn  41:2
Hughes, William P.  107:2
Hughesville, MT  319:8
Hulbert, J. H.  184:9
Hulin, Lester  232:3
Hull, Orley  150:2
Hultberg, Nels O.  28:1
  281:21
Human, W. C.  212:6
Humason, Orlando  179:1
  229:4  264:1
Hume, George  86:8
Hume, Johnny  176:6
Hume, Robert Deniston
  86:257  258:13
Humes, Thomas  58:3
  234:7
Hummel, John J.  289:2
Humphrey, G. O.  319:4
Humphrey, George  150:1
Humphrey, W. E.  41:1
Humphries, John E.  234:1
Humptown, ID  102:2
Humptulips, WA  305:1
Hungate, Harrison H.  150:1
Hungate, J. W.  94:6
Hungerford, Kenneth E.
  117:3
Hunsaker, Andrew J.  174:6
  303:6
Hunsaker, J. T.  150:2
Hunsaker, Jacob  57:3
  266:3
Hunsaker, Thomas H.  97:2
Hunt, Forest J.  130:1
Hunt, Frank W.  43:1  118:2
Hunt, James M.  246:5
Hunt, Leigh S. J.  234:1
  243:10
Hunt, William H.  133:6
Hunt, Wilson Price  33:3
  43:4  84:2  198:7
Hunter, Celia  115:8
Hunter, Frederick M.  232:3
Hunter, J. Ware  266:2

Hunter, ID  33:1  SEE ALSO
    Meridian, ID
Huntington, David Lynde
    106:5
Huntington, Harry Darby
    200:4  220:2
Huntington, John Webster
    Perit  30:2  230:3
Huntington, OR  4:1  12:5
    75:4  114:3  152:1
Huntley, William  289:3
Huntley, WA  267:1
Huntoon, Berton Waldron
    266:2
Huntsville, WA  119:4
    305:1
Hurd, Maynard P.  266:2
Hurd, Owen  12:7
Hurley, Daniel  138:5
Hurley, Jack  178:2
Hurley, R.  23:5
Hush-Hush-Cute (Chief)
    26:3
Huson, MT  112:30
Hussey, Charles  23:3
    192:2  212:4
Hussey, Warren  23:5
    118:1
Hustler, J. G.  295:6
Huston, Joseph W.  87:3
Huston, Lee  32:6
Huston, Thad  266:3
Hutchens, Martin K.  299:4
Hutchinson, H. M.  311:1
Hutchinson, R. M.  230:3
Hutchinson, Richard Ashton
    288:4
Huth, Anton  266:3
Hutton, Levi W.  58:8
    108:15
Hutton, May Arkwright  41:1
    58:10  108:31  252:1  278:2
Hyatt, Glen C.  266:1
Hydaburg, AK  130:9  269:6
Hyde, Charles H.  266:2
Hyde, Mattie  108:5
Hyder, AK  63:1  148:1  241:1

Hylak, Anton  266:2
Hyland, T. A.  295:2
Hyner, Matthew E.  266:2
Hyskell, Charles M.  152:3


Idaho City, ID  23:8  33:37
    36:44  87:19  118:15
    164:5  223:8  249:3
    259:2  308:8  SEE ALSO
    Bannock City, ID
Idaho Falls, ID  23:12  24:6
    118:7  180:3  213:5
Idaho Springs, ID  268:4
Idanha, OR  228:3
Ide, Chester D.  150:1
Ide, Clarence W.  266:2
Iditarod, AK  63:1
Iktigalik, AK  77:6
Ilia, WA  119:1  280:2
Iliff, T. C.  227:9
Illim-Spokanee (Chief)  108:3
Ilo, ID  23:3  24:1
Ilwaco, WA  14:1  97:7
    109:20  198:1  202:31
    229:4  272:7  305:1
Imbler, Jesse  150:1
Imbrie, James J.  150:2
Imnaha, OR  12:2
Imoda, John B. C.  34:4
Inchelium, WA  305:1
Independence, ID  59:4
Independence, MT  319:3
Independence, OR  68:3
    75:10  187:2  229:2
    300:2
Index, WA  180:1  225:2
    305:1
Ingalls, David  295:3
Ingalls, Henry  119:1  199:1
Ingalls, Rufus  197:11
Ingalls, Theodore P.  119:2
Ingersoll, Charles E.  130:1
Ingham, G. W.  245:8
Ingle, Elijah  199:2
Ingraham, E. S.  38:3

Inkom, ID 164:1
Inskip, G. W. 134:4
Insula (Chief) 93:4 249:1
Ione, OR 152:3
Ione, WA 225:2 305:1
Ipalook, Percy 128:3
Irby, I. 157:2
Ireland, DeWitt Clinton
 295:6 300:17
Iron Springs, ID 223:1
Irrigon, OR 198:1 300:2
Irvin, WA 39:4
Irving, George 130:1
Irving, Joseph 57:25
Irving, Peter 266:2
Irwin, Don L. 148:7
 226:17
Irwin, F. G. 211:7
Irwin, John N. 43:1 95:3
Irwin, Mason 203:1 266:2
Isaacs, Henry Perry 150:1
 156:2 199:3 257:4
Isaacs, Walter F. 41:1
Isle, Walter W. 94:3
Ismay, MT 312:1
Israel, George C. 266:3
Issaquah, WA 14:1 152:1
 305:2 SEE ALSO Gilman,
 WA
Itjen, Martin 63:1 148:1
Ives, George 1:5 25:12
 76:6 97:1 133:12 155:7
 256:12 319:4
Ives, WA 267:1
Izee, OR 251:3


Jack, John 234:1
Jackman, E. R. 251:4
Jackson, C. S. "Sam" 207:38
 300:9
Jackson, D. B. 246:3
Jackson, Granville R. 137:7
Jackson, Henry Martin 54:26
 83:2 128:5 129:3 130:7
 178:5 241:2 245:6 248:2

265:360 293:3
Jackson, John R. 203:2
 220:3 222:4
Jackson, Otis C. 199:2
Jackson, Sheldon 8:3 18:2
 28:2 31:4 48:3 55:5
 63:3 90:2 125:5 130:8
 149:25 159:12 160:2
 161:11 171:4 190:218
 269:4 281:21 290:1
Jacksonville, OR 41:2
 75:3 97:9 114:2 152:2
 187:5 196:1 225:4 249:4
 261:2 264:10 297:10
 300:5 317:7
Jacobs, Charles A. 199:2
Jacobs, Cyrus 33:3
Jacobs, John M. 292:10
Jacobs, Locke 66:9
Jacobs, Orange 29:7 31:2
 38:2 119:7 150:1 163:3
 234:2 243:10 266:4
 276:2
Jacobs, R. 119:9
Jacobs, Samuel 119:11
Jacobsen, Berne 176:1
Jacobson, Berthe Poncy
 69:15
Jacquet, Aloysius 34:3
James, Burton 69:6 70:35
James, Florence Bean
 278:1
James, Francis Wilcox
 203:1
Jameson, Grover 114:4
Jamestown, WA 273:6
Jamieson, Archibald 229:3
Jamieson, Edward Herbert
 288:3
Jamieson, Tom 40:5
Janeck, L. O. 305:1
Janes, Leonard 274:8
Jantzen, Carl 114:3
Jaqueth, A. L. 173:6
Jardine, MT 308:10
Jarvis, David H. 130:2
Jasper, Charles 289:2

Jaussaud, Leon F. C.  199:1
Jeffers, Nelson  175:8
Jefferson City, MT  46:3
   319:4
Jefford, Jack  263:22
Jeffries, John T.  179:3
Jeffs, Richard  150:1
Jenkins, David C.  266:2
   308:3
Jenkins, David P.  39:5
   108:2  288:4
Jenkins, Frank  232:1
Jenkins, William  5:3
Jennings, Jefferson  199:1
Jennings, Judson T.  169:21
Jennings, Robert W.  130:2
Jennings, MT  48:3  215:4
   319:6
Jericho, MT  319:6
Jerome, ID  23:4  164:1
   180:2
Jerry, WA  305:1
Jerusalem, ID  223:1
Jesmond, BC  47:1
Jesson, Ed  310:2
Jessop, John  260:6
Jessup, Theodore H.  199:2
Jessup, Wilford  176:2
Jette, J.  311:2
Jewell, Moro  70:3
Jewett, Robert S.  287:2
Jewett, W. F.  9:10
Jewitt, John Rodgers
   140:17
Joe, Norman  140:5
Johanson, Nils A.  203:1
John, Jacob R.  179:1
John Day, OR  251:8  264:4
Johns, Bennett W.  266:4
Johns, Helen  169:29
Johns, James S.  207:3
Johnson, Albert  130:4
   261:1
Johnson, Albert G.  303:12
Johnson, Arlien  278:2
Johnson, Byron Ingemar
   253:3

Johnson, C. Gardner  236:4
Johnson, Carl J.  59:4
Johnson, Daniel  150:1
Johnson, Dorothy M.  214:2
Johnson, Elvira  93:4
Johnson, Forrest  274:22
Johnson, Frank  150:1
Johnson, Frank F.  23:14
   24:3
Johnson, George  97:5
Johnson, H. V. V.  187:6
Johnson, Harvey L.  266:2
Johnson, Hezekiah  303:6
Johnson, James  97:12
   202:12
Johnson, James "Bohemia"
   97:2
Johnson, James L.  266:2
Johnson, John W.  153:1
   232:4
Johnson, Joseph French
   96:13
Johnson, Julius C.  293:11
Johnson, Lee A.  279:5
Johnson, P. B.  119:5
Johnson, P. W.  99:16
Johnson, Phil  161:1
Johnson, R. G.  251:5
Johnson, Rae  175:26
Johnson, Robert H.  199:1
Johnson, Samuel  179:2
   199:2
Johnson, Thomas  150:1
Johnson, W. Lon  245:4
Johnson, William  84:3
Johnston, A. B.  173:6
Johnston, David S.  266:4
Johnston, Eric A.  96:8
   108:1  124:1  176:2
   293:6
Johnston, Nora Anne  278:1
Johnston, Tex  178:2  252:3
Jones, Alden  175:19
Jones, Arthur D.  288:2
   293:4
Jones, Charles Herbert
   266:2

Jones, Harvey 31:6
Jones, Henry E. 187:7
Jones, J. Clarence 2:6
Jones, Jimmy 246:3
Jones, L. DeFloyd 211:5
Jones, Lewis Newton 266:2
Jones, Nard 96:1 283:5
Jones, Nelson 150:2
Jones, Robert Vinton 176:4
Jones, Roy 137:4 263:2
Jones, Seth 103:4
Jones, Sherman L. 266:2
Jones, Strachan 77:4
Jones, W. B. 161:2
Jones, Walter A. 212:9
Jones, Walter William
134:7
Jones, Wesley L. 16:2
52:1 57:2 83:4 128:3
130:7 188:3 243:1
245:10 261:1 293:28
Jones, William C. 176:1
Jones, William R. 199:1
Jonson, Axel E. 237:4
Jordan, Alvah H. B. 266:2
Jordan, Len B. 12:6
118:1 259:3
Jordan, Michael M. 134:3
Jordan Valley, OR 134:44
Joseph (Chief) 11:12
26:366 27:63 36:30
43:8 91:6 96:3 102:11
103:15 114:15 118:8
132:4 133:18 139:6
164:7 172:23 198:7
252:6
Joseph, George W. 49:5
261:1
Joseph, ID 102:2
Joseph, Or 12:5 300:2
Josephi, Simeon Edward
150:2 187:17
Joset, Joseph 11:3 27:9
34:21 93:7
Joslin, Falcon 281:6
Joslyn, Herm 137:2
Josslin, William 49:3
Joy, George 175:12

Joy, Harper 88:2
Juanita, WA 305:1
Judell, Hermann L. 87:3
Judge, Thomas L. 214:24
Judge, William H. 309:3
Judson, Edward B. 266:2
Judson, John P. 38:5
Judson, Lewis Hubbell
84:3 193:7
Juliaetta, ID 23:3
Junction City, MT 78:4 319:6
Junction City, OR 300:4
Juneau, Joseph 130:2
143:4 311:1
Jura, BC 47:1
Justice, John G. 119:10


Kadiak, AK 77:27 SEE
ALSO Kodiak, AK
Kadlec, Harry R. 96:2
176:2
Kahlotus, WA 305:1
Kailin, Leo 108:1
Kake, AK 63:1 130:5
269:8
Kaktovik, AK 115:6
Kalahan, Clyde 175:10
Kalama, WA 14:1 75:3
151:9 198:1 229:5
243:1 295:3 305:4
Kale, C. Stewart 266:2
Kalispell, MT 1:2 45:3
135:5 183:4 247:6
319:11
Kalitee, Andrew 103:11
Kallander, Rudy M. 195:3
Kaltag, AK 63:1
Kamiah, ID 4:4 23:4 24:2
26:5 91:6 102:13 103:5
Kamiakin (Chief) 6:4 11:5
17:3 27:27 141:4 188:4
220:4
Kamloops, BC 3:17 5:7
20:2 92:2 123:16 204:8
235:2 238:5 253:5 SEE
ALSO Fort Kamloops

Kamm, Jacob  68:3  109:4
  172:2  179:1  197:2  202:5
  229:6  285:2  297:3
Kammisgaard, Ed  137:5
Kanakanak, AK  8:6
Kanasket, WA  50:2
Kandle, George B.  266:3
Kane, Clement A.  71:5
Kane, Thomas F.  38:1
Kane, William  264:1
Kane, William Herbert
  138:2
Kanim, Pat  80:5  SEE
  ALSO Patkanim
Kantishna, AK  115:3
Karlson, A. E.  281:5
Karluk, AK  8:3  19:3  28:2
  130:4  149:5
Karstens, Harry P.  233:20
Kartar, WA  267:1
Kasaan, AK  269:5
Kaslo, BC  47:2
Katalla, AK  130:1  146:6
  310:3
Katlian (Chief)  161:1
Kauffman, John Jacob  199:2
Kaufman, Joseph  102:3
Kaufman, W. H.  191:6
Kay, Thomas  194:15
Kay, Wendell P.  129:4
  241:1
Kayler, Thomas H.  150:1
Keach, Philip  203:1
Keady, William F.  150:1
Kealey, Lawrence  256:6
Keane, James E.  157:2
Keane, John  243:7  276:7
Kearney, Joseph F.  266:1
Keasey, OR  307:4
Keatingville, MT  46:1
Keefe, Dion  199:1
Keeney, Joseph B.  150:2
Keenleyside, H. L.  316:14
Keerins, Sam  251:4
Kehoe, George  274:20
Keil, William  36:21  41:1
  144:30  153:1  203:1
  252:2  304:3

Keiser, Charles F.  116:2
Keith, Thomas  238:6
Keller, Josiah P.  179:1
Keller, WA  225:1  293:1
  305:1
Kelley, Cornelius Francis
  167:4  214:4  216:75
Kelley, Hall Jackson  4:5
  16:3  45:8  50:15  84:1
  151:4  153:1  162:5
  177:4  188:11  198:2
  261:3  272:5  284:3
  304:3
Kelley, J. K.  198:1
Kelley, Louis M.  71:7
Kelley, Matthew A.  64:3
Kelling, Deitrick  150:1
Kellogg, Charles H.  150:1
Kellogg, G. E.  300:4
Kellogg, George  150:2
Kellogg, Jay A.  150:2
Kellogg, John Jay  230:1
Kellogg, Joseph  150:2
  284:3
Kellogg, Lucien E.  119:2
  157:3
Kellogg, Noah S.  96:3
  99:1  108:6  118:5  150:1
  172:16  188:2  192:3
  212:7  259:2
Kellogg, Orrin  150:2
Kellogg, ID  23:7  96:3
  98:16  108:2  118:4
  164:1  172:3  180:4
  205:5
Kellogg, OR  230:1
Kellough, George E.  199:2
Kelly, Clinton  150:1  179:3
Kelly, Fred J.  264:1
Kelly, Hampton  179:3
Kelly, James Kerr  51:120
  119:14  150:2  163:2
  179:10
Kelly, John  150:3  176:3
Kelly, Joseph "Bunco"
  151:2
Kelly, Martin F.  199:1
Kelly, Milton  29:5

Kelly, Penumbra 150:1
Kelly, Peter 260:8
Kelly, Peter R. 140:5
  189:16
Kelly, Thomas 179:5
Kelly, Thomas J. 57:2
Kelly, William B. 119:6
Kelowna, BC 5:3 204:4
Kelsay, John 51:50
Kelsey Bay, BC 165:10
Kelso, WA 14:1 151:6
  176:1 180:3 229:3
  305:4
Kelty, Paul 232:1 300:5
Kemano, BC 275:4
Kemmer, Louis 202:1
Kemp, Fred 116:4
Kemp, Randall 107:3
Kemper, John 319:3
Kempster, Arthur L. 266:1
Kenai, AK 130:2
Kendall, Benjamin F.
  245:14
Kendall, Thomas S. 153:1
Kendall, MT 78:4 224:4
  319:11
Kendall, WA 225:1 305:1
Kendrick, ID 23:5 24:6
Kenna, Howard J. 71:13
Kennedy, Arthur Edward
  3:8 126:5 238:3
  253:8 281:2
Kennedy, Henrietta Baker
  278:1
Kennedy, James B. 294:2
Kennedy, John H. 150:1
Kennedy, Robert 199:2
Kennedy, Robert C. 157:3
Kennedy, Will 60:17
Kennewick, WA 82:2 96:2
  198:2 252:4 305:2
Kenney, Frank M. 245:4
Kennicott, Robert 63:1
  77:11 159:2 161:2
  168:50 311:2
Keno, OR 97:2
Kent, WA 14:1 41:1 89:1
  305:1

Kenworthy, Mary 234:14
  276:5
Ker, David Russell 126:8
Ker, Robert 126:4
Kerbyville, OR 225:3
  264:2
Kerchival City, MT 25:2
  78:2
Keremos, BC 3:3 123:4
  204:2
Kern, John Tully 179:1
Kern, Paris I. 157:2
Kerr, F. M. 156:2
Kerr, R. C. 38:5
Kershaw, J. Frederick
  199:1
Kershaw, James S. 199:1
Kershaw, John H. 199:1
Kershaw, Tunis R. 266:3
Kershon, George 18:4
Kesler, Harry 183:6
  213:3
Kesling, James 150:2
Kessler, George 200:3
Ketcham, Robert 274:5
Ketchell, Stanley 67:5
Ketchikan, AK 28:4 52:4
  128:11 130:47 146:6
  148:6 159:7 241:10
  263:7 269:30 271:7
  275:4 290:7
Ketchum, Frank E. 77:22
  168:4
Ketchum, Howard 175:11
Ketchum, ID 23:6 118:4
  164:1
Kettenbach, Frank W. 23:8
Kettle Falls, WA 39:2
  58:3 96:1 198:11 291:3
  293:24 305:1
Keturi, Elmer 66:5
Ketzler, Alfred 54:6 66:3
Keuterville, ID 102:21
Keyes, William C. 266:2
Keystone, MT 78:1 SEE
  ALSO Carter, MT
Keyzer, R. 212:4
Kiana, AK 63:1 263:4

Kieley, Matty 67:10
Kila, MT 319:2
Kilbourne, William K.
  284:3 297:5
Kildall, Simon F. 266:2
Killisnoo, AK 18:3
Kimball, Harold G. 70:6
Kimber, Chris 281:4
Kimberly, ID 23:6
Kimberly, OR 251:3
Kimble, D. E. 314:3
Kincaid, Harrison Ritten-
  house 150:2 232:10
  300:5
Kincaid, John Francis
  150:1
Kincaid, Orvin 150:1
Kincaid, Robert 266:3
Kindred, B. C. 150:2
Kindred, William S. 203:1
Kineth, John 150:1
King, A. N. 150:2
King, Charles B. 96:4
  99:3
King, Clement B. 39:2
King, F. B. 102:3
King, George E. 80:2
King, George W. 150:1
King, Sarah Fairbanks
  150:2
King, Stoddard 83:2
  96:17 108:1
King, Thomas 151:3
King, W. A. 266:1
King, W. L. Mackenzie
  238:11
King, Will R. 49:7
King, William 157:4
  284:3
King Hill, ID 23:1 87:5
Kingegan, AK 311:1
Kingsbury, Edward P.
  266:1
Kingsley, Ceylon S. 87:2
  94:7 118:2
Kingston, ID 39:1 108:1
  212:3 223:1

Kinkead, John Henry 19:6
  130:3 149:21 190:5
Kinnear, E. M. 150:1
Kinnear, George 178:3
  243:4 276:3
Kinnear, Roy John 113:2
  243:9
Kinney, Alfred Coleman
  187:10
Kinney, Marshall J. 37:1
Kinney, Robert Couch 51:8
  150:2
Kinney, Samuel 150:2
Kinnison, J. P. 150:1
Kiona, WA 305:1
Kipling, Thomas Fiske
  202:6
Kipling, WA 267:1
Kirk, Peter 203:1 243:5
Kirk, T. J. 150:1
Kirkland, Joseph E. 150:1
Kirkland, WA 14:1 217:1
  243:8 305:1
Kirkman, William 119:3
  199:2 203:1 257:4
Kirkpatrick, John A. 266:2
Kirkpatrick, Minor P.
  266:3
Kirkpatrick, William D.
  266:2
Kirkville, MT 308:5 SEE
  ALSO Clark, MT
Kirkwood, Jay W. 103:2
Kitimat, BC 186:7 204:4
  275:5
Kitsap (Chief) 7:14
Kitselas, BC 186:5
Kittilsen, A. N. 281:18
Kittson, William 39:4
Kivalina, AK 52:1
Kizer, Benjamin H. 58:4
  108:1
Kizer, Carolyn 278:1
Kjeldsen, Carl 112:7
Kjellman, William A.
  190:8 281:2
Kjelsberg, Magnus 281:2

Klamath Falls, OR   17:4
    41:3   75:9   82:4   97:8
    114:4   152:2   180:5   187:7
    229:2   300:12   303:7
    317:5
Klamathon, OR   9:8
Klawock, AK   130:14   149:3
    241:2
Klein, J. P.   108:2
Kleinschmidt, Albert   103:3
Klickitat, WA   242:30
Kline, Robert L.   266:3
Klippel, Henry   150:1
Klondike City, YT   255:2
Kluck, Jack   276:2
Knapp, Frank E.   157:4
Knapp, Ivan   97:2
Knapp, Louis   258:4
Knapp, Lyman E.   10:1
    149:3   281:2
Knapp, Sewell M.   150:2
Knappton, WA   109:2
    202:2   225:1   SEE ALSO
    Cementville
Kneeland, Ammi H.   266:2
Kneeland, W. H.   266:5
Knight, Mary M.   266:2
Knighton, Elizabeth J.
    302:1
Knighton, Henry M.   119:3
    284:9   318:8
Knippenberg, Henry   319:5
Knoff, John J.   191:7
Knowles, Hiram N.   60:4
    133:9   209:9   286:9
Knowles, Joe   305:1
Knowlton, WA   267:1
Knox, James   266:2
Knox, W. N.   102:3   103:3
Knudsen, Morris H.   118:1
Knutson, Carl   274:6
Knutzen, Will   315:3
Koch, Elers   103:12
Kodiak, AK   21:8   125:5
    128:6   130:19   143:4
    146:5   148:4   159:40
    226:6   241:4   262:4

281:25   SEE ALSO Ka-
    diak, AK
Koehler, Mark L.   124:12
Koelsch, Charles   127:11
Koerner, Leon   260:4
Koerner, Otto   260:3
Koerner, Walter   260:4
Koger, Marion   199:1
Kohlhauff, William   119:12
Kohlhire, Phil   134:3
Kohrs, Carston Conrad
    46:3   48:10   133:14
    155:25   214:4   292:6
    298:3
Koonah (Shaman)   311:4
Koontz, James H.   150:1
Koontz, William A.   199:2
Kooskia, ID   23:6   24:2
    102:8   103:6   SEE ALSO
    Stuart, ID
Kootenai, BC   198:2   238:2
    253:13
Kopczynski, August   102:9
    103:4
Koponen, Niilo   241:2
Korell, Franklin F.   49:2
Kosmos, WA   225:1   305:1
Kotata (Chief)   272:7
Kotlik, AK   8:4
Kotzebue, AK   8:10   52:10
    63:2   137:10   263:17
Koyukuk, AK   8:3   63:1
    52:6
Kraby, Peter D.   57:2
    266:3
Kralman, William   199:1
Kratt, Jacob   303:6
Krauss, Michael   161:1
Kremer, J. Bruce   298:3
    299:8
Krestova, BC   152:1
Krieger, J. B.   102:12
Kroeger, William   102:6
Kroll, Henry   263:4
Kruger, Theodore   5:3
Kruse, John   258:3
Kuhl, Henry   199:1

Kuhn, Albert H.   266:3
Kuhn, Joseph A.   150:1
Kuna, ID   23:8
Kunkel, Paul W.   2:10
Kuppens, Francis X.
   254:8
Kupro, ID   102:3   SEE
   ALSO Lorena, ID
Kuratli, John   2:7
Kurtz, M. A.   33:7
Kuykendall, E. V.   280:4
Kuykendall, George Ben-
   son   150:2   280:3
Kuykendall, William   187:5
Kwah (Chief)   235:17
Kwan, Arthur   138:2
Kwong Lee   238:15
Kydd, John   199:1
Kyger, Daniel T.   199:2
Kyle, Cecil   195:6
Kyle, Charles O.   157:2
Kyle, George A.   266:2
Kyle, William   73:18
Kyle, ID   98:4


Laberee, O. G.   288:4
Labonte, Louis   162:10
La Center, WA   305:1
Lacey, WA   305:1
LaConner, WA   14:1   89:1
   150:2   203:3   305:1
   314:14   315:13
Lacy, O. P.   119:12
Ladd, Henry W.   202:1
Ladd, John R.   150:2
Ladd, William Sargent
   119:3   150:3   152:2
   179:1   197:3   201:4
   210:9   222:2   297:15
   302:3   304:3
Ladue, Joseph   81:4   159:5
   255:5   309:11
Ladysmith, BC   122:7
   165:8
Lafayette, OR   35:3   68:8
   187:6   229:3   284:3   SEE
   ALSO Fort Lafayette
Laffoon, Reuben F.   266:2
La Fleur, WA   267:1
Lafortune, Joseph   199:1
La Grande, OR   4:1   12:3
   75:3   119:1   150:2   180:3
   187:5   264:1   300:7
   303:3
La Grande, WA   305:1
La Grave, Dennis   199:2
Laidlaw, Andrew   289:2
Laidlaw, James   118:1
Laidlaw, W. A.   42:1
Laidlaw, OR   42:4
Laing, John A.   82:9
Laird, Eli   99:8
Laird, J. E.   279:4
Laist, Frederick   216:13
Lake Oswego, OR   68:11
   SEE ALSO Oswego, OR
Lake Pershing, WA   267:1
Lakeport, OR   258:5
Lakeside, OR   97:1   258:6
Lakeview, OR   75:3   97:3
   114:4   300:6
Lamb, Frank   152:1
Lamb, George   71:7
Lamb, James M.   119:1
   199:1
Lamb, John D.   199:1
Lambert, Edward   112:5
Lambert, Russ S.   266:2
Lambert, Ted   159:1
Lambuth, Letcher   200:7
Lame, Charlie   97:9
Lamley, Job   202:3
Lamonta, OR   42:3
La Motte, George de   34:4
Lamping, George B.   266:2
Lampkin, Fred W.   207:6
Lampman, Ben Hur   152:3
Lancaster, Columbia   119:5
   150:2   188:3   203:2   220:2
   245:4   306:3
Lancaster, OR   68:8
Land, T. C.   258:3

Lander, Edward M.   80:3
141:5   220:6   245:7
306:7
Lander, Frederick W.
150:2
Lander (Fort), WA   31:3
Landes, Bertha Knight
41:1   176:1   278:1
Landes, Henry   38:3   41:1
150:2   293:4
Landon, William B.   308:1
Landore, ID   223:1
Landusky, Powell "Pike"
61:24
Landusky, MT   61:18
78:9   224:8   312:1
319:15
Landvoight, George   5:8
Lane, Charles D.   52:2
161:1   311:2
Lane, Clarence R.   283:5
Lane, George B.   266:3
Lane, Harry   49:7   187:8
210:6
Lane, Joseph   4:2   6:3
16:6   35:12   51:25
84:2   85:4   119:6
139:1   145:274   147:2
150:2   172:3   176:3
177:2   188:17   208:3
220:7   249:3   252:1
261:3   305:3
Lane, Lafayette   145:8
163:2
Lane, Louis   161:2
Lane, Thaddeus S.   289:4
Langdale, BC   204:2
Langdon, Abram   230:2
Langdon, John W.   257:2
Langdon, Lucius   42:3
Lange, J. Malcolm   274:16
Langford, Edward E.   3:7
20:5   126:6
Langford, Nathaniel Pitt
25:4   48:4   133:14
283:4   286:7
Langford, William G.   119:10

Langhorne, William Whit-
field   266:2
Langille, William   198:1
Langley, BC   20:3
Langley, WA   191:5
Langlie, Arthur B.   41:4
70:10   92:2   169:10
176:3   178:7   184:4
234:2   244:6   245:21
248:3   261:3   276:2
293:4
Langlois, Anthony   208:14
Langlois, OR   258:4
Lanham, Z. A.   157:2
Lannin, Joseph   279:4
Lansdale, Richard H.
179:2   181:3
Lansing, Gulian V.   266:1
Lantz, Patricia Taylor
278:1
La Pine, OR   42:4
LaPray, Joseph   39:2
La Push, WA   305:1
Lapwai (Fort), ID   118:4
147:4   SEE ALSO Fort
Lapwai
Lapwai Mission, ID   12:4
17:10   23:3   26:10   27:3
36:2   39:4   43:3   87:4
91:6   93:9   102:4   118:9
119:5   132:4   172:10
187:3   188:9   192:15
198:3   296:7   317:5   SEE
ALSO Spalding Mission
Larabie, S. E.   133:7
Largey, Patrick A.   167:2
Larkin, James E.   191:5
Larkin, Ken   175:7
Larpenteur, Charles   48:10
Larrivie, Henry   112:6
Larsen, Enoch T.   303:8
Larsen, Lewis P.   288:2
Larson, John J.   266:1
Larson, Peter   294:2
La Salle, William   266:2
Lasater, Harry   199:2
Lasater, James H.   119:9

150:1 199:2
Last Chance, MT 78:10
319:33
Latah, WA 89:1
Latham, John 266:2
Latham, Thomas 47:1
Lathrop, Austin E. 129:5
130:3 148:2 159:4
160:2 241:2 262:12
Latimer, John R. 112:6
Latourette, Howard 49:7
Latourette, Kenneth Scott
303:4
Latta, Marion C. 266:2
Laumeister, Frank 138:3
Laure, Augustine 34:2
Laurel, MT 1:1 299:2
312:1
Lauridsen, G. M. 100:7
266:1
Laurier, Wilfred 238:28
Laurin, MT 46:5 78:3
224:2
Laursen, Allan 274:6
Lausmann, Anton A. 307:254
Lausmann, Jerry 307:16
Lava Hot Springs, ID 23:5
Lavoie, Henry 112:9
Lawler, George 266:4
Lawrence, John 309:9
Lawson, B. K. 152:4
Lawton, OR 264:2
Lawyer (Chief) 4:4 6:4
11:2 26:5 27:7 36:2
102:3 150:1 155:3
172:3 176:5 177:3
188:6 198:7
Layton, Davis 119:3 179:2
Leach, Frank 137:2
Leadore, ID 23:3 164:1
Learned, Alphonso Fowler
150:2
Leary, John 234:3
243:21 246:1
Leask, David 10:5
Leasure, Daniel W. "Web"
212:8

Leasure, John C. 150:1
Leavenworth, WA 98:9
157:4 293:1 305:1
Leavitt, Erasmus Darwin
286:2
Leavitt, H. L. 234:2
Leavitt, Scott 156:2
Leavy, Charles H. 293:48
Lebam, WA 152:2 305:1
Lebanon, OR 147:2 187:5
300:2
Lebarge, Michael 77:8
Le Breton, George W.
119:7 193:8 198:1
Ledbetter, Chris C. 237:4
Ledgerwood, Joseph 280:3
Ledoux, Damien 112:6
Ledyard, Ray 274:5
Lee, Daniel 4:8 16:5
44:25 84:1 93:25
101:2 119:3 153:2
177:11 187:8 188:6
193:15 198:2 272:3
302:3
Lee, Dorothy McCullough
41:1
Lee, Henry A. G. 119:6
199:2
Lee, James B. 30:1
Lee, Jason 4:21 6:5
16:8 17:14 44:348
45:17 50:6 84:2 93:24
101:3 119:7 144:4
150:2 153:3 162:13
177:56 187:13 188:23
193:100 198:6 220:5
232:4 249:6 261:3
272:5 284:2 297:16
302:10 317:13
Lee, Joseph D. 150:2
Lee, Norman 47:1
Lee, Robert Charlton 114:6
Lee, Robert Ormond 114:6
Leechtown, BC 47:1
Lees, Frank W. 293:6
Leesburg, ID 118:1 164:2
223:2 308:6 SEE ALSO

Grantsville, ID
Leese, WA 267:1
Leeson, Michael A. 319:9
Lefevre, Pierre 39:6
Legaic (Chief) 10:11
Legg, Gordon T. 275:16
Legris, Lionel O. 112:3
Lehman Hot Springs, OR 207:2
Lehnherr, Christian 258:3
Leigh, John 173:5
Leigh, Richard 59:5
Leighton, George 140:3
Leitch, Harriett 169:11
Leiter, O. Clarke 300:5
Lejacq, J. M. 235:4
Leland, Alonzo F. 29:15 102:10 103:4 145:7 192:1
Lemhi (Fort), ID 118:4 164:1 SEE ALSO Fort Lemhi
Lemon, Millard 245:6
Lennep, MT 319:3
Leonard, Albert P. 266:2
Leonard, Frank 173:5
Leonia, ID 319:2
Lequerica, John 134:7
Lequime, Eli 5:4
Lermond, Norman Wallace 191:15
Leschi (Chief) 7:18 32:17 41:1 58:10 139:1 141:5 176:2 222:5 234:3 245:11 273:1 301:6 306:4
Leslie, David 44:8 84:4 93:5 119:8 150:2 193:16 198:1
Leslie, Preston H. 286:13
Leveridge, W. K. 86:2
Levine, Louis 156:2
Levinson, Newman J. 300:5
Levy, Max 203:2
Lewelling, Henderson 261:2
Lewes, John Lee 108:1
Lewis, Carey E. 191:8
Lewis, Cicero Hunt 297:4
Lewis, Dave 103:6
Lewis, Elisha H. 150:1
Lewis, Freeborn S. 191:4
Lewis, George F. 199:1
Lewis, Haman C. 150:2
Lewis, Hamilton 176:1
Lewis, J. Hamilton 163:2
Lewis, J. R. 87:14
Lewis, Joe 4:5 93:4 132:2 252:5 296:8
Lewis, Reuben 84:3
Lewiston, ID 12:25 17:7 23:17 24:4 27:6 29:15 34:7 39:11 76:7 87:13 96:17 97:12 103:15 117:15 118:26 133:5 164:3 172:3 180:4 192:13 198:14 205:4 213:5 215:5 229:8 256:8 259:8
Lewistown, MT 1:1 156:4 215:5 319:15
Lewisville, OR 84:1
Lexington, OR 152:2 207:1
Libby, Daniel B. 161:6 281:3 309:3
Libby, Isaac Chase 108:1
Libby, S. D. 246:5
Libby, MT 48:2 151:3 215:4 319:29
Libby, WA 267:1
Libbysville, AK 161:2 311:2 SEE ALSO Port Clarence
Liberty, WA 225:3 308:10
Lichtenstadter, Sam 108:1
Lichty, H. M. 279:4
Lichty, Guy C. 279:8
Lidy Hot Springs, ID 97:1
Liebig, Frank 135:5
Liesk, Joyce 140:5
Lieuallen, C. L. "Buck" 207:4
Likins, Calvin T. 266:2
Lilley, George 38:3

Lilliwaup, WA  152:2
Lillooet, BC  3:16  47:4
  123:5  138:97
Linck, Alaska  241:1
Linck, John W.  266:3
Lincoln, MT  319:7
Lincoln, OR  68:9
Lind, Edmund  231:4
Lind, WA  82:5  293:8
  305:1
Lindblom, Eric O.  281:11
Lindeberg, Jafet  28:2
  161:1  281:11  310:5
  311:2
Linden, Robert J.  106:5
Linderman, Frank Bird
  214:2
Lindley, Ernest Hiram
  117:21
Lindsay, A. S.  157:2
Lindsay, John A.  185:2
Lindsay, William  283:7
Lindsley, Aaron L.  91:11
Linfield, Frances Eleanor
  Ross  174:8
Linkville, OR  41:1
Linn, Ethan A.  199:2
Linn City (Linnton), OR
  68:20  84:2  284:4
  287:2  297:4
Linville, Harrison  68:3
Lion City, MT  78:2
  319:7
Lionnet, Louis  202:4
  272:2
Lippincott, B. C.  38:2
Lister, Alfred  266:2
Lister, David  150:2
Lister, Ernest  38:2  58:18
  83:3  184:10  222:6
  245:25  266:2  293:3
  305:1
Lister, Samuel G.  266:3
Listmann, George John
  266:2
Litchfield, Gilbert C.  30:3
Little, Andrew J.  118:2

Little, Frank  252:4
Little, Frank W.  156:1
  299:8
Little, Sidney Wahl  232:5
Little Dalles, WA  229:5
Littlefield, David  264:2
Littlefield, H. R.  187:5
Littlejohn, P. B.  4:6  84:1
Littler, C. Vard  2:10
Livengood, Jay  137:1
Livengood, AK  63:1  115:2
  137:7  309:5  SEE ALSO
  Brooks, AK
Livermore, Lot  150:1
  207:8
Livingston, MT  1:1  48:3
  60:3  183:3  215:5  247:7
  312:1  319:10
Lloyd, John Plummer Der-
  went  266:2
Lloyd, Tom  233:24
Locke, Harrison P.  318:6
Locke, Phil S.  266:2
Lockhart, F. G.  51:15
  258:6
Lockley, Fred  300:5
Lodge Grass, MT  312:1
Logan, David  35:3  51:80
  145:3
Logan, Edward  199:2
Logan, WA  243:1
Logie, James  287:4
Logsdon, Clarence M.
  266:2
Loiselle, Philias  112:5
Lolo, MT  312:1
Lomas, W. H.  189:13
Lombard, MT  46:2
Lomen, Alfred  137:11
Lomen, Carl  8:2  161:11
Lomen, G. J.  137:1  160:4
  161:6
Lomen, Ralph  137:4
Londborg, Maynard D.  290:1
Lonergan, W. D.  175:8
Lonerock, OR  308:5
Loney, Samuel K.  199:2

Long, Edward  150:2
Long, George S.  175:9
  195:7  200:6
Long, J. Grier  289:2
Long, Jacob  150:2
Long, R. A. "Reub"  251:4
Long, Robert Alexander
  58:2  195:3  200:15
  305:1
Long, Thomas  161:2
Long Beach, WA  109:15
  202:9  305:2
Longden, George R.  266:2
Longmaid, John  319:4
Longmire, Elcaine  203:1
Longmire, James  203:1
  252:5  261:1  305:3
Longpre, Dan J.  112:13
Longpre, Peter  112:5
Longstaff, Frank  203:2
Longtain, Andre  162:12
Longview, WA  17:4  41:7
  58:2  152:3  172:2  176:3
  180:4  195:3  198:1
  200:158  305:5  317:5
Looking Glass (Chief)  6:3
  11:2  26:14  27:7  36:3
  102:4  103:4  118:4
  132:4  133:5  155:3
  172:5  176:2  198:1
Looking-Glass, OR  152:1
Lookout, WA  SEE Alger,
  WA
Loomis, Edwin G.  202:7
Loomis, Lewis Alfred
  109:14  150:1  202:17
Loomis, WA  109:3  225:2
  267:1  305:1
Loop, WA  267:1
Loop Loop, WA  267:1
Loose, Ursinus K.  266:3
Lopez, WA  14:1
Lopp, William T.  160:2  190:4
Lord, C. J.  217:7  245:18
  266:2
Lord, William P.  150:2
  153:1

Lorena, ID  102:2  SEE
  ALSO Kupro, ID
Loring, AK  18:1  63:1
Lorrain, John Baptiste
  25:2
Lorraine, M. J.  151:6
Loryea, A. M.  187:6
Lost River, ID  223:1
Lott, Mortimer H.  46:3
Louisville, MT  78:2
  112:5  319:4
Loundagin, George W.  199:2
Lovejoy, Asa Lawrence
  4:5  41:1  51:15  68:4
  119:12  150:2  177:6
  179:1  198:2  210:5
  257:4  264:1  284:4
  300:6
Lovelady, Thomas J.  30:1
Loveland, Charles  23:6
Lovewell, Samuel Harrison
  199:2
Low, John N.  7:4  31:9
  80:9  306:13
Lowden, Francis M.  176:1
  199:2
Lowden, Marshall J.  199:1
Lowden, WA  305:1
Lowe, William Hamilton
  5:5
Lowe, ID  102:5  SEE AL-
  SO Winona, ID
Lowell, ID  102:3  103:2
Lowell, WA  57:1
Lowery, R. T.  47:1
Lownsdale, Daniel H.  150:2
  179:1  210:4  264:1  284:5
Lownsdale, J. P. O.  150:1
Lowry, D. C.  118:3
Lucas, Jay P.  150:2
Luchtefeld, Barney  102:6
  103:3
Lucier, Etienne  84:4
  114:4  162:14  198:1
Lucile, ID  102:6
Luckey, J. L.  42:3
Luckey, Joe S.  232:3

Ludden, William Henry
288:2
Luddington, R. S.   157:2
Ludlow, J. P.   246:2
Lueddemann, Max  300:4
Luelling, Henderson  41:1
284:3
Luellwitz, Gustav  288:3
Lugenbeel, Pinkney  33:3
Luhn, Henry Bernard  289:3
Lukeen, Ivan Simonsen
77:8
Lump City, MT  46:3  319:2
Lund, BC  204:4
Luse, Harry  9:4
Lutz, Harry E.   266:3
Lyda, William H.   195:6
Lyle, George  242:4
Lyle, WA  198:1  242:15
Lyman, Horace  150:1
Lyman, William Denison
198:8  199:3  257:13
Lyman, ID  59:6
Lyman, WA  314:5  315:5
Lynch, Frank  234:1
Lynch, Marjorie  278:1
Lynch, P. M.  199:2
Lynch, Robert E.  199:2
Lynden, WA  14:1  305:3
Lyng, Howard  128:5
Lyng, R. T.  281:2
Lyon, Caleb  33:9  43:1
87:13  118:6  134:2
147:2  164:1  188:3
211:3  259:4  304:2
Lyon, George C.  41:1
Lyons, Hays "Haze"  133:6
256:7
Lyons, Patrick  119:2
176:1
Lyons, Thomas  199:1
Lytle, Elmer  75:3
Lytle, Joseph  203:1
Lytle, Robert F.  203:1
266:1
Lytton, BC  3:12  204:3
253:5

Mabry, Emeline J.   199:2
Mabry, Robert  289:2
Mabton, WA  252:1
McAdow, Perry W.  46:2
319:5
McAfee, J. W.  187:6
McAllister, D. A.  150:2
McAllister, George  32:5
McAllister, H. C.  86:5
McAllister, James J.  32:16
33:4
McAllister, Ward  149:3
190:7
McArdle, L. D.  245:7
McArthur, Lewis A.  82:14
McArthur, Neil McLean
33:2  181:4
McAulay, George B.  212:8
McAuliff, James  119:21
179:1  199:2
McBean, Gerald  275:12
McBean, John  119:4  179:2
McBean, William  119:3
177:15  179:2  198:4
235:7  296:5
McBeth, Kate  102:12
103:8
McBeth, Sue  102:12
McBoyle, A. P.  102:3
McBride, Henry  245:11
261:1  266:3
McBride, J. S.  308:1
McBride, James  150:3
McBride, John R.  30:1
51:25  87:17
McBride, Richard  126:3
140:1  238:11  253:50
260:4  294:1
McCabe, C. A.  280:3
McCaffery, M. P.  185:5
McCaffree, Mary Ellen
278:1
McCall, John Marshall
150:1
McCall, Thomas  49:4
195:7  265:4  307:3
McCall, ID  23:8  103:3

118:5 164:1 259:3
McCallum, AK 63:1
McCammon, ID 23:3
McCann, Edwin W. 199:1
McCarthy, AK 63:1
McCarthyville, MT 78:4
McCarty, J. W. 150:1
McCarty, John 150:2
McCarty, William 84:2
202:12
McCarver, Morton Matthew
31:2 32:3 119:8 150:4
152:2 179:3 203:1
266:6 284:3 305:2
McChesney, John T. 57:9
McClain, Alva J. 279:6
McClanahan, E. J. 232:4
McClane, John Birch
150:2
McCleary, Henry 176:1
McCleary, WA 152:2
176:2 305:2
McClellan, Jib 76:11
McClelland, J. M. 200:6
McClelland, John 41:1
McCloskey, Sol J. 258:3
McClung, D. R. 82:9
McClung, J. H. 232:5
McClure, Alexander
286:3
McClure, Andrew 56:14
McClure, Charles D.
319:7
McClure, Charles M.
150:2
McClure, James A. 12:8
259:3
McClure, John 272:3
McClymont, Thomas 185:5
McCollough, Frank T.
288:4
McConaha, George N.
220:2
McConkey, J. D. 102:4
McConnaughey, John W.
266:2
McConnell, Beverly Brown

278:1
McConnell, Robert Ervie
38:1 231:29
McConnell, William J.
43:1 95:7 117:4 118:3
134:2 170:3 197:6
205:3 259:2
McCool, Robert 199:1
McCord, O. H. P. 264:2
McCord, S. B. 150:1 264:2
McCormick, Robert Laird
222:3
McCormick, S. J. 51:16
McCormick, Washington
Jay 133:4 155:4 181:8
286:2
McCormick, WA 152:2
McCornick, W. S. 23:4
McCoy, George 266:2
McCoy, James C. 119:1
McCoy, John D. 199:1
McCoy, Joseph H. 199:2
McCoy, Thomas K. 119:2
150:1
McCoy, William 68:4
McCracken, John 179:2
McCrae, Wallace 207:3
McCready, Norman Sylves-
ter 266:3
McCreight, John Foster
238:7 253:4
MacCrimmon, J. C. 150:2
McCroskey, R. C. 184:13
McCullagh, J. A. 189:7
McCully, A. A. 229:3
McCully, Frank M. 38:4
119:9 266:2
McCurdy, H. W. 246:1
McCurdy, Samuel M. 150:2
McCush, Daniel 266:2
McCush, William 266:1
McCutcheon, Isaac D. 286:8
McCutcheon, John T. 245:3
McCutcheon, Stanley J.
66:2 129:7 241:1
McDermott, Fred 157:3
McDermott, Harvey 175:14

McDevitt, William 191:10
McDonald, Angus 20:5
McDonald, Archibald 39:8
    108:6 305:3
MacDonald, Betty Bard
    Heskett 32:3 41:1 152:1
    176:2 252:1 278:1
McDonald, Donald 262:6
McDonald, Duncan 135:5
McDonald, E. D. 99:7
McDonald, Finan 27:7
    42:4 50:4 72:7 135:4
    155:3
McDonald, H. 150:2
McDonald, J. R. 243:3
McDonald, John A. 238:33
McDonald, John B. 199:2
MacDonald, Ranald 39:40
    50:4 176:4 203:1 272:4
McDonald, Robert 255:5
    311:3
McDonald, Thomas W.
    266:2
McDonald, William H.
    150:1
McDonald, William J.
    238:4
McDonnell, Edward 199:2
McDonnell, Steve J. 293:3
McDougal, D. C. 219:3
McDougall, Duncan 4:2
    72:11 108:2 176:2
    198:6 272:24
McDougall, James 235:7
McDowell, Ella R. 169:23
McEachern, Daniel Victor
    240:246
McEachern, John A.
    240:19
McEachran, William E.
    124:7
McElroy, E. B. 150:2
    153:1
McElroy, Thornton F.
    41:2 245:10
McEvoy, Joseph 199:3
McEwen, James 134:14

McFadden, Obadiah B. 119:6
    203:3 245:3
McFarland, Amanda 149:4
McFarland, Frank 150:2
McFarlane, E. G. 103:5
McFarlin, Charles Dexter
    258:4
McGee, Homer 9:11
McGee, I. L. 127:8
McGeer, Gerald G. 236:4
    238:2
McGhee, John W. 119:4
    199:2
McGill, Henry C. 38:1
McGillicuddy, J. A. 195:2
MacGillivray, Duncan J.
    289:2
McGillivray, Joseph 72:4
McGilvery, Napoleon 150:1
McGilvra, Hugh 195:2
McGilvra, John J. 31:5
    119:2 163:3 243:14
McGinnis, David R. 279:5
McGinnis, Emery 266:2
MacGinniss, John 167:2
    209:20
McGlinchey, Neil 119:4
McGlynn, John 150:2
McGoldrick, J. P. 99:1
McGonagall, Charles 115:1
    233:18
McGovern, James E.
    293:16
McGowan, Edward "Ned"
    3:7 20:4
McGowan, George 41:1
    110:2
McGowan, Patrick J. 202:9
McGowan, William 245:4
McGowan, WA 109:3 202:4
McGown, Eva 52:5 148:1
    309:2
McGrady, Kyle 103:9
    229:1
McGrane, Frank 102:19
    103:8
McGrath, I. N. "Newt" 293:11

McGrath, AK  63:1  137:6
  263:13
McGraw, John H.  31:4
  38:2  94:6  163:7  176:2
  178:4  222:10  234:9
  243:11  245:5  276:4
McGregor, Daniel  266:2
McGregor, Henry J.  266:2
McGuinness, Michael Joseph
  266:2
McGuire, Francis  150:2
Machetanz, Fred  129:3
  290:3
McIlhany, James S.  266:2
McInnes, Thomas R.  238:6
McInnis, Malcolm  203:1
McInroe, Charles  199:2
McIntire, Horace J.  287:3
McIntosh, Harold  308:3
McIntosh, R. L.  185:2
McIntyre, J. Lincoln
  175:6
McIntyre, James  203:2
McIteeny, John S.  35:2
McKaig, Ray  213:5
MacKay, Albert Edward
  187:9
McKay, Alexander  50:7
  72:6  177:3  198:2  272:5
McKay, Charles Richard
  84:5
McKay, Dan  156:7
MacKay, Donald D.  124:12
McKay, Douglas  49:8
  195:3  261:1
McKay, George L.  266:2
Mackay, Gordon  245:10
McKay, Jean Baptiste Des-
  portes  162:14
McKay, Joseph William
  3:11  20:15
McKay, Robert  185:2
McKay, Thomas  4:12  33:6
  44:6  50:8  97:2  101:4
  119:7  162:10  177:13
  272:4
McKay, William Cameron

119:4  150:4  179:2
  187:7  207:4  272:4
MacKay, ID  23:8  164:1
McKee, Paul B.  82:42
McKenna, WA  305:1
McKenny, T. I.  245:7
Mackenzie, Alexander  52:2
  55:2  63:2  130:2  311:13
MacKenzie, Donald  6:4
  33:14  39:4  72:8  119:5
  132:8  198:4  259:3
MacKenzie, George F.  82:6
MacKenzie, K. A. J.  187:19
McKenzie, Norman  260:6
MacKenzie, Roderick  289:2
Mackin, Charles  34:3
McKinley, Archibald  4:8
  177:5  198:1
McKinney, Thompson M.
  199:2
McKinney, William  199:1
McKinney, William E.  199:1
McKinnon, Alexander Balone
  266:3
McKnight, Orlando  284:1
McKone, Archie  122:15
McLain, Minor  266:3
MacLane, John F.  127:11
Maclaren, James Barnet
  294:2
McLaren, R. N.  297:6
McLean, Alexander  161:5
McLean, Clark N.  199:2
McLean, Daniel  161:2
McLean, Donald  3:6
  235:13
McLean, James Alexander
  117:55
McLean, John  235:7
MacLean, John Duncan
  253:8
MacLean, Laughlin  96:1
  288:4
McLean, Malcolm A.  236:4
  238:3
McLean, Roderick  5:4
McLean, Samuel  286:7

McLeary, James H.   286:4
Macleay, OR  75:4
McLeod, C. H.   181:4
McLeod, Jarvis  185:2
McLeod, John  4:16   101:13
   177:20
McLeod (Fort), BC  235:3
   SEE ALSO Fort McLeod,
   BC
McManus, John E.   266:4
McManus, O. C.   157:2
McMillan, Christopher C.
   266:2
McMillan, Duncan Neil
   266:2
MacMillan, Harvey Reginald
   122:6   260:6   294:13
McMillen, H. D.   293:5
McMillen, James H.   150:2
McMinnville, OR  68:5
   75:8   174:10   187:11
   300:7   303:12   317:3
McMordie, S. P.   185:2
McMorris, Lewis  119:5
   199:3
McMullen, Fayette  7:3
   245:4
McMunn, H. I.   175:9
McMurray, John  213:7
McMurray, John L.   266:4
McMurray, WA  315:8
McMurry, Fielding  232:4
McMurry, James Scott
   232:1
McMynn, W. G.   47:1
McNary, Charles L.   49:10
   162:9   195:3   198:1
   205:6   207:4   244:5
   261:3   293:7
McNary, James  56:5
McNary, Wilson D.   207:5
McNaught, James H.   243:13
McNaught, Joseph  234:1
McNeeley, Edwin J.   266:2
McNeill, Hobart W.   163:4
McNitt, Frank T.   266:3
McPherson, J. L.   130:2

McQuade, Peter  126:3
McQueen, Stuart V.   307:11
McQuesten, Leroy Napoleon
   "Jack"  63:5  81:2  149:7
   159:5   255:14   309:23
   310:5   311:6
MacQuinn, Sutcliffe  266:2
Macquinna (Chief) SEE
   Maquinna
McRae, Donald  57:55
McRae, John  32:4   266:2
McReavy, John  203:1
McRedmond, Luke  203:1
McRoy, Peter  161:1
McTavish, Donald  72:3
   120:3   196:3
McTavish, John George
   72:6  108:3  119:2  120:4
   188:6
McUne, George  114:3
McVay, Alfred  176:4
McWhorter, Lucullus V.
   27:4  305:1
McWilliams, Robert J.
   150:1
Maddock, Frank  36:3
Madison, Helene  278:1
Madras, OR  42:16   56:4
   82:5   300:2
Madsen, Charles  161:5
Magallon, Adrien  199:2
Maginnis, Martin  48:3
   60:17   133:26   155:4
   156:1   214:4   215:4
   254:3   286:26   298:4
Magnuson, Warren G.   41:2
   83:3   96:2   129:6   130:5
   178:8   234:1   241:2   244:1
   245:13   248:2   265:30
   276:2   293:7   301:5
Magruder, Lloyd  76:3
   103:5   118:2   256:3
Maguire, John  67:6
Mahaffey, Pierce A.   150:1
Maher, Michael  212:4
Mahoney, Dan "Dapper Dan"
   9:6

Mahoney, Mike 161:2
Mahoney, Thomas R. 49:7
Mahoney, Willis 49:7
Maiden, MT 78:8 156:1
  224:5 319:14
Major, Charles George 5:5
Maki, Joseph 4:3
Malad City, ID 23:10 24:2
  45:2 87:3 118:2 164:1
Maley, W. B. 68:5
Malheur City, OR 225:2
  264:3
Mallon, Carl 212:5
Mallory, C. M. 150:2
Mallory, Henry 266:2
Mallory, Rufus 150:2
Malloy, William J. 266:1
Malloy, William S. 199:1
Malo, WA 225:2
Malone, Francis M. 283:8
Malone, Patrick J. 300:8
Maloney, M. 119:4
Maloney, Thomas 191:15
Malott, Connor 96:3
Malott, WA 267:1 305:1
Malta, MT 215:3 247:3
Mammoth, MT 319:4
Manders, John E. 241:2
Mangan, Edward H. 199:2
Mangan, Joseph J. 199:2
Manion, John 199:1
Manley Hot Springs, AK
  137:2
Mann, Irvin 207:4
Mann, Lee 102:4
Mann, William H. 199:2
Manning, E. C. 294:2
Manning, Lucius R. 266:2
Manning, WA 267:1
Mannion, Joseph 236:8
Mansfield, Francis W.
  266:2
Mansfield, Mike 129:9
  214:3 215:8 216:3
  265:10
Manson, Alexander M.
  238:4

Manson, Donald 162:11
  235:16
Mantle, Lee 60:18 133:4
  167:2 286:2
Manwaring, Hyrum 59:6
Maple, Jacob 80:3 306:4
Maple, Samuel 306:5
Maple Falls, WA 305:1
Maquinna (Chief) 121:5
  140:20 165:6 313:2
Mara, John A. 107:6
Marblemount, WA 305:1
  314:7 315:5
March, Hiram Alfred 266:2
Marchisio, Jocelyn 278:1
Marcus, WA 107:3 151:3
  225:2
Marcy, Benjamin W. 199:2
Mardesich, August 245:3
Marengo, WA 119:7 280:2
Mariaville, BC 20:2
Mariner, William 257:3
Marion, Joseph E. 112:9
Markham, Edwin 153:1
Markley, Lemon R. 266:2
Marlin, WA 305:1
Marple, Perry P. 51:110
Marquam, Philip A. 150:2
Marsh, Calvin Lacon 266:1
Marsh, David 150:1
Marsh, Ernest P. 57:95
Marsh, S. P. 150:2
Marshall, Hugh J. 134:2
Marshall, AK 8:2 63:1
  SEE ALSO Fortuna Ledge,
  AK
Marshfield, OR 41:1 75:3
  104:9 180:2 187:4
  258:15 300:6 SEE ALSO
  Coos Bay, OR
Marsing, ID 23:1
Marsten, M. R. 52:2
Martin, A. W. W. 237:4
Martin, Bedford W. 150:1
Martin, C. Victor 116:2
Martin, Charles H. 49:15
  244:10 261:3 293:3 302:1

Martin, Clarence D.    38:2
  41:2    58:13    83:4    92:2
  100:3    169:10    184:20
  195:3    222:8    231:3
  234:5    244:7    245:27
  248:2    261:2    293:20
Martin, David    71:10
Martin, Frank    213:4
Martin, George M.    169:11
Martin, Harry S.    288:3
Martin, J. A.    227:13
Martin, Joseph    238:14
  253:11
Martin, Michael    199:2
Martin, Mungo    140:1
  260:4
Martin, Patrick    199:2
Martin, Samuel N. D.
  91:3
Martin, William    150:2
Martin, William J.    145:5
Martin, ID    223:1
Martina, MT    112:5
Martinsdale, MT    156:1
  319:5
Maryhill, WA    151:9    152:2
  198:1    203:2    305:2
  308:1
Marysville, ID    23:1
Marysville, MT    76:3    78:4
  214:1    224:8    247:4
  319:13
Marysville, OR    251:4
Marysville, WA    14:1
  305:2
Masik, August    161:5
Mason, Allen C.    150:2
Mason, Charles Henry
  80:5    119:7    141:3
  150:1    179:3    220:9
  234:2
Mason, Coridon Z.    203:1
Mason City, WA    244:3
  267:1    293:2    305:1
Masset, BC    204:4
Masterson, Andrew C.
  199:3

Masterson, Henry    108:3
Mastick, E. B.    191:10
Mastin, W. H.    150:2
Matanuska, AK    148:17
  159:15    171:10    226:329
  241:1    262:9    271:6
  281:22    290:5
Matheny, Jasper N.    39:6
Matheny, N. W.    41:1    108:4
Mather, Edward K.    10:4
Mathes, Edward T.    38:1
  266:2
Matheson, George    279:5
Matheson, Harvey E.    279:8
Mathew, William L.    199:1
Matlock, E. L.    150:1
Matlock, William F.    207:4
Matson, J. Albert    258:4
Matson, John    196:35
Matson, Ralph C.    187:11
Matthew, Otto L.    266:2
Matthews, Alexander G.
  266:2
Matthews, James Skitt    260:5
Matthews, Mark A.    113:4
  124:11    234:7    245:5
Matthews, W. Gale    244:3
  293:31
Matthias, Franklin    306:5
Matthieu, Francis Xavier
  22:3    68:5    84:2    114:7
  153:1    162:15    198:1
Matthieu, Stephen W.    114:6
Mattice, Henry    179:3
Mattison, M. M.    234:3
Mattoon, Charles H.    303:25
Mattson, Helmi    278:1
Matzger, William O.    51:11
  119:5
Maudlow, MT    46:2
Maupin, Howard    42:10
Maupin, OR    75:2
Maxey, Carl    265:8
Maxey, Chester Collins
  257:2
Maxson, Samuel R.    199:2
Maxwell, Bedford    46:2

Maxwell, George R.  238:9
Maxwell, George W.  179:1
Maxwell, J. W.  217:6
Maxwell, Samuel L.  41:1
Maxwelton, WA  305:1
May, Percy  113:4
May, Walter W. R.  96:2
May, ID  23:1
Maybury, Charles R.  245:9
Mayfield, William  256:10
Mayflower, MT  319:3
Mayhew, Lewis  266:1
Maynard, Charles W.  266:2
Maynard, David Swainson
    6:3  7:21  31:20  41:1
    50:20  80:7  121:4  172:5
    178:25  187:6  234:50
    243:3  252:1  276:10
    301:2  304:2  305:3
    306:19
Maynard, Hannah Hatherly
    123:2
Mayo, Alfred  63:4  149:4
    255:4  309:5  311:4
Mays, F. W. D.  119:2
Mayview, WA  119:1  280:2
Mayville, MT  78:2  319:4
Mazama, WA  267:1
Meacham, A. B.  87:5  153:1
Meacham, Harvey  87:3
Mead, Albert E.  243:1
    245:11  266:3
Mead, Elwood  279:3
Mead, Eugene H.  157:2
Mead, Fred M.  266:3
Meade, William J.  266:2
Meaderville (Butte), MT
    67:10  167:4  209:3
    319:7
Meadows, ID  23:3
Meagher, Thomas Francis
    13:182  25:13  48:15
    112:6  133:29  155:2
    156:5  183:5  214:7
    215:5  247:8  254:6
    286:20  298:6
Meany, Edmond Stephen

    38:10  152:1  178:3
    203:1  245:6
Meath, Edward  266:1
Mecklenburg, G.  227:5
Medbury, A. R.  303:5
Medford, OR  17:4  41:6
    75:5  82:3  104:9  114:5
    152:2  180:4  187:2
    196:2  300:10  303:4
Medfra, AK  263:2
Medical Lake, WA  27:3
    39:3  305:1
Medimont, ID  212:2
Meeds, Lloyd  12:6
Meek, Fred  162:6
Meek, Helen Mar  172:5  296:9
Meek, Joseph L.  4:10
    6:4  50:5  76:6  84:11
    119:14  145:8  150:2
    162:8  172:18  177:29
    179:3  188:10  193:4
    198:1  252:3  264:3
Meek, Stephen Hall L.
    42:4  56:50  97:5  193:2
    264:2  318:45
Meeker, Ezra  45:13  141:6
    151:3  195:1  203:1
    217:1  222:12  245:10
    252:4  301:3  305:11
Megler, Joseph C.  202:1
    245:3
Megler, WA  109:8  198:1
    202:3
Mehling, Theodore J.  71:14
Meier, Julius L.  49:5
    153:1  261:3  293:2
Meier, William F.  157:2
Meigs, C. R.  51:30
Meigs, G. A.  7:8
Meigs, L. O.  245:5
Meikle, S. M.  23:7
Meiners, Martin  199:1
Meisner, Clara  231:5
    278:1
Mekoryuk, AK  290:1
Melba, ID  23:2
Melgard, Hawkin  23:8  24:4

Melrose, MT  46:3  319:5

Melsing, L. F.  281:5

Menan, ID  23:4

Menetrey, Joseph  34:6
181:4  254:6

Mengarini, Gregory  34:10
93:9  155:5  214:3  249:2
254:5

Menlo, WA  36:1  152:1
203:1  305:1

Menne, Frank R.  187:8

Mentor, WA  119:2  280:3

Mercer, Asa Shinn  6:2
31:25  38:3  41:2  64:45
121:4  176:7  178:7
188:3  197:10  234:5
252:2  304:4  306:15

Mercer, Thomas  31:19
32:4  80:2  150:1  176:2
197:1  234:2  305:1
306:10

Mercier, A. C.  311:2

Mercier, Moses  309:4

Meredith, William L.
234:9

Meridian, ID  23:4  33:10
164:1  SEE ALSO Hunter,
ID

Merriam, C. K.  150:3

Merriam, George S.  157:2

Merriam, H. G.  152:1

Merrick, C. H.  187:10

Merrill, Dennis D.  57:5

Merrill, Russel  137:17
263:3

Merritt, Mark Wood  289:2

Merwin, L. T.  82:5

Mesa, ID  164:1

Mesplie, Toussaint  87:5
179:1  249:5  272:3

Messerly, Elias  157:3

Metaline Falls, WA  225:2
305:2

Metcalf, Lee  214:3  215:8
247:3

Metcalf, Ralph  266:2

Metcalfe, James B.  163:3

Methow, WA  225:1  267:1
305:4

Metlakatla, AK  3:7  10:30
18:7  28:1  63:1  90:3
125:3  130:3  146:10
149:5  189:6  241:1
253:3  269:9  SEE ALSO
New Metlakatla and Old
Metlakatla

Metolius, OR  42:4

Metschan, Phil  49:3  251:4

Metzdorf, Dewey  263:5

Metzger, Eugene M.  266:2

Meyer, Frederick  266:3

Meyers, Henry L.  133:7

Meyers, Jacob A.  39:5

Meyers, Louther W.  107:2

Meyers, Victor Aloysius
15:1  41:2  176:4  178:4
234:10  244:17  245:20
252:1  261:2

Meyersville, OR  SEE
Myrtle Point, OR

Michaelsen, Helen  231:3

Michel, Justus  199:1

Midas, ID  102:2

Middleton, George H.  199:2

Middleton, ID  23:3  33:10
118:1

Middleton, OR  207:1

Midland, WA  305:1

Midvale, ID  23:2

Mihnos, Frank O.  2:7

Miklautsch, Tom  52:2

Milam, Robert E.  303:10

Miles, John  266:2

Miles City, MT  1:3  34:3
48:6  60:5  133:7  156:4
214:3  215:7  227:5
247:13  292:7  299:2
312:1

Milford, OR  225:2

Milhollin, James Halsey
266:3

Milhollin, John Henkle
266:3

Miller, A. E.  113:8

Miller, Alexander Cyrus
266:2
Miller, Cincinnatus Heine
(Joaquim) 41:1 43:2
87:7 96:1 102:7 104:11
153:2 159:3 258:5 264:4
300:7
Miller, Fred 127:7
Miller, Fred C. 266:3
Miller, G. W. 119:5
Miller, Gene 137:11
Miller, George H. 266:2
Miller, George J. 157:3
Miller, George Melvin
232:5
Miller, George T. 134:5
Miller, Gustav Adolphus
266:2
Miller, H. Lloyd 279:17
Miller, Henry W. 112:6
Miller, Herbert C. 2:15
Miller, Jack SEE Dalton,
Jack
Miller, Jacob H. 116:2
157:3
Miller, James D. 68:7
Miller, James Knox Polk
46:6
Miller, Joaquim SEE Miller,
Cincinnatus
Miller, John F. 179:1
Miller, John H. 266:1
Miller, John P. 307:8
Miller, Jonathan 236:7
Miller, Joseph L. 199:2
Miller, Keith 54:10
Miller, Leonard Emile
266:2
Miller, Magnus 305:1
Miller, Max 57:2
Miller, Milton A. 162:11
Miller, Minnie Myrtle
258:5
Miller, Philip 116:3 157:2
Miller, Sam C. 157:4
Miller, Samuel 203:1
266:2

Miller, Sebastian 229:4
Miller, W. Clayton 106:19
Miller, William Frederick
266:2
Miller, William L. 266:2
Millican, OR 42:2
Milligan, Fred 263:6
Milligan, George 114:6
Milliken, William T. 303:17
Million, Elmer C. 266:4
Mills, Edward D. 199:2
Mills, George 245:5
Mills, Jacob 227:9
Mills, James H. 48:3
133:9 286:17
Mills, Z. C. 150:1
Milltown, WA 315:5
Milner, Moses E. 102:5
103:4
Milner, ID 23:2 103:2
164:1
Milot, Leon 116:2
Milroy, Robert Houston
255:5
Miltner, Charles C. 71:17
Milton, OR 119:4 207:6
284:7 SEE ALSO Milton-
Freewater, OR
Milton-Freewater, OR
207:5 303:2 SEE ALSO
Freewater, OR and Mil-
ton, OR
Milwaukie, OR 41:1 68:6
172:3 210:5 228:4
229:12 284:17 297:4
300:2 303:2
Mineral, ID 223:1
Mineral, WA 225:4 305:1
Minesinger, James 292:11
Ming, John H. 319:5
Minidoka, ID 23:4
Minkler, Bird D. 203:1
Minkler, WA 315:2
Minor, T. T. 243:6
Minter, Charles McClellan
230:2
Minto, John 150:3 172:2

194:13  222:8
Minton, John Clark  266:2
Mission, WA  267:1
Missoula, MT  1:3  39:3
48:14  60:18  76:10
108:5  112:20  133:10
155:15  181:128  183:6
215:13  247:10  254:10
299:15  319:20
Mitchell, Faye Langellier
278:1
Mitchell, Frank W.  266:3
Mitchell, George Monroe
266:2
Mitchell, Homer  242:4
Mitchell, Hugh B.  41:1
245:4
Mitchell, John H.  29:5
85:3  86:5  150:3  188:2
197:16  261:5  302:3
Mitchell, P. W.  219:4
Mitchell, Sidney Zollicoffer
82:18  266:2
Mitchell, William H.  266:3
Mitchell, OR  42:10  225:4
300:2
Mix, Annie M.  199:2
Mix, G. P.  213:11
Mix, J. D.  119:9
Mizner, Wilson  161:4
Moar, Jonathan  287:3
Moar, Thomas A.  287:1
289:2
Moberly, Walter  3:4  5:9
Mock, John  71:4
Mock, William H.  266:3
Mohler, Carl  245:4
Mohler, ID  23:1
Mohler, WA  305:1
Mohn, Jacob E.  266:2
Mohr, Paul F.  150:2
Moldstad, N. J.  217:2
Molkins, Iwa S.  199:1
Moller, Fred  263:17
Molson, John  308:1
Molson, WA  203:1  225:1
267:1  308:8

Monaghan, James  27:3
39:16  96:4  99:2  107:6
212:5  288:3
Monaghan, John Robert
288:4
Monarch, ID  SEE  Black
Cloud, ID
Monarch, MT  319:5
Monida Station, MT  46:4
Monitor, WA  157:2  203:1
Monmouth, OR  75:2  300:3
Monroe, Hugh  135:8
Monroe, OR  75:2
Monroe, WA  14:1  305:1
Monse, WA  267:1
Monsen, Al  263:2
Montana City, MT  78:2
215:3  319:4
Montandon, George E.  266:3
Montavilla, OR  75:2
Montborne, WA  315:3
Monte Cristo, WA  57:3
152:1  225:4  315:2
Monteith, Charles  91:6
Monteith, John B.  26:7
91:17  102:3  172:4
Monteith, Thomas  41:1
Monteith, William J.  91:9
Montesano, WA  14:1  41:1
89:1  152:1  203:4  305:5
Monticello, WA  41:2  50:2
172:1
Montour, ID  23:3
Montpelier, ID  23:6  24:3
45:2  101:1  164:1  180:2
Montreal, MT  112:4
Moody, Charles  275:7
Moody, Richard Clements
3:20  20:9  123:3  236:6
253:12  260:9
Moody, Sewell Prescott
236:13  260:5  294:7
Moody, Zenas Ferry  150:3
153:1
Moody, WA  315:2
Moodyville, BC  73:5  122:7
131:4  158:5  236:8

Moon, Harley D.   266:1
Mooneyville, WA   202:1
Moore, Christopher W.
    23:10   87:10
Moore, Crawford   23:14
    24:6
Moore, Frank Rockwood
    106:28
Moore, Isaac   68:4
Moore, John T.   303:25
Moore, Marshall F.   119:5
Moore, Miles Conway
    119:6   150:1   163:2
    199:2   203:1   222:8
    245:2   257:3
Moore, Robert   68:7   84:5
    284:2
Moore, Terris   148:1
    233:10
Moore, Thomas   199:1
Moore, William   149:7
    268:2
Moore, William Hickman
    234:2
Moore, MT   319:2
Moorehouse, OR   119:1
Moores, Isaac R.   51:7
    147:2   197:3
Moores, John H.   150:2
Moorhouse, Lee   150:2
    207:4
Moose City, ID   223:1
Moosetown, MT   319:3
Moran, Margaret   278:1
Moran, Robert   150:2
    163:2   178:4   203:1
    234:5   243:3   305:4
Moran, Thomas   266:2
Mordaunt, A. P.   281:6
More, Marion   23:2
    36:2
Moreau, Basil Anthony
    71:8
Morehouse, Henry L.
    303:5
Moreland, Jesse   150:2
Morford, Russell B.   87:3

Morgan, Harry E.   175:29
    305:1
Morgan, Hiram D.   150:2
    266:3
Morgan, Howard   49:13
Morgan, Jenkins   266:2
Morgan, John H.   38:3
    231:9
Morgan, John T.   95:10
Morgan, Murray   240:7
Morgan, W. H. H.   287:5
Morganville, WA   282:4
Moriarty, M. F.   289:3
Morice, A. G.   186:2
Moricetown, BC   186:2
    235:3
Morison, John Robert
    185:3
Morlan, M. J.   150:1
Moro, OR   295:2
Morris, A. L. "Al"   116:2
Morris, B. F.   102:7   103:3
Morris, B. Wistar   153:1
Morris, Carl   41:1
Morris, S. M.   200:15
Morris, William C.   96:6
Morris, William Wardner
    319:3
Morrison, Aulay   238:3
Morrison, B. K.   147:4
Morrison, Edward H.   107:3
Morrison, Harry W.   118:2
    240:5
Morrison, John L.   84:4
Morrison, John T.   43:1
Morrison, Robert Wilson
    150:2
Morrow, J. H.   199:1
Morrow, Jackson L.   111:16
    150:2
Morse, Davis W.   266:2
Morse, Eldridge   57:2
Morse, Frank C.   266:2
Morse, Franklin B.   199:1
Morse, Olney N.   150:2
Morse, Robert I.   266:2
Morse, Roy F.   200:5

Morse, Wayne L.   12:9
  41:4   49:15   85:6   129:16
  130:4   232:2   261:3
Morss, Willard   175:8
Mort, Richard   114:1
Morton, James F.   41:1
  191:18
Morton, John   236:5   260:6
Morton, WA   305:2
Morvillo, Anthony   103:3
Morwick, William   235:3
Moscow, ID   23:13   24:6
  27:3   96:1   97:2   117:10
  118:12   164:1   192:3
  198:1   205:4   212:1
Moses (Chief)   36:8   108:1
  150:1
Moses Lake, WA   41:2
  172:4   252:2   293:27
  305:1   SEE ALSO Nep-
  pel, WA
Mosher, LaFayette   145:9
  150:2
Moss, A. B.   95:1
Moss, Sidney Walter   22:2
  150:1   177:4
Mosser, Jonas   114:5
Mossyrock, WA   305:1
Mott, James W.   162:4
Mottet, Frederic   266:2
Mottman, George A.   245:20
  266:3
Moultray, William R.   266:2
Mount, Margaret S.   231:3
Mount, Wallace   266:2
Mt. Angel, OR   75:8
Mount Idaho, ID   23:1
  91:4   102:20   103:4
  164:1   172:2   223:1
Mount Vernon, WA   14:1
  41:2   89:1   191:5   246:3
  305:2   314:11   315:11
Mountain Home, ID   23:6
  118:4   164:1
Mountain Village, AK   8:4
Mowell, John Wilson   266:2
Moxee, WA   305:1

Moyer, Charles H.   99:2
Mud Lake, ID   23:5
Muir, Andrew   260:3
Muir, John   20:8   275:11
Mukilteo, WA   92:1   220:2
  305:3
Muldoon, ID   223:1
Mulkey, Johnson   150:2
Mulkey, Marion Francis
  150:1
Mullan, John   27:21   39:5
  43:2   45:8   48:12   96:2
  99:5   108:4   112:8   118:7
  133:46   139:3   141:5
  155:34   181:9   188:8
  212:4
Mullan, ID   23:2   98:13
  108:1   118:3   164:1
  212:8
Mullerleile, Louie   237:5
Mulligan, Charnel   232:8
Multnomah, OR   68:10
  153:1   284:1
Mulville, Samuel   60:5
Munge, Asahel   177:1
Munks, William   150:2
  314:6   315:3
Munn, Clarence Emerson
  266:2
Munro, Henry L.   266:2
Munro, William J.   266:2
Munsel, Patrice   96:5
Munson, Albert J.   266:3
Munson, John P.   231:7
Munson, L. R.   1:2
Munson, Lyman   119:3
  179:2   286:8
Munson, Mark C.   230:2
Munter, Herb   178:3   252:2
Murdock, John   161:2
Murfin, A. M.   279:4
Murkowski, Frank   54:3
Murphy, Bob   52:16
Murphy, Horace J.   199:1
Murphy, Jeremiah   67:17
  167:3
Murphy, John L.   87:2

Murphy, John Miller 245:52
Murphy, Martin 208:7
Murphy, Thomas G. 149:7
Murphy, ID 23:1 36:3
118:2 134:4
Murray, Alexander 157:3
Murray, David 150:2
Murray, E. J. 300:5
Murray, James A. 67:6
209:2
Murray, James E. 214:6
215:12 241:1 247:5
Murray, Margaret Lally
138:1
Murray, ID 23:8 24:2
39:3 96:5 98:5 99:4
108:7 118:7 172:7
212:6 223:2
Murrow, Lacey V. 176:1
245:4
Murtaugh, ID 23:3
Musgrave, Anthony 20:2
126:3 238:3 253:10
260:3
Musgrove, William H.
287:3
Musselshell, MT 78:6
Muzzall, Ernest 231:7
Myers, George L. 82:5
Myers, George T. 203:1
Myers, Guy C. 82:25
Myers, Henry L. 299:7
Myers, Jake 61:35
Myers, Jefferson 49:3
Myers, John L. 266:2
Myers, William H. H.
179:4
Myrtle Point, OR 258:10
Mystery Town (Camp), MT
224:6

Naches, WA 305:1 SEE
ALSO Natchees
Nahcotta, WA 109:26
202:12 305:1

Nailor, Madge Haynes
278:1
Nakusp, BC 151:4 316:5
Nampa, ID 23:11 24:3
33:40 36:5 117:5 118:5
134:3 164:1 205:8
Nampuh (Chief) 43:1 164:2
Nanaimo, BC 3:20 20:11
120:5 122:3 123:4
131:6 165:40 204:5
253:11 260:4 275:13
Nancarrow, Bill 115:8
Napavine, WA 14:1 152:1
Naselle, WA 202:3 305:1
Nash, George Williston
38:1
Nash, I. H. 219:2
Nash, Lucius 252:4
Natchees, WA 198:1 SEE
ALSO Naches
Nation, AK 309:4
Naught, F. M. 150:2
Neah Bay, WA 100:20
176:2 203:1 246:3
305:3
Neale, Mervin Gordon
117:43
Needham, Arthur 266:2
Needham, Joseph 3:4
126:2
Neel, Daisy 140:6
Neely, Aaron S. 203:2
Neely, David A. 150:3
Neff, Jesse B. 173:4
Neher, John A. 266:3
Neihart, James L. 319:4
Neihart, MT 60:3 319:11
Neil, Edith 196:5
Neil, John Baldwin 87:2
95:3
Neil, Nellie 129:2
Neill, Roy K. 106:8
Neils, Gerhard 242:15
Neils, Paul 242:12
Nelson (Chief) 31:3
Nelson, A. J. 25:2
Nelson, Charles 203:1

Nelson, Cyrus T.
　199:3
Nelson, Elvon　274:13
Nelson, Hiram　199:2
Nelson, Hugh　294:5
Nelson, Jasper　203:1
Nelson, M. B.　200:9
Nelson, Otto　263:4
Nelson, Vaughn
　274:12
Nelson, BC　107:9　123:2
　198:3
Nenana, AK　52:3　63:2
　137:8　233:4　263:8
Neppel, WA　293:12
　SEE ALSO Moses
　Lake, WA
Nera, WA　267:1
Nerland, Andrew　128:6
　241:1
Nesmith, James Willis
　35:7　85:5　119:17
　145:30　147:2　150:3
　153:1　179:9　194:6
　198:4　220:4　296:2
　300:5　302:2
Nespelem, WA　27:3
　36:1　198:3　252:2
　267:1
Neterer, Jeremiah　266:2
Nethercutt, George M.
　289:2
Neubauer, Nathaniel L.
　116:3
Neuberger, Maurine　49:3
Neuberger, Richard L.
　12:10　41:4　49:15
　88:2　129:7　261:3
Neufeldt, Tony　114:5
Neuhausen, Thomas
　49:6
Nevada City, MT　25:16
　46:3　48:3　78:5
　133:15　215:5　256:3
　308:4　319:14
Neverstill, OR　152:1
Nevins, George F.

　82:5
New Chicago, MT　76:3
　78:4　224:2
New Denver, BC　47:1
New Hazleton, BC
　186:3　SEE ALSO
　Hazleton, BC
New Jerusalem, ID
　33:3
New Kamilche, WA
　9:2
New Meadows, ID　23:5
New Metlakatla, AK
　140:13　SEE ALSO
　Metlankatla and Old
　Metlakatla
New Plymouth, ID　23:3
　164:1
New Westminister, BC
　3:50　5:22　20:11
　122:8　123:6　126:5
　158:9　246:4　253:21
　260:5　275:5
New Year, MT　319:3
New York, MT　78:1
　SEE ALSO York,
　MT
Newberg, OR　75:3
　300:2
Newbery, Arthur A.
　107:6
Newburn, Harry K.
　232:2
Newcastle, WA　163:9
Newdale, ID　23:3　59:4
Newell, Charles　203:1
Newell, Robert　43:1
　68:9　84:6　91:3
　103:3　119:12　150:1
　162:17　193:18
Newell, William A.
　245:9
Newell, William H.
　29:4　119:6　245:4
Newelsville, OR　162:3
Newhalem, WA　315:2
Newhouse, F. I.　23:4

Newkirk, Israel A.
266:2
Newland, John T.
266:3
Newman, James
274:12
Newman, William
B. C. 150:1
Newman, WA 267:1
Newmarket, WA 100:5
SEE ALSO Tumwater,
WA
Newport, OR 75:4
228:10
Newport, WA 293:5
305:1
Newquist, Lori 178:6
Newschwander, William
231:3
Newsome, ID 102:2
223:1
Newton, Seville M.
185:8
Newton, Tom 100:3
Nezperce, ID 23:3
Niagra City, BC 47:1
Nicholas, Amander M.
199:1
Nicholia, ID 164:1 223:1
Nichols, Frank 42:4
Nichols, Samuel H.
245:5 266:3
Nicholson, Leo 231:6
Nickel Plate, BC 47:1
Nickell, Charles 150:1
Nickerson, G. W. 185:3
Nickerson, William J.
288:3
Nicola, BC 47:1
Nicolai, H. E. 279:9
Nieminen, Matt 137;8
Nighthawk, WA 267:1
Nikolski, AK 290:2
Nind, Philip H. 20:3
Nine Mile Falls, WA 39:3
Ninilchik, AK 63:1
Niorada, MT 319:2
Nisqually, WA 14:1 31:3

84:2 93:11 187:5
194:15 198:1 249:5
SEE ALSO Fort Nisqually
Nisqually Flats, WA 152:1
Nobili, John 34:8 208:9
235:3
Noble, John F. 119:5
179:3
Noble, William A. 199:2
Nobles, Edward T. 266:2
Noel, Jacqueline 169:12
Noggle, David 87:11
Nolan, C. B. 133:7
Noland, Pleasant Cal-
vin 150:2
Nolte, Grover C. 191:4
Noltner, Anthony 163:2
300:11
Nome, AK 8:16 28:9
52:45 55:10 63:4 66:4
115:4 130:27 137:22
143:4 146:15 148:6
159:16 160:8 161:11
190:4 196:3 241:6
271:11 281:30 290:40
310:20 311:36
Nookmute, AK 130:1
Nooksack, WA 14:1
Noorvik, AK 8:6 52:3
63:1
Nootka, BC 20:6 121:15
123:4 165:9
Norblad, Albin Walter
153:1
Nordale, Alton 226:1
Nordale, Hjalmar 263:1
Norman, Fred 245:5
Norman, Nelson R. 199:1
Norman, William S. 106:5
Norris, MT 46:3
North Bend, OR 41:1
75:3 104:4 258:11
300:2 SEE ALSO
Yarrow, OR
North Bend, WA 305:1
Northport, WA 96:1 97:2
107:16 151:3 225:2
305:1

Northrop, N.  119:4
Northrup, Emanuel  174:13
Norton, Marianne Craft
  278:1
Norton, Z. C.  150:2
Norvall, John W.  150:1
Norwood, William  25:2
Norwood, MT  319:2
Noti, OR  251:1
Notti, Emil  54:14  130:1
Notus, ID  23:1
Nowell, Charles  140:10
  189:4
Nowikakat, AK  77:2
Noyes, Alfred  161:1
Noyes, Arthur H.  52:2
  55:4  63:1  130:2  143:1
  159:4  161:2  309:2
  310:5  311:12
Noyes, Fred  103:5
Noyes, Harold J.  2:12
Nugent, John F.  127:7
  213:7  219:2  261:1
Nuklukahyet, AK  77:6
  310:4
Nulato, AK  19:6  63:1
  77:24  81:3  125:3
  130:6  137:4  159:7
  161:5  168:5  281:2
  309:2  310:4  311:4
Nushagak, AK  19:3
Nutter, Donald  214:2
Nuxoll, Francis G.  102:6
  103:5
Nye City, MT  78:3  319:3
Nyssa, OR  4:1  244:2


Oak Bay, BC  165:12
Oak Harbor, WA  14:1
  305:2
Oakley, ID  23:6
Oakridge, OR  75:2
Oakville, WA  14:1
Oatman, Harrison B.  150:1
Oberg, A. T.  2:7

O'Brien, George  255:5
O'Brien, John L.  245:5
O'Brien, Michael G.  71:6
O'Brien, R. G.  245:6
O'Brien, Thomas  212:11
O'Brien, OR  225:1
O'Bryant, Hugh D.  41:1
  264:1
Ocean Falls, BC  122:6
  275:14
Ocean Park, WA  14:1
  109:12  202:6  203:1
Oceanside, WA  202:3
O'Connell, Jerry J.  214:2
  215:4  244:11
Ocosta, WA  152:4  203:1
  305:2
Odegaard, Charles  276:11
Odell, B. F.  191:4
Odell, Elwyn  231:4
Odessa, WA  305:1
Odle, George  103:9
Odle, James  103:4
O'Donahue, Jim  114:5
O'Donnell, H. E.  102:2
O'Donnell, William  119:2
  199:1
O'Farrell, Patrick A.
  209:5
Offner, Winfield S.  199:2
Ogilvie, William  255:12
Ogle, Hal  97:8
O'Hara, Edwin V.  261:2
Ohida, ID  103:1
Ohlson, Otto F.  129:11
  130:2  226:24  262:4
  281:3
Okanogon, WA  198:5
  225:1  267:1  293:12
  305:1
O'Keeffe, Cornelius C.
  112:4  155:4  181:11
O'Keeffe, David  155:6
  181:6
Olalla, WA  14:1  191:7
  203:1
Oland, John C.  212:4

Olcott, Ben W.   153:1
261:1
Old Metlakatla, AK   140:8
SEE ALSO Metlakatla
and New Metlakatla
Old Toroda, WA   225:2
308:6   SEE ALSO Toroda,
WA
Olds, Martin   51:26
Olds, W. H.   147:1
O'Leary, Thomas   245:4
Olema, WA   267:1
Olinger, Jay   57:6
Olive, Walter   116:3
Oliver, A. J.   25:10   46:3
Oliver, Ed   41:1   110:9
114:5   152:1   172:5
Oliver, Frank   251:6
Oliver, Fred H.   289:2
Oliver, Herman   114:8
251:4
Oliver, Joe C.   264:2
Oliver, John   238:4   253:30
Oliver, Turner   150:1
Oliver, William Forest
266:1
Olley, James   193:6
Ollicut (Chief)   11:2   26:8
27:2   133:3   SEE ALSO
Alokut
Olmstead, Hannah J.   150:1
Olmstead, Harrison   188:3
Olnes, AK   137:1   281:2
309:3
Olney, Clinton Edward
266:2
Olney, Cyrus   51:80   179:2
Olney, Nathan   56:3   119:7
179:6
O'Loughlin, James   150:1
Olson, Charles A.   203:2
266:1
Olympia, WA   7:10   15:9
16:16   17:6   29:10
31:12   32:12   38:5
41:3   58:10   64:4   73:6
80:16   104:8   108:5

141:8   152:6   163:3
172:10   178:11   191:6
222:32   234:6   243:3
245:50   246:66   252:17
257:4   266:2   276:6
293:40   305:16   317:12
SEE ALSO Smithfield and
Smithter, WA
Olzendam, Roderic   195:3
Omak, WA   92:2   97:1
267:1   293:9   305:1
O'Malley, M. G.   152:1
O'Mara (Judge)   67:2
O'Meara, James   30:1
145:18   163:4   197:1
300:9
Omineca, BC   40:2
Onalaska, WA   305:1
Onderdonk, Andrew   238:20
O'Neal, Dan   181:4
Oneida, ID   211:2
O'Neil, B. F.   23:6
O'Neil, Hugh   25:6
O'Neil, James A.   84:4
198:1
O'Neill, Charles W.   212:8
O'Neill, James H.   98:40
O'Neill, Thomas   266:2
O'Neill, Wiggs J.   186:3
Ontario, OR   12:2   134:8
251:4   300:7
Opal City, OR   42:2
Opdyke, David   197:4
Ophir, AK   63:1   137:2
263:3   309:4
Ophir, MT   25:1   78:2
Ophir, WA   267:1
Oppenheimer, Charles   5:4
Oppenheimer, David   236:4
238:13   275:2
Oppenheimer, Isaac   236:2
238:6   275:3
Opsund, O. N.   303:5
Opsvig, Peter L.   266:2
Orchard, Harry   43:1
99:2   118:4   127:25
132:3   134:2   205:14

252:1   259:3
Orchards, WA   305:1
Ordway, Lizzie   306:3
O'Reagan, Barney SEE
    Murphy, Thomas G.
Oregon City, OR   17:13
    22:13   35:3   41:4   44:9
    68:24   75:16   84:8
    104:22   151:6   162:20
    172:19   187:4   194:30
    198:8   208:38   229:33
    249:18   264:4   272:4
    284:7   295:16   296:4
    297:38   300:7   317:10
    318:17
O'Reilly, Peter   5:14
    20:8
Orem, Con   25:13
Orient, WA   225:2   305:1
    315:1
Orkiszewski, Erwin W.
    71:5
Orley, Bud   175:12
Orman, Robert   319:3
Ormsby, Norris   266:2
Oro Grande, ID   102:3
    164:1   223:3
Orofino, ID   23:3   39:2
    87:8   108:1   119:3
    132:1   152:2   164:1
    192:7   223:4
Orondo, WA   157:4   305:1
O'Rourke, Phil   108:4
    118:4   172:4   212:3
Oroville, WA   5:3   203:1
    225:6   267:1   305:1
Orting, WA   14:1
Orton, C. W.   184:7
Osborn, George W.   266:3
Osborn, Josiah   296:6
Osborn, Obadiah   199:3
Osborn, Robert H.   199:1
Osborne, William   152:1
Osburn, S. V. William
    212:3
Osburn, W. F.   232:1
Osburn, William T.   232:2

Osburn, ID   23:4   98:5   212:6
Osgood, Frank H.   203:1
    305:1
Osoyoos, BC   5:6   204:2
Ostner, Charles Leopold
    118:2
Ostrander, Nathaniel   203:1
Ostrander, WA   14:1   305:1
O'Sullivan, James   58:3
    172:15   252:8   293:100
Oswego, OR   68:11   75:5
    SEE ALSO Lake Oswego,
    OR
Othello, WA   198:1   293:6
Otterson, O. C.   212:3
Otto, Filis   278:1
Ouellette, Paul E.   71:6
Ouimette, Esdras N.   150:2
Outhouse, John T.   30:1
Overfelt, Tom   110:4   134:6
Overton, William   198:1
    284:2
Owen, Gue   102:2
Owen, Henry   152:2
Owen, Hezekiah S.   266:3
Owen, John   1:3   46:2
    133:7   155:17   181:10
    211:11   259:2   286:4
Owens, Frank Lester   37:4
Owens, Henry C.   110:2
Owens, James W. F.   150:1
Owens, John   119:5
Owens, Richard   97:3
Owens, S. A.   199:1
Owens, Thomas   150:3
Owens-Adair, Bethenia
    150:5   252:2   304:3
    SEE ALSO Adair, Beth-
    enia
Owhi (Chief)   27:11   50:5
Ownbey, Nicholas   56:6
    318:14
Owsley, Barney   280:2
Oxford, ID   23:5
Oysterville, OR   30:7
Oysterville, WA   14:1   97:4
    109:7   202:26   203:4

272:1 305:1
Ozette, WA 152:1
Ozment, G. W. 150:1


Pacific City, WA 119:2
272:2
Pack, Charles Lathrop
305:1
Packer, Paul C. 232:2
Packwood, Robert 12:14
49:2
Packwood, Samuel 163:3
Packwood, William H.
51:35 97:5 264:5
305:1
Packwood, WA 305:1
Padilla, WA 314:4 315:5
Padoshek, Martin 157:2
Page, C. H. 295:3
Page, R. G. 279:5
Page, Thomas P. 119:7
Pagwhite (Chief) 211:14
SEE ALSO Bannock Jim
Paine, F. W. 119:7
Paine, Joseph 39:4
Painter, Robert M. 179:1
Painter, William Charles
119:6 150:2 179:1
199:5
Paisley, OR 152:1
Palladino, Lawrence Bene-
dict 34:2 93:3 112:2
155:15
Palmehn, John A. 42:2
Palmer, Joel 30:3 36:4
56:17 68:6 87:4
145:13 179:2 188:8
198:1 220:4 239:5
272:2 297:11 318:44
Palmer, Joseph 281:1
Palmer, Loring 163:3
Palmer, AK 148:3 159:9
226:25 281:12 290:2
Palouse, WA 27:3 39:3
96:2 119:4 305:1

Palux, WA 203:1
Pambrun, Pierre C. 4:20
101:5 177:28 198:1
208:3 235:3
Pamphlet, Tom 294:3
Pandosy, Charles Marie
5:6 179:1 260:4
Pangborn, Clyde 16:3
252:4
Pantages, Alexander 41:3
104:6 196:100 203:1
234:9
Panton, Andrew C. 187:9
Paquet, Francis Xavier
150:2
Paradise, MT 319:4
Pardee, Alfred Day 102:3
Pardee, James K. 319:2
Pardee, ID 102:3 223:1
Pardee, MT 78:1 319:3
Paris, ID 23:4 164:1
Parkdale, OR 239:1
Parker, Aaron F. 29:4
102:15 103:20
Parker, Carlton 32:3
Parker, Frank J. 119:2
163:2
Parker, Frederic C. N.
303:6
Parker, Gilman 303:6
Parker, Hollon 199:7
Parker, J. G. 246:6
Parker, Jared C. 266:2
Parker, John Allen 266:3
Parker, Samuel 4:12 16:4
56:45 93:4 96:4 97:4
101:3 119:4 150:1
153:2 177:45 188:10
291:2 296:5 318:24
Parker, Stanley E. 185:2
Parker, Wilder W. 150:2
295:4
Parkersburg, OR 258:4
Parkland, WA 305:1
Parks, George A. 130:4
Parks, Samuel C. 43:1
Parks, William 266:2

123                           PARKSVILLE

Parksville, BC  165:4
Parma, ID  23:3  33:6
  213:3
Parr, Charles  115:1
Parr, William O.  116:2
  157:2
Parrent, Henry  319:3
Parrington, Vernon Louis
  176:1  276:11
Parrish, Charles W.  264:2
Parrish, George W.  157:3
Parrish, Josiah Lamberson
  44:6  84:4  147:1  150:1
  193:4  194:4  198:1
  272:3
Parrish, Philip H.  152:1
Parrot, R. B.  319:2
Parrot, MT  224:2  319:3
Parry, W. E.  103:12
Parry, Will  163:4  243:7
Parsons, Frank  23:5
Parsons, W. H.  217:3
Parsons, William  103:6
Pasco, WA  16:6  96:3
  151:3  198:13  229:5
  252:8  293:18  305:4
  317:3
Pastolik, AK  77:7
Pataha, WA  119:5  150:1
  280:9  305:1
Pate, William N.  157:3
Pateros, WA  176:3  267:1
  305:2
Paterson, R. B.  96:3
Patkanim (Chief)  7:15  50:2
  150:2  220:5  306:5
Pattee, David  181:8
Patterson, A. W.  232:5
Patterson, Don S.  94:7
Patterson, Ferd  36:20
Patterson, Isaac Lee
  153:1
Patterson, Otis  150:2
Patterson, Thomas  163:5
Pattison, John  150:1
Patton, Edward  136:6
Patton, Matthew  150:2

Patton, Thomas M.  150:2
Pattullo, Thomas Dufferin
  185:9  253:30  260:5
Patty, Ernest  137:1
Paul, William  54:4
Paul, ID  23:4
Paulhamus, William S.
  245:7
Paulina (Chief)  42:5
Paull, Andrew  140:3
  189:13
Paull, William  140:1
Paulsen, August  96:2
  127:3
Paulson, Paul A.  288:6
Paxon, Edgar S.  181:7
Paxon, AK  63:1
Payette, Francois  33:4
  43:2  118:1
Payette, ID  23:5  24:3
  164:1  180:2
Payne, Martin  150:1
Payne, WA  267:1
Payton, Daniel  187:8
Peabody, Alexander  79:4
  245:5
Peale, Langford  76:14
Pearl, Phil  113:5
Pearse, B. W.  126:4
Pearson, Daniel O.  150:1
  203:2
Pearson, Grant  115:5
Pearson, Hans  266:2
Pearson, W. H.  198:2
Pearson, Walter J.  49:8
Peavy, Dan  176:9
Peck, Ebeneezer M.  199:1
Peck, Origin O.  118:2
  212:3
Peck, ID  23:3
Pedro, Felix  28:1  63:1
  281:3  290:1  309:4
  310:6  311:3
Peebles, John C.  51:28
Pe Ell, WA  14:1  152:2
  252:1  305:1
Pegg, Wellington  116:2

Pegues, John E.  148:3
Pelican, AK  130:1
Pelkey, Robert  181:5
Pelly, Thomas M.  178:4
  241:1
Pelton, G. E.  "Ed"  152:2
  191:20  315:2
Pemberton, August F.  3:6
Pemberton, Joseph Des-
  pard  3:7  126:8
Pemberton, William Young
  60:6  133:6  155:3
  286:1
Pemberton, BC  204:2
Pender Harbor, BC  275:10
Pendleton, Frank R.  266:3
Pendleton, OR  12:3  17:4
  36:6  39:2  82:4  104:5
  119:8  152:3  198:1
  207:50  251:5  300:14
  303:8  317:3
Penewawa, WA  119:2
Pengra, B. J.  197:3
  232:4
Pennell, John  234:5
Pennock, William  245:5
Pennoyer, Sylvester  150:2
  153:1  163:4  210:10
  302:3
Penrose, Stephen B. L.
  41:1  88:5  96:1  176:1
  243:4  257:80
Penticton, BC  5:10  123:3
  204:3
Peola, WA  119:1  280:1
Peone, Baptiste  39:2  93:4
  108:4
Peopeomoxmox (Chief)
  4:5  6:5  118:1  119:14
  198:6  252:1
Peoria, OR  68:5  229:4
Peratrovich, Frank  128:5
  129:5  130:2  241:2
Percival, Daniel F.  94:8
  150:2
Percival, John C.  245:2
Percival, Samuel  245:5

Perham, B. A.  184:16
Perkins, Henry Kirk White
  4:4  44:12  93:9  119:4
  193:10  198:1  302:21
Perkins, James Allen  150:1
  288:4
Perkins, Perry C.  199:1
Perkins, Sam  245:5
Perrine, Ira B.  259:3
Perry, Alfred F.  199:2
Perry, Edith  308:1
Perry, Henry George Thom-
  as  253:5
Perry, John H.  41:1
Perryville, AK  63:1
Pershbaker, John  258:4
Peshastin, WA  157:2
Peters, Evan  176:1
Petersburg, AK  63:1
  128:4  130:12  148:4
  269:6
Petersen, Ray  137:2
Peterson, Hans O.  266:2
Peterson, Henry  263:2
Peterson, John H.  266:2
Peterson, William H.
  150:2  199:1
Pettet, William  289:3
Pettibone, Alfred W.  266:2
Pettibone, George A.  99:2
  127:5  212:12
Pettibone, N. B.  102:19
  103:10
Pettygrove, Francis W.
  41:2  73:6  150:1  151:2
  152:2  179:1  198:1
  252:1  264:1  284:15
  297:12
Pettyjohn, Jonathan  199:3
Pfouts, Paris S.  25:5
  133:3  155:1
Phair, Caspar  138:3
Phelps, Byron  163:2
  243:1
Phelps, Ira A.  300:5
Phelps, John E.  266:1
Philbrook, George  71:7

125          PHILIPSBURG

Philipsburg, MT  60:6
  76:6  214:3  224:12
  308:6  319:16
Phillips, B. D.  319:3
Phillips, Charles W.
  199:2
Phillips, David  306:4
Phillips, David Lucas
  38:3
Phillips, Fred  251:4
Phillips, S. A.  266:2
Phillips-Wolley, Charles
  5:10
Philomath, OR  72:5
  300:3
Phoenix, BC  47:1
Picabo, ID  23:4
Picard, John  199:1
Pickering, William  31:3
  41:1  64:7  197:2
  245:6  305:3  306:3
Pickernell, John Edmunds
  84:2  202:10
Pickett, Charles E.
  304:2
Pickett, George Edward
  41:2
Pickett, James Tilton
  41:1
Pidcock, Richard H.
  189:6
Pidduck, George Albin
  266:2
Pidduck, Thomas Henry
  266:2
Piedalue, Joseph  112:3
Pierce, Edward Allen
  187:5
Pierce, Elias Davidson
  43:1  76:6  96:2  97:2
  108:1  118:8  132:1
  192:7  259:2  280:3
Pierce, Frank R.  152:1
Pierce, Mary  278:1
Pierce, Walter M.  49:20
  207:3  261:4
Pierce, William Henry

  186:3
Pierce, ID  23:1  43:2
  96:2  118:10  164:2
  192:8  212:2  259:3
Pietrzycki, Marcellus
  Marcus  150:1
Pike, Enoch W.  150:2
Pike, Warburton  40:6
Piles, Samuel H.  106:5
  243:4  245:3
Pillow, Charles B.  179:5
Pillsbury, J. H.  185:2
Pilot Rock, OR  11:1  119:1
  207:4
Pilz, George E.  149:5
Pinckney, William H.  266:2
Pincus, Isaac  266:2
Pine Grove, ID  223:1
Ping, Elisha  119:11  150:1
  245:1
Pinkham, Elsa M.  278:1
Pinkham, Joseph  95:3
Pinkham, Sumner  36:6
Pinkney City, WA  27:5
  108:2  119:1  SEE ALSO
  Colville, WA
Pinnell, John  245:5
Pioneer, MT  78:6  224:2
  319:6
Pioneerville, ID  118:1
  223:2  308:2
Piper, Edgar B.  300:7
Pipes, Martin L.  300:6
Pitcher, Alexander  116:2
  157:3
Pitcher, Hamilton  266:1
Pitt, WA  242:7
Pittman, Anna Maria  44:8
Pittock, Henry Lewis  41:2
  96:12  179:1  195:2
  210:6  239:1  300:8
Placer, OR  225:1  308:6
Placerville, ID  33:5  118:8
  164:1  223:4  308:3
Plainville, WA  119:1
Plano, ID  59:6
Plante, Antoine  27:10

Platinum, AK 63:4
Platt, V. W. 23:5
Plaza, WA 39:4
Plentywood, MT 214:2
Plourde, Donat 112:5
Plummer, Alfred A.
  150:2
Plummer, Charles 306:13
Plummer, Fred 173:6
Plummer, Henry Amos
  1:5 25:16 36:2 46:3
  76:9 97:3 118:2
  132:4 133:20 155:13
  156:1 188:3 197:4
  214:4 247:4 256:57
  280:4 308:1 319:13
Plummer, O. P. S. 150:2
  187:9
Plummer, ID 23:3 164:2
Pluvius, WA 152:2
Plymouth, OR 198:1 284:2
Pocatello (Chief) 43:1
  211:9
Pocatello, ID 12:3 17:4
  23:14 24:5 45:7 117:6
  118:7 164:2 172:3
  211:20 213:7 268:3
Pocock, George 176:1
Pogue, WA 267:1
Pohlatkin (Chief) 27:3
Pohlman, Arthur H. 116:2
Pohlman, Dorothy Prewitt
  278:1
Poindexter, Miles C. 16:3
  57:1 83:5 243:3 245:4
  261:2 293:4
Poindexter, Phil 46:3
Point, Nicholas 34:12
  43:1 48:3 93:8 99:3
Point Barrow, AK 8:9
  14:1 55:5 65:2 66:3
  77:10 190:11 281:4
  290:14 SEE ALSO
  Barrow, AK
Point Hope, AK 52:3 63:1
  137:4 160:2 190:11
  290;5

Pokegama, OR 75:3
Polaris, MT 224:3 319:4
Pollock, Lawrence 274:6
Pollock, ID 223:1
Polson, Alexander 195:3
  266:3 305:1
Pomeroy, Joseph M. 119:4
  280:28
Pomeroy, Thomas 181:3
Pomeroy, Walter 162:7
Pomeroy, WA 82:5 119:9
  280:188 305:1
Pomona, ID 223:1
Pomona, WA 305:1
Ponderay, ID 23:2
Pony, MT 78:5 224:3
  308:8 319:6
Pooley, Charles Edward
  5:3
Poor, Henry Varnum 176:1
Pope, Andrew 195:2
Pope, James 213:24 244:5
  259:6 261:1
Porro, Thomas J. 169:7
Port Alberni, BC 122:3
  165:7 204:4 SEE ALSO
  Alberni, BC
Port Alice, BC 165:9
  275:6
Port Angeles, WA 14:1
  16:5 41:1 89:1 120:4
  142:5 152:5 191:40
  246:4 252:3 273:5
  305:3 SEE ALSO Cher-
  bourg, WA
Port Blakeley, WA 9:6
  73:4 121:3 246:10
  305:1
Port Clarence, AK 77:5
  161:5 281:6 SEE ALSO
  Libbysville, AK
Port Douglas, BC 3:5
  47:2
Port Edward, BC 186:3
Port Essington, BC 186:10
  275:4
Port Gamble, WA 9:6 32:4

73:9  89:1  195:9  203:5
246:8  265:3  273:8  305:2
Port Gardner, WA  41:2
  89:1
Port Hadlock, WA  73:6
Port Hardy, BC  165:13
  275:11
Port Ludlow, WA  9:5
  32:3  73:5  89:1  97:5
  195:6  246:6  305:3
Port McNeill, BC  122:8
  165:10
Port Madison, WA  7:8
  73:10  89:1  121:3
  246:9  305:1  306:4
Port Moody, BC  158:5
  236:5  238:16  253:5
Port Neville, BC  275:6
Port Orchard, WA  14:1
  73:4  89:1  191:2  246:7
  305:3
Port Orford, OR  97:7
  104:3  258:23
Port Renfrew, BC  47:2
  122:3  165:3  204:4
Port Simpson, BC  10:3
  186:7  275:5  SEE AL-
  SO Fort Simpson, BC
Port Townsend, WA  14:1
  16:6  18:2  32:14  41:4
  50:5  73:6  97:3  121:4
  130:4  142:4  150:3
  152:7  191:4  195:2
  203:14  234:2  245:9
  246:21  252:8  273:9
  276:4  305:5  317:4
Portage, WA  305:1
Porter, A. L.  80:6
Porter, Arthur  59:9
Porter, Charles O.  49:4
  261:1
Porter, E. W.  23:5
Porter, Henry L.  281:5
Porter, McCauley  150:1
Porter, WA  305:1
Porthill, ID  22:6
Portman, Edward N. Bar-

clay  5:3
Post, Frank T.  293:10
Post, Frederick  27:8
  39:6  41:1  106:4  180:10
Post, John  266:2
Post Falls, ID  23:2  39:3
  96:1  97:3  106:9  108:2
  164:1  212:1
Potlatch, ID  23:2  96:1
  118:2  164:1
Potlatch, WA  305:1
Potomac, MT  319:2
Potosi (Chief)  153:1
Potter, Bill  36:16
Potter, Clyde F.  53:10
Potter, E. O.  232:1
Potts, Benjamin Franklin
  46:2  48:10  133:30
  155:4  214:6  247:4
  286:80
Pottsville, ID  212:6
Pouce Coupe, BC  40:16
Poulin, A. Z.  33:4
Poulsbo, WA  305:1
Powell, Charles F.  211:6
Powell, E. L.  119:1
Powell, Israel Wood  189:14
  253:4  260:6  294:2
Powell, Joab  36:17  153:1
  303:8
Powell, John  292:11
Powell, Leonard J.  38:3
Powell, R. L.  274:33
Powell, William  266:2
Power, James  314:4
Power, Thomas C.  60:9
  133:11  155:3  214:6
  215:6  247:6  286:6
  319:5
Powers, Albert  258:6
Powers, Joseph L.  71:8
Powers, Truman  150:1
Powers, OR  258:6
Poxleitner, Charles J.
  103:15
Poynton, Joseph F.  212:10
Prairie, WA  315:3

Prairie City, OR  75:3
  225:3  251:7  264:1
Prando, Peter P.  254:4
Prather, Leander Hamil-
  ton  289:6
Pratt, Edwin T.  58:5
Pratt, L. E.  195:24
Pratt, Orville C.  145:16
Pratt, W. B.  173:7
Prefontaine, Francis X.
  266:2
Prescott, Charles H.
  150:1
Prescott, WA  119:2  280:1
Preston, Charles B.  199:2
Preston, Dale  199:1
Preston, Harold  243:3
Preston, Josephine Corliss
  38:2
Preston, Platt A.  119:3
  199:2
Preston, William B.  59:5
Preston, William G.  119:3
  199:4
Preston, ID  23:7  24:2
  164:1
Preusse, Herman  288:3
Prevost, J. L.  311:2
Prevost, James Charles
  3:11
Priaulx, Arthur W.  195:2
Price, Andrew  217:70
Price, Barrington  5:6
Price, Clayton S.  41:3
Price, Gabriel W.  281:5
Price, John E.  217:9
Price, Littleton  95:6
Prichard, Andrew  96:2
  97:2  99:3  106:9  108:3
  118:2  188:3  212:4
Prichard, Arthur G.  266:2
Prichard, ID  118:2
Prickett, Henry E.  87:9
Pride, David Porter Baker
  29:2  95:9
Priest Rapids, WA  198:7
Priest River, ID  23:1  96:1

Prim, Pain Page  51:20
  150:1
Prince George, BC  40:6
  123:5  137:5  204:19
  253:2  SEE ALSO Fort
  George, BC
Prince Rupert, BC  63:2
  123:5  130:5  185:228
  186:15  204:6  238:4
  253:10  269:5  275:58
Princeton, BC  3:2  5:15
  47:1  204:2
Princeton, MT  319:3
Prindle, WA  305:1
Prine, Francis Barney
  42:4  147:5  152:1
Prineville, OR  36:3  42:25
  56:3  75:3  82:3  187:3
  196:4  228:20  300:2
  303:3  318:3  320:4
Pringle, Alexander David
  5:8
Pringle, Clark Spencer  296:6
Pringle, Virgil  172:6
Prior, Edward Gawler
  126:6  238:3  253:3
Pritchard, Charles H.
  266:1
Pritchett, Harold J.  244:3
Pritchett, Kintzing  153:1
Proebstel, Frederick  150:1
Prosch, Charles  41:1
  176:2  178:3  197:1
  245:9
Prosch, Thomas  50:7
Prosser, William F.  150:3
  163:6  243:7  266:2
Prosser, WA  150:1  305:2
Prowell, W. R.  157:3
Prudhoe Bay, AK  54:16
  115:14  136:20  160:6
Pruner, George D. C.
  266:2
Puckett, Gladys S.  169:27
Pulaski, Edward C.  98:19
  118:1
Pullen, Daniel  100:8

Pullen, Harriet "Ma"  63:1
  129:2  234:1  268:2
  309:4
Pullman, WA  27:3  96:1
  108:3  119:2  198:1  252:3
  305:1
Putnam, George  96:2  300:6
Puyallup, WA  14:1  31:3
  80:5  89:1  222:6  252:1
  305:4
Pysht, WA  100:9


Quadra, BC  20:1
Qualchien (Chief)  11:2
  27:13  220:4
Qualicum, BC  165:3
Quartz, MT  78:3
Quartzburg, ID  223:1  308:1
Quartzville, OR  225:1
Quayome, BC  3:2
Queets, WA  152:1  305:2
Quesnel, BC  3:12  47:2
  123:15  161:1  204:2
  235:3
Quick, James  114:3
Quiemuth (Chief)  176:1
  220:2  245:5
Quigley, F. Leo  98:6
Quigley, Harold  231:6
Quigley, MT  78:3
Quilcene, WA  152:3  305:1
Quinault, WA  152:2
Quincy, WA  172:2  198:1
  237:383  293:37  305:1
Quinlan, Michael A.  71:5
Quinn (Parson)  280:8
Quinn, Thomas  119:1  199:3
Quithlook, AK  8:3
Quivey, G. W.  300:3
Quivira, OR  258:3


Rabbeson, A. B.  150:3
Raboin, Louis  119:6

Race Horse (Chief)  211:5
Racetrack, MT  319:3
Rad, Frank  102:7
Rader, L. E.  191:5
Rader, Ruben  46:2  319:1
Rader, William  319:3
Radersburg, MT  46:7
  224:3  319:4
Ragaru, Aloysius  34:1
Ragless, William  237:4
Rainier, OR  300:5
Rains, Gabriel  176:1
Rains, James P.  103:4
Raley, J. Roy  207:6
Raley, James H.  150:1
  207:10
Ralston, J. C.  293:7
Ramey, John  103:3
Rampart, AK  63:1  130:3
  137:2  148:3  309:7
  311:4
Rampart House, YT  255:2
Ramsay, MT  46:2
Ranck, William  150:2
Rand, Ed  152:2
Randall, Reino  231:2
Randle, WA  305:1
Randolph, OR  97:4  225:1
  258:3
Rank, Ira M.  161:1
Rankin, Jeannette  46:1
  181:5  214:7  215:6
  299:6
Rankin, John  181:7
Rankin, Wellington D.
  214:4  215:5  299:4
Rappagliosi, Philip  34:4
Rasin, Unit  243:5
Rasmuson, Elmer E.  66:1
  128:3  130:1  136:3
Ratcliffe, Edward M.  266:2
Ratekin, Sam  173:11
Rathbun, John C.  245:4
  266:3
Rathdrum, ID  23:5  39:4
  99:4  108:3
Rathert, W. H.  242:10

Rathvon, Henry Agustus
  266:1
Rattenbury, Francis  260:6
Raught, A. L.  175:19
Ravalli, Anthony  1:3  34:18
  93:7  96:1  133:4  155:20
  181:6  249:2
Ravensdale, WA  225:1
Raver, Paul J.  82:10
Rawn, C. C.  181:3
Rawson, M. R.  102:2
Ray, Dixy Lee  178:4  278:1
Ray, Jack  112:9
Ray, Ned  256:6
Rayburn, Barbara Jean
  278:1
Raymer, John  289:2
Raymond, Narcisse  179:4
Raymond, Rossiter W.  319:3
Raymond, W. W.  272:3
Raymond, WA  152:3  195:2
  305:2
Raymur, James A.  236:8
Rea, Oscar E.  266:2
Read, Will F.  212:3
Reardan, WA  305:1
Reavis, James B.  150:2
  163:2  266:2
Rebmann, James  34:2
Rector, William H.  194:11
  318:19
Red Bluff, MT  308:6
Red Lion Mt  308:3  319:3
Red Lodge, MT  1:2  214:2
  319:1
Red Mountain City, MT
  78:6  319:3
Red Wolf (Chief)  141:3
Redelsheimer, Julius  203:1
Redington, J. W.  300:5
Redman, John T.  150:1
  266:2
Redmond, Frank T.  42:2
Redmond, OR  42:10  75:2
  300:2
Redmond, WA  203:1  305:1
Redondo, WA  305:1

Redpath, N. J.  245:6
Reed, Alexander  119:2
Reed, Charles B.  116:1
  157:3
Reed, Henry E.  300:12
Reed, Henry W.  197:2
  211:4
Reed, John  33:10  72:7
Reed, John B.  266:2
Reed, John H.  51:27
Reed, Mark  58:16  176:2
  195:4  245:13  246:2
  293:2
Reed, Samuel G.  97:4
Reed, Simeon Gannett  6:3
  41:1  95:1  107:4  119:4
  152:2  179:1  188:7
  192:6  197:3  212:2
  264:2  285:3  297:9
  302:2  304:3
Reed, Walter J.  150:2
Reeder, James Lawrence
  287:3
Reed's Fort, MT  78:7
Reedsport, OR  75:2  104:3
  152:1
Reedy, James  173:6
Rees, Denton J.  2:5
Rees, Raymond R.  119:8
Reese, Willard Hall  222:3
Reese, Frank W.  203:1
Reese, I. T.  119:12
Reeve, Robert  137:4  241:1
  263:21
Reeves, Belle  15:1  245:9
Reeves, Charles Francis
  38:1  76:9  276:2
Reeves, Elza A.  266:2
Reeves, Frank  157:2
Reeves, I. W.  116:3  157:2
Reeves, Moise  112:16
Rehorn, John  199:2
Reid, Albert E.  199:1
Reid, Cecil  140:2
Reid, Frank H.  130:1
  255:3  268:12  311:2
Reid, James  235:3

Reid, Robert A.  266:1
Reilly, Edward J.  245:7
Reinhard, Jacob P.  181:3
Reinhart, Caleb S.  266:3
Reiter, E. D.  289:1
Reith, Jacob  150:2
Remote, OR  152:2
Remsberg, Charles Edward
  266:2
Renata, BC  316:3
Renova, MT  319:2
Renton, William  9:7  73:10
  80:2  217:2  282:6  306:4
Renton, WA  14:1  178:5
  252:2  276:6  282:183
  305:2
Replogle (Reverend)  52:2
Republic, WA  203:1  225:5
  305:1
Reser, John L.  199:1
Reser, William P.  199:2
Reuben, James  103:5
Reubens, ID  23:8
Revelstoke, BC  3:2  50:2
  107:4  151:7  198:5
  316:6
Revenue Flat, MT  319:3
Rex, R. G.  187:8
Rexburg, ID  23:9  24:3
  59:7  118:1  164:1
Rexford, Fenton  115:1
Rexford, MT  319:3
Rexville, WA  315:3
Reynolds, Allen H.  199:2
Reynolds, Almos H.  119:13
  150:1  199:1
Reynolds, George  99:10
Reynolds, Harry A.  257:7
Reynolds, James S.  87:15
Reynolds, Maryan E.
  169:15
Reynolds, Rasselas  199:3
Reynolds, City, MT  78:3
  319:2
Rhett, William  103:2
Rhoades, James M.  283:7
Rhodes, A. J.  113:3

Rhodes, B. H.  266:2
Rhodes, William  97:3
Ricard, Pascal  179:1
Rice, Alonzo E.  266:2
Rice, (Mrs.) Cliff  152:2
Rice, G. M.  207:6
Rice, Ren H.  96:4
Rice, Thomas  266:2
Rich, Irene  96:1
Richards, Albert N.  238:4
Richards, Frank  311:3
Richards, Frank H.  163:3
Richards, George H.  120:7
Richards, John S.  169:38
Richardson, Charles  266:4
Richardson, Charles B.
  199:1
Richardson, G. W.  150:1
Richardson, George Thomas
  203:1
Richardson, H. G.  266:3
Richardson, James A.
  150:1  187:6
Richardson, Simeon Childs
  264:4
Richardson, Simon Peter
  266:2
Richardson, Thomas L.
  266:3
Richardson, Wilds P.  63:2
  130:5  160:4  311:2
Richardson, William E.
  289:3
Richardson, AK  63:1
Richfield, BC  3:6
Richfield, ID  23:3
Richland, WA  41:7  96:3
  198:1  252:4  305:1
Richmond, John P.  44:9
  93:6  193:3
Richmond, Volney  148:2
Richmond, ID  102:3  SEE
  ALSO Warren, ID
Richmond, OR  225:1  308:8
Richter, Frank  5:6
Rickard, G. L. "Tex"  63:1
  161:4  309:2  311:1

Rickards, John E.   60:13
133:8
Rickey, Henry C.   305:1
Rickman, C. C.   157:3
Ricks, Thomas E.   59:18
Ricksecker, Eugene   266:2
Ricord, John   44:12
Riddell, Crockett M.   266:2
Ridenbaugh, W. H.   95:2
Ridgeway, WA   315:3
Ridley, William   10:6   140:4
186:4
Ridpath, William H.   96:2
106:2
Riffe, WA   305:1
Riffle, Elihu G.   199:2
Riffle, Richard   274:9
Rigby William F.   59:6
95:2
Rigby, ID   23:6   24:2
164:1
Riggin, F. A.   227:16
Riggins, R. L.   "Dick"
102:6
Riggins, ID   12:3   23:2
102:6   103:5
Riggs, H. C.   33:3
Riggs, Thomas   130:11
Rigley, Maurice   71:7
Rigney, John L.   203:1
Rigsby, James W.   119:2
Riley, Cleveland C.
303:5
Riley, Frank Branch
210:2
Riley, Jean F.   266:2
Riley, Leonard W.   174:6
303:17
Rimini, MT   224:5   319:3
Rinehart, Henry   150:1
Rinehart, J. H.   150:1
Rinehart, Louis B.   150:1
Rinehart, W. V.   250:3
Ring, George V.   103:12
Ringer, L. M.   119:3
150:1
Riparia, WA   92:2   198:1

Riplinger, John   266:3
Rippentoe, J. J.   38:1   94:7
Ririe, ID   23:2
Risdon, D. M.   232:9
Riske, L. W.   47:1
Ritchey, William Lowery
33:3
Rithet, R. P.   126:11
Ritz, Philip   119:7   199:2
203:1   217:2   257:1
Ritz, Will A.   184:27
203:1
Ritzville, WA   108:2   203:1
293:7   305:1
Rivais, Antoine   179:4
Riverdale, OR   75:3
Rivers, Ralph J.   128:11
129:5   130:6   241:6
Rivers, Victor   128:5
129:5
Riverside, OR   134:4
Riverside, WA   267:1   305:1
315:4
Riverton, OR   258:3
Roach, Harry   275:10
Robar, MT   78:2
Robaut, Aloysius   34:3
Robb, James R.   84:2
Robbins, Charles H.   106:7
Robbins, Herbert E.   266:3
Robbins, S. E.   137:1   266:3
Robbins, William L.   266:3
Roberts, Alexander C.   38:1
57:2
Roberts, Alvin B.   179:2
Roberts, Andrew   150:2
Roberts, Edward J.   106:23
107:24   203:1
Roberts, John E.   300:5
Roberts, Lloyd S.   288:2
Roberts, Mary L.   195:6
Roberts, ID   23:4   164:1
Robertson, Frank C.   118:1
Robertson, J. A.   127:7
Robertson, James   266:2
Robertson, W. H.   242:5
Robertson, W. W.   293:6

Robertson, William Fleet
40:6
Robie, Albert H.   110:3
119:4   141:4
Robinson, A. E.   "Nimrod"
309:4
Robinson, Alver   266:2
Robinson, Joseph William-
son   163:2   266:1
Robinson, Kinsey M.   12:6
82:3   293:13
Robinson, Martin   266:3
Robinson, Thomas   266:1
Robinson, William   264:1
Robinson, William Fears
266:3
Robinson, MT   319:3
Robinson, WA   267:1
Robinsonville, OR   264:3
Robson, Ebenezer   3:4   5:2
Robson, John   3:12   5:8
107:8   238:35   253:7
260:5
Robson, BC   107:4   151:4
198:1   209:2
Roche Harbor, WA   246:3
Rochester, Al   178:4
Rochester, H. B.   185:2
Rochester, MT   224:2   319:4
Rochester, WA   152:1
Rock, Harold   63:1
Rock, Howard   54:1   66:2
Rock, Mike   36:3
Rock Bay, BC   275:7
Rock Island, WA   293:7
305:1
Rocker, MT   78:1
Rockfellow, John S.   25:11
Rockford, WA   97:2
Rockland, ID   23:1
Rockport, WA   315:8
Rockwell, Kathleen Eloisa
"Klondike Kate"   196:305
234:1
Rockwood, J. H.   Jess"   175:9
Rocky Bar, ID   23:5   87:4
Rocky Point, MT   156:2   319:2

223:3
Rodebaugh, Jimmy   137:20
263:8
Roderick, Al   173:9
Roderick, Matt   47:1
Rodgers, Andrew   4:4
177:16   296:11
Rodgers, David   113:4
Rodgers, William H.   286:5
Roe, James   266:2
Roe, Jonas L.   150:1
Roe, Percy D.   294:4
Roedel, Charles Ottmar
199:2
Roeder, Henry   150:2
305:4
Roeder, Otto B.   266:3
Roehl, Charles F.   266:2
Roehl, William F.   266:2
Roettger, WA   267:1
Rogers, Al   203:1
Rogers, Cornelius   4:8
17:3   93:4   119:3   177:11
Rogers, E. M.   150:1
Rogers, George W.   241:2
Rogers, J. V.   "Jack"   116:2
Rogers, Jeremiah   236:5
260:2   294:4
Rogers, John R.   38:2
57:3   58:4   94:5   191:4
222:6   234:1   243:1
245:21   252:1   305:5
Rogers, Nelson S.   195:6
Rogersburg, WA   305:1
Rogerson, ID   23:2
Roggensberger, Joe   173:5
Rohn, J. Fred   199:2
Rohn, J. J.   199:1
Roice, Edward A.   266:2
Rolla, BC   40:8
Romaine, Jerome W.   266:3
Rome, OR   134:4
Romney, Miles   214:4
Ronald, James T.   203:1
234:3   243:5   276:6
Ronald, Walter G.   293:3
Ronald, WA   305:1

Ronan, Peter 133:7 155:32
181:5 292:7
Ronan, MT 112:1
Roney, Nels 232:2
Roney, Thomas 266:1
Rooper, H. C. 42:3
Roosevelt, ID 102:5 164:3
Rosalia, WA 27:8 39:6
198:1 305:3
Rosario, WA 203:1 314:3
315:3
Rose, Aaron 150:2
Rose, Charles 112:7
Rose, Conrad 116:2 157:5
Roseberry, ID 23:2
Roseburg, OR 75:5 82:2
180:2 187:3 229:2
303:2 317:6
Rosellini, Albert D. 203:1
245:22 248:2 261:1
265:3
Rosene, John 161:7
Rosling, Eric Edward 266:1
Roslyn, WA 150:2 163:10
180:2 225:4 243:3 305:2
Ross, Alexander 6:3 108:5
176:2 198:7 221:5
272:11 291:6 305:3
Ross, Charles Benjamin
105:13 117:4 205:4
213:191 219:4 259:11
Ross, Donald H. 202:2
Ross, Edward S. 289:2
Ross, Frank C. 266:4
Ross, James Delmadge 82:7
113:5 244:16 293:17
305:2
Ross, John E. 150:1
Ross, John O. D. 173:6
Ross, Terry L. 116:2
Ross, Victor 137:5
Ross, William M. 266:2
Rosser, Al 244:3
Rossland, BC 96:1 106:3
107:10 209:4
Rossman, J. H. 2:10
Roswell, ID 33:4 118:1

Rothschild, David C. H.
203:1
Rottenbelly (Chief) 93:2
177:6
Rouge, Stephen de 34:6
Rounds, Nelson 38:3
Rounds, Ruel 205:4
Roundup, MT 1:2 247:3
Roust, Tom 137:1 263:2
Routhe, E. A. 96:1
Rowan, James 57:3
Rowe, Lewis S. 266:3
Rowe, Peter Trimble 63:1
137:3 146:3 268:1
311:3
Rowell, Fred Rice 266:3
Rowland, Christian 279:10
Rowland, Harry G. 266:2
Rowland, L. L. 150:1
187:9
Roy, Donald Francis 234:5
Roy, WA 305:1
Roza, WA 305:1
Ruble, Schuyler 308:1
Ruble, William 308:1
Ruby, AK 63:1 137:4
263:4
Ruby, MT 308:6 319:4
Ruby, WA 225:1 267:1
305:1
Ruby City, ID 23:5 118:5
134:10 147:3 164:1
223:1
Rucker, Bethel J. 41:1
Rucker, (Mrs.) J. M. 266:3
Rucker, Wyatt 41:1
Ruckle, J. S. 229:4 264:3
Rudd, Irby H. 199:1
Rudderham, G. W. 185:2
Ruhl, Robert W. 96:3
Ruhlman, John 274:25
Ruick, Norman 205:5
Rulaford, George A. 199:1
Rumsey, MT 319:3
Rupert, ID 23:10 164:1 180:2
Russel, Thomas A. 199:2
Russell, Ambrose J. 266:1

Russell, Charles 119:8
199:2
Russell, Charles J. W.
202:3
Russell, E. Shepard 199:2
Russell, Osborne 84:7
119:4
Russell, Patrick 199:2
Russell, Samuel F. 127:3
Russell, Walter E. 199:1
Russian Mission, AK 63:1
Rust, Frank A. 113:7
Rust, Henry 150:1 264:2
Rust, William R. 266:3
Rustic, ID 102:3
Ruth, A. S. 203:1 245:13
Ruthburg, ID 223:1
Rutledge, Edward 118:1
Rutter, R. L. 70:4 83:4
Ryan, George 203:1
Ryan, John C. 241:1
Ryan, John D. 167:4
209:5 214:6
Ryder, W. F. 200:5
Ryderwood, WA 41:2 305:1
Ryther, Ollie 278:1


Saanich, BC 3:4 165:15
Sabot, Simon 242:5
Sachs, Morris Benedict
266:4
Sackett, Sheldon F. 258:3
300:4
Sacred Heart Mission, ID
34:29 93:9 118:3 212:7
SEE ALSO Cataldo, ID
Sager, John C. (and family)
4:7 93:4 172:4 177:40
252:4 296:30
Sagwitch (Chief) 211:4
Sagwon, AK 115:7
Sahinen, Uuno M. 319:9
Sailey, Ralph 173:6
St. Anthony, ID 23:8 24:2
164:1 180:2

St. Eugene Mission, BC
47:2
St. Francis Mission, WA
305:1
St. Germaine, Mike 175:14
St. Helens, OR 151:3
163:3 187:4 210:4
229:7 284:12 300:3
302:1 303:3
St. Ignatius Mission, MT
34:16 48:9 93:6 112:2
133:7 155:2 181:8 214:3
St. Ignatius Mission, WA
34:11 305:1
St. James (Fort), BC 235:5
SEE ALSO Fort St. James,
BC
St. Joe, ID 23:4 97:4
98:4 99:22
St. John, Arthur Charles
266:2
St. Johns, OR 284:3
St. Joseph, OR 75:4
St. Joseph's Mission, ID
34:12
St. Joseph's Mission, WA
34:10 305:3
St. Louis Mission, OR
208:3
St. Maries, ID 23:7 97:6
98:4 99:11 118:5 164:1
St. Mary's Mission, MT
34:19 48:8 133:9
155:14 181:5 298:4
SEE ALSO Stevensville,
MT
St. Mary's Mission, WA
34:5 93:12 96:1 119:3
305:1
St. Michael, AK 8:6 28:4
52:4 77:12 130:9 143:2
146:8 159:12 161:14
190:8 281:22 309:5
310:13
St. Onge, Peter Louis Na-
poleon 179:1
St. Paul, AK 19:13 77:13

161:9
St. Paul, ID 33:3
St. Paul's Mission, MT
  34:4
St. Paul's Mission, OR
  34:3  68:3  75:4  93:5
  208:5  249:5
St. Paul's Mission, WA
  34:8
St. Peter's Mission, MT
  34:12  48:4
St. Regis, MT  319:5
Sale, Anderson  179:1
Salem, ID  59:6
Salem, OR  17:10  30:10
  35:7  39:4  44:11  68:6
  75:20  104:24  145:8
  152:5  172:9  187:11
  194:5  197:10  198:2
  210:23  229:13  249:5
  297:12  300:14  303:23
  SEE ALSO Chemeketa,
  OR
Saling, Isham E.  150:2
Salmo, BC  204:2
Salmon City, ID  23:10
  45:3  46:3  103:9  118:3
  164:1
Salmson, Edward J.  266:2
Salomon, Edward S.  245:5
Salter, James M.  57:9
Saltese (Chief) 108:1
Saltese, MT  98:12
Salubria, ID  23:2  223:1
Sampson, Arthur  137:6
  263:3
Sampson, Hiram C.  38:2
Sampson, Lammon E.
  266:3
Samuels, H. F.  24:3  289:4
Samuelson, Donald W.
  259:3
Samuelson, E. E.  231:6
Sanborn, Homer  285:7
Sanburn, I. B.  212:4
Sand Ridge, OR  302:1
Sander, C. A.  150:1

Sanders, Addison  286:2
Sanders, Wilbur Fiske  1:2
  25:23  48:11  60:16
  133:35  155:24  156:4
  214:7  247:9  256:4
  286:30  319:9
Sanderson, Albert E.  191:10
Sanderson, Henry  199:2
Sandon, BC  47:2
Sandpoint, ID  23:7  39:3
  96:1  117:5  118:2  164:2
Sanford, Deforest  191:5
Sanger, OR  264:2
Santa, ID  118:1
Santee, Eva  169:17
Saportas, Billy  268:7
Sapperton, BC  3:7
Sappho, WA  152:1
Sappington, MT  46:4
Sargent, John H.  266:2
Satsop, WA  14:1  152:2
Sauk City, WA  315:6
Saule, James D.  202:5
Saunders, Henry  131:5
Saunders, J. C.  203:2
Saunders, Schuyler S.
  203:1
Saunders, Steve  266:2
Sauvie, Laurent  284:1
  287:6
Savage, Austin  87:5
Savage, Charles R.  245:13
Savage, George  176:1
  191:5
Savage, W. D.  173:7
Savage, William  30:1
  150:2
Savidge, Clark  245:10
Savoonga, AK  8:8  161:1
Sawtooth City, ID  164:1
  223:2  308:6
Sawyer, George C.  82:5
Sawyer, Robert W.  293:2
Sawyers, John Jacob  230:2
Saylor, Conrad G.  150:2
Saylor, William Henry
  187:13

Sayre, J. Willis 222:5
Sayre, Thompson D. 266:2
Sayward, J. A. 126:4
Sayward, William R. 294:3
Sayward, BC 107:2 275:6
Scallon, William 156:3
  209:4 216:7 299:4
Scaman, Jack 116:2
Scanlon, M. J. 294:4
Scappoose, OR 152:1
Scarborough, James 97:4
  272:3
Scenic, WA 98:25 305:2
Schade, Fred 245:3
Schafer, Albert 203:1
Schafer, Peter 9:9
Schaible, Arthur 52:3
Schanck, Don 173:8
Schatz, Phillip 237:4
Scheberle, John W. 71:7
Scheble, Francis M. 116:2
  157:2
Scheffer, Peter 112:15
Scheffer, Tom 112:10
Scheiffelin, Ed 311:1
Schelbrede, C. A. 268:5
Schenk, Gretchen Knief
  169:18
Scherneckau, August 308:2
Schively, John H. 245:5
  266:2
Schlitz, John M. 299:3
Schmidt, Hugo 242:8
Schmidt, Joe 102:5
Schmidt, Leopold F. 245:8
  266:2
Schnabel, William F. 134:3
Schneble, Frederick D.
  119:3
Schnebly, David J. 150:1
  284:2
Schnebly, Frederick D.
  150:2
Schneider, Chris 114:6
  264:2
Schoenberg, Wilfred P. 39:8
Scholl, Louis 199:2

Scholz, Richard F. 152:1
Schorr, George F. 150:1
Schreiner, S. H. 279:4
Schricker, W. E. 266:4
Schroeder, John Edward
  195:9
Schrum, Nicholas 35:1
Schulte, Arthur A. 71:6
Schultz, James Willard
  214:2
Schulze, Paul 279:6
Schumacher, Carl 199:2
Schwabacher, Sig 119:3
Schweikert, Martin 308:1
Schwellenbach, Lewis B.
  96:1 129:2 206:3 244:7
  245:2 293:7
Scio, OR 75:3 300:2
Scobey, J. O. 266:2
Scobey, MT 156:1
Scoggin, James 280:1
Scott, Alvin B. 266:2
Scott, Dan 293:11
Scott, Douglas W. 12:16
Scott, Harvey Whitefield
  41:2 44:9 49:3 84:1
  86:3 96:16 153:1 172:3
  197:3 210:9 261:3
  295:2 300:18 302:8
  303:9 304:11 305:1
Scott, James B. 266:2
Scott, John Tucker 150:2
  252:1
Scott, Jonathan Hoeten
  138:2
Scott, Leslie M. 162:10
Scott, Levi 51:5
Scott, Lyman S. 30:67
Scott, Rudolph Bowman
  289:4
Scott, Thomas Fielding
  153:1
Scott, U. B. 229:7 246:8
Scott, William D. 289:2
Scottsburg, OR 187:5
  225:2 230:4 264:3
  297:5

Scow, William 140:12 189:9
Scranton, John M. 246:4
Scranton, S. 28:10 39:10 41:1 108:6
Seabeck, WA 73:15 100:6 203:1 246:6 305:1
Seabold, WA 305:1
Seaborg, B. A. 202:7
Seaborg, Ernest A. 266:2
Sealand, WA 203:3
Sealth, Noah (Chief) 7:390 176:3 178:18 234:8 252:7 276:5 301:10 SEE ALSO Seattle (Chief)
Searight, George 95:2
Searls, Paul 175:10
Seaside, OR 41:1 75:5 229:6 300:2
Seattle (Chief) 31:21 32:4 273:1 304:3 306:17 SEE ALSO Sealth, Noah
Seaview, WA 109:3 202:7
Seavy, James 150:1
Sebern, O. V. 127:8
Sechelt, BC 275:16
Secrest, J. H. 200:4
Seddall, John Vernon 5:3
Sedro Woolley, WA 14:1 89:1 305:1 314:12 315:10 SEE ALSO Woolley, WA
Seeber, John F. 150:2
Seeke, Marshall C. 199:2
Seelig, Ray 293:6
Seghers, Charles H. 254:5 311:1
Seil, Nicholas 199:1
Seitz, John P. 199:2
Sekiu, WA 100:5 152:1
Selah, WA 305:1
Selawik, AK 8:6 63:1
Seldovia, AK 63:1 146:2
Selland, Severt O. 199:1
Sells, H. L. 264:3
Sellwood, James R. W. 150:1

Sellwood, OR 228:5
Selway, James 46:2
Semlin, Charles Augustus 238:12 253:3
Semple, Eugene 100:3 150:1 163:195 243:7 261:1 266:5 276:3
Seneca, OR 251:4
Sengstacken, Henry 258:5
Sequim, WA 100:4 152:1 180:2 305:2
Servis, Francis G. 286:3
Sessons, Hugh 9:6
Settle, A. J. 5:3
Settle, John 179:1
Settlemier, J. H. 150:2
Sewall, WA 267:1
Seward, AK 115:5 130:21 137:4 146:3 148:3 159:12 160:2 226:9 241:3 263:4 281:7 290:3 SEE ALSO Fort Seward
Sewid, James 140:11
Seymour, Frederick 3:40 5:8 20:5 236:3 253:20 283:5
Seymour, BC 3:4 20:2
Shadden, Thomas J. 150:2
Shafer, Harry M. 38:1
Shaft, Charles 181:3
Shain, Clarence B. 245:4
Shakan, AK 63:1
Shakespeare, Noah 238:27
Shaktolik, AK 8:4 52:2 77:5
Shangrila, OR 307:11
Shaniko, OR 42:10 75:2 114:5 196:2 225:3 308:5 SEE ALSO Cross Hollows, OR
Shannahan, Barney 67:4
Shannon, Davis 51:5
Shannon, George D. 150:2
Sharples, Abram W. 187:9
Sharpstein, Arthur P. 203:1

Sharpstein, Benjamin L.
119:9  163:2  199:1
243:4
Shattuck, Allen  128:3
Shattuck, Erasmus D.
51:22  150:1  210:3
Shaw, A. C. R.  68:3
Shaw, Benjamin Franklin
119:8  141:14  198:1
220:5
Shaw, Dave C.  49:4
Shaw, Dudley  40:5
Shaw, Ellsworth E.  199:2
Shaw, Hilyard  232:9
Shaw, Le F. A.  199:2
Shaw, R. W.  179:3
Shaw, Reginald  231:7
Shaw, T. C.  150:2
Shaw, William  296:21
Shazer, George  157:2
Shea, Con  134:9
Sheakley, James  130:1
149:5  190:3
Shearer, George M.  103:4
Shearer, Joe  264:1
Shearer, Wallace C.  2:7
Sheaville, OR  134:2
Sheehan, John F.  150:1
Sheely, Ross  226:7
Shelathwell (Chief)  272:7
Shelby, Aaron D.  145:4
Shelby, MT  214:2  299:2
Sheldon, Don  66:3
Sheldon, Henry D.  232:3
Sheldon, Robert  262:2
Sheller, J. B.  279:5
Sheller, Roscoe  279:6
Shelley, ID  23:4  164:1
Shelton, David  150:2
176:1  266:1
Shelton, Joseph M.  150:1
Shelton, William H.  199:1
Shelton, WA  14:1  58:6
100:5  152:2  163:1
176:6  195:5  203:1
246:10  305:1
Shenkenberg, Theodore  266:2

Shepard, Cyrus  38:1
44:15  93:20  188:5
193:5
Shephard, L. B.  281:4
Sheppard, Ernest  275:10
Sherar, Joseph  42:7
Sherfey, J. W.  280:2
Sheridan, MT  46:3  319:9
Sheridan, OR  75:6  187:3
Sheridan, WA  225:2  308:7
Sherwood, Elmer Ellsworth
266:2
Sherwood, James K. O.
107:6
Shiel, George K.  179:3
Shilling, W. N.  95:10
Shine, Patrick C.  289:2
Shipley, Maynard  57:5
Shirk, David L.  118:4
134:23
Shishmaref, AK  8:11
Shissler, Franklin  102:7
103:1
Shorb, C. J.  300:5
Short, Robert V.  51:11
Short, William  113:4
234:1
Shortess, Robert  84:8
119:6  162:5  193:8
198:1  272:6
Shorts, Bruce C.  217:10
Shoshone, ID  23:6  108:1
164:1  180:2
Shotbolt, Thomas  126:5
Shotwell, Harry S.  116:2
Shotwell, Jacob A.  157:2
Shoudy, George  163:2
Shoup, George L.  29:4
43:4  87:3  95:17  117:4
118:8  205:2  259:3
Showalter, Noah D.  38:7
94:6  169:4  245:4
Shrewsbury, Homer H.
266:2
Shroyer, William  274:6
Shuck, William  103:2
Shulberg, William  23:4

Shungnak, AK 130:3 263:9
Shutt, Sloan P. 300:8
Sichel, Sigmund 150:1
Sick, Emil 276:2
Sidney, BC 165:6
Sidney, WA 14:1
Sieg, Lee Paul 38:1
Siglin, J. M. 258:4
Silcott, J. M. 119:3
Silcott, Jane 118:4
Silcott, WA 305:1
Siletz (Blockhouse), OR
  30:5
Siliquowya, Enoch 91:12
Sill, Jasper 266:2
Sillitoe, Acton Windeyer
  5:6
Silver, WA 267:1
Silver Bow, MT 48:7
  60:6 67:6 76:3 78:4
  133:3 215:9 216:3
  319:8
Silver City, ID 11:1
  23:10 24:5 36:25
  87:33 118:18 127:4
  134:52 164:3 223:9
Silver City, MT 76:2
  78:2 319:5
Silver City, WA 225:2
Silver City, YT 255:3
Silver Lake, OR 42:14
  152:1
Silver Star, MT 46:2
  319:5
Silverman, Samuel I. 102:8
  106:6
Silverton, OR 75:9 187:4
  225:2 300:3
Silverton, WA 225:2 304:2
Silvertooth, Felix W. 114:2
  308:2
Silvertooth, John 114:5
Similkameen, BC 5:5
Simmer, A. G. 28:1
Simmons, Charles 97:3
Simmons, Herman S.
  157:3

Simmons, Michael T. 7:7
  16:7 31:4 100:4 141:6
  150:3 172:18 178:3
  188:10 195:3 203:3
  221:3 222:8 234:10
  245:9 305:5
Simms, John A. 119:7
Simpson, Asa M. 9:12
  258:6
Simpson, Benjamin 30:9
  68:5
Simpson, Francis I. 199:2
Simpson, John 266:2
Simpson, John P. 36:1
  293:18
Simpson, L. J. 258:5
Simpson, Mary 231:2
Simpson, Samuel Leonidas
  153:1 300:5 302:4
Simpson, Sol G. 9:6
  58:7 195:3
Sims, Ed 245:16
Sims, Marx 115:1
Sims, W. S. 212:7
Sinclair, Bartlett 106:4
Sinclair, J. E. 57:2
Sinclair, James 119:4
  179:4
Sincock, Frank 279:3
Sing, Dong 185:2
Singiser, Theodore F. 95:7
Singleton, John 119:2
  199:4
Siringo, Charles A. 127:8
  212:12 SEE ALSO Al-
  lison, C. Leon
Sisemore, John 42:5
Sisson, Edward Octavius
  38:2 299:11
Sisson, Grant 70:4
Sisters, OR 42:10
Sitka, AK 18:6 19:26
  21:5 28:14 52:5 55:6
  66:4 77:25 90:8 120:9
  125:9 130:53 143:18
  146:50 148:8 149:35
  159:35 160:15 161:18

190:20  241:8  262:5
269:17  271:8  272:5
281:35  290:11  302:9
310:15
Sitton, Charles  285:13
Sitton, N. K.  150:1
Skagit City, WA  314:6
315:5
Skagway, AK  14:1  55:4
130:14  143:5  146:5
148:2  159:14  190:5
196:9  255:9  268:80
269:5  275:15  309:9
310:20  311:4
Skamania, WA  198:1
Skamokawa, WA  14:1  305:1
Skarland, Ivar  290:1
Skidmore, Stephen G.
285:152
Skiff, Nolan  207:3
Skiles, Oral  279:3
Skinner, Alonzo A.  119:3
145:4  179:2
Skinner, Cyrus  155:5
181:5  256:6
Skinner, David E.  113:3
130:4  276:4
Skinner, Eugene F.  41:1
150:2  232:17
Skinner, Gilbert W.  130:5
Skinner, Silas (Sam)
134:13
Skinner, Thomas James
126:4  253:7  260:4
Skipworth, G. F.  232:3
Skookum Jim  281:1
Skykomish, WA  98:5
305:1
Slabtown, WA  41:1
Slacum, William A.  4:3
44:13  84:2  162:10
188:8  272:5
Slade, Joseph Alfred "Jack"
256:11
Slater, James Harvey  150:2
Slater, Seth S.  103:2
118:1

Slater, Thomas  266:2
Slaterville, ID  223:1
Slaughter, Samuel C.  266:2
Slentz, Samuel D.  266:2
Slickpoo, ID  103:3
Slisco, Martin  137:1
Sloan, F. C.  176:2
Sloan, Gordon  294:2
Sloan, W. A.  274:9
Sly, Ben  97:3
Smails, George  199:1
Small, D. W.  150:2
Small, Rainie Adamson
266:3
Smith, Addison T.  213:4
293:8
Smith, Alden R.  309:13
Smith, Alexander C.  87:4
Smith, Alvin T.  84:6
Smith, Amadee M.  68:4
Smith, Andrew C.  187:14
Smith, Asa Bowen  4:8
17:4  93:6  119:4  177:22
192:1
Smith, C. DeWitt  33:2
Smith, Charles J.  49:3
Smith, Clareta Olmstead
278:1
Smith, Delazon  35:4  51:60
145:18  154:2
Smith, E. L.  150:2
Smith, Edward S.  150:3
Smith, Edwin A.  96:1
Smith, Eugene D.  150:1
Smith, Ezekiel  199:2
Smith, Frank  161:2
Smith, Frank L.  289:4
Smith, George Belding
266:2
Smith, George Venable
100:7  152:3  163:2
191:35  234:5  243:8
276:5
Smith, Green B.  150:2
Smith, Green Clay  13:2
25:4  48:12  133:10  183:3
214:2  283:2  286:14

Smith, Harvey 293:4
Smith, Helen 150:2
Smith, Henry A. "Harry"
  7:5 31:5 150:1 234:2
  306:9
Smith, Hiram Francis
  150:2 203:1
Smith, Hugh 12:20
Smith, I. N. 87:3
Smith, J. C. 119:5 198:1
Smith, Jefferson Randolph
  "Soapy" 55:2 196:5
  234:2 255:4 268:244
  309:7 310:10 311:4
Smith, John C. 199:1
Smith, John Minard 266:1
Smith, Joseph E. 58:3
Smith, "Kentucky" 95:18
Smith, Leta May 203:1
Smith, Levi Lathrop 32:2
  41:1 234:1
Smith, Norman R. 100:9
  266:4
Smith, Robert Burns 60:15
  133:5 155:3 156:1
  214:3
Smith, Samuel J. 199:2
Smith, Sidney A. 84:5
  119:4 179:2
Smith, Silas B. 272:5
Smith, Silas Turner 266:2
Smith, Solomon Howard
  44:3 84:6 150:2 272:5
Smith, Sylvester S. 102:6
  103:4
Smith, Thomas H. 150:4
  284:4
Smith, Victor 100:18
Smith, Wesley O. 300:4
Smith, William N. 119:6
Smith, William S. 199:2
Smith, Winfield D. 199:1
Smithe, William 238:9
  253:5
Smithers, C. Owen 167:7
Smithers, Erasmus M.
  282:10

Smithers, BC 123:2 186:6
  204:2
Smithfield (Smithter), WA
  41:1 234:2 SEE ALSO
  Olympia, WA
Smithville, ID 223:1
Smitkin (Chief) 97:1
Smohalla 36:9
Smylie, Robert E. 117:4
  259:3
Smyser, Selden 231:7
Smythe, William E. 283:6
Snedden, William C. 241:6
Snell, Earl 195:1
Snell, Marshall King 266:2
Snipes, Benjamin E. 41:1
  203:1 250:4
Snively, Henry 163:4
Snodgrass, M. D. 226:9
Snohomish, WA 14:1 58:8
  150:1 246:4 305:1
Snoqualmie, WA 14:1 305:2
Snow, Herman H. 179:1
Snyder, John 266:3
Snyder, Wilson McLean 266:3
Soap Lake, WA 293:26 305:1
Soda Springs, ID 23:8
  211:18
Soelberg, Axel 69:13
Soer, Aloysius 34:2
Sogge, George 231:2
Sointula, BC 165:4
Sol Duc Hot Springs, WA
  100:7 305:2
Soldier, ID 211:1
Solie, Hans 57:6
Solloway, R. L. 275:6
Solomon, AK 63:1
Somerville, Robert 266:2
Sooke, BC 3:8 47:3
  122:5 165:9
Sooyoos, WA 267:1
Sorensen, C. P. 99:11
South Bend, WA 14:1
  109:6 163:2 202:3
  305:1
Southard, W. E. "Ed" 293:58

Southern Cross, MT  78:1
    319:5
Spalding, Ely T.  288:2
Spalding, Henry Harmon
    4:71  16:15  27:5  33:4
    43:4  91:50  93:35  96:4
    101:17  102:5  108:5
    118:14  119:28  132:4
    150:2  172:11  177:34
    188:20  192:4  198:11
    249:5  252:2  296:23  305:4
Spalding, ID  164:1
Spalding Mission, ID  4:14
    118:4  SEE ALSO Lap-
    wai, ID
Spanaway, WA  305:1
Spangle, William  39:1
Spangle, WA  27:3  39:6
    96:2  108:2  305:2
Spangler, James W.  113:4
Sparks, Loren Darius
    231:14
Sparta, OR  264:1
Spaulding, J. H.  99:6
Speck, Clayton S.  279:7
Speirs, George  266:2
Spellman, John  178:2
Spencer, George Albert
    266:3
Spencer, John Clark  186:3
Spencer, Matthew Lyle
    38:3
Spencer, Robert R.  217:28
Spencer, William Valentine
    30:1
Sperry, James B.  150:2
Spithill, Alexander  266:3
Splawn, A. J.  27:11  36:3
    155:1  203:1
Splawn, Charles A.  150:1
Splawn, Moses  33:3  118:1
    132:1
Spokane House, WA  27:10
    72:4  108:19  119:5
    132:4  198:2  252:4
    317:6
Spori, Jacob  59:7

Sprague, Charles A.  49:4
    261:1
Sprague, Frank S.  266:3
Sprague, Robert W.  217:2
Sprague, WA  39:3  92:1
    108:1  305:1
Spratt, Joseph  131:7
Spray, OR  42:1
Sprenger, Jacob B.  30:1
Spriggs, A. E.  133:2
    298:2
Springdale, WA  305:1
Springer, Alva  110:8
Springer, C. H.  266:2
Springfield, OR  41:2  68:2
    82:2  232:6  300:2
Springtown, ID  164:2
Springtown, MT  319:3
Springville, OR  68:6
Springwater, OR  228:7
Sproat, Gilbert Malcolm
    3:4  5:4  107:1  253:6
    294:4
Sproat's Landing, BC  107:2
Sproul, Robert  50:2
Spurbeck, Don  274:6
Spurgeon, Sarah  231:3
Squamish, BC  275:10
Squire, Watson Carvosso
    31:5  163:4  178:4  217:2
    234:1  243:11  245:10
    266:8
Staats, W. H.  42:5
Stacy, Martin Van Buren
    203:1
Stadelman, Charles H.
    266:3
Stahlhut, William H.  279:3
Staines, Robert John  3:9
    126:4  165:3  253:6
Stalker, A. R.  95:3
Stallcup, John C.  266:2
Stamp, Edward  158:2
    236:11  260:3  294:11
Stampfler, Jacob  266:2
Stanbra, Charles  266:2
Standifer, Jeff  132:2

Stanfield, Joseph 177:15
296:9
Stanfield, Robert N. 49:5
Stanfield, OR 207:2
Stanford, Lyman 134:2
Stanford, Thomas C. 24:5
Stanford, MT 156:1
Stanley, E. J. 227:7
Stanley, J. H. 150:1
Stanley, John Mix 198:1
Stanley, Marjorie 278:1
Stanley, ID 164:1
Stanrod, Drew W. 23:9
95:3 205:3
Stansfield, G. A. 246:4
Stanton, Sewell 97:2
Stanton, ID 223:1
Stanup, Peter C. 273:1
Stanwood, WA 14:1 203:1
246:3 305:1
Stapleton, George Wash-
ington 133:4
Star, ID 23:4 33:3
Starbuck, Nell 176:2
Starbuck, WA 119:1
280:2
Stark, Benjamin 179:1
198:1 210:5 284:7
297:6
Stark, MT 112:3
Starkweather, Harvey
49:6
Starkweather, William A.
51:17
Starr, E. A. 246:7
Starr, John W. 30:4
Starr, Noah A. 30:1
Starr, Philip M. 30:1
Starrett, George E. 119:2
203:1
Starring, Francis W. 303:7
Startup, Jeremiah Gibson
266:2
Startup, WA 305:1
Stateler, L. B. 227:10
Stauffer, Joseph E. 266:3
Stearns, Al 242:8

Stearns, Josiah O. 203:1
266:1
Stearns, Rollin 242:7
Stebbins, AK 8:3
Stedman, William L. 157:2
Steel, George A. 150:1
Steel, William Gladstone
239:4 302:2
Steele, Alden Hatch 150:2
203:1
Steele, Edward 266:1
Steele, Samuel B. 255:10
268:4
Steele, William L. 133:5
Steen, Enoch 110:1
Steese, James G. 63:2
Stegall, Steve 114:4
Steilacoom, WA 7:7 32:5
50:5 80:5 89:1 92:2
119:9 121:5 203:2
222:7 246:7 305:5
Stein, Henry W. 191:6
Steiner, R. S. 157:3
Steitz, Augustus 107:2
Steiwer, Frederick 207:3
293:4
Stella, WA 152:1 305:1
Stemple, MT 319:2
Stephan, Frank 213:5
Stephen, Fred M. 169:8
Stephens, James B. 150:1
179:2 210:5 284:2
Stephens, Melvin McKay
185:3
Stephens, William 119:7
Stephens, William T. 231:3
Stephenson, F. L. 186:3
Stepovich, Mike 128:3
129:6
Steptoe, Edward J. 11:30
108:2 119:13 141:5
198:6 305:2
Steptoeville (Walla Walla),
WA 41:1 119:1
Sterling, S. F. 157:4
Sterling, MT 78:4 319:5
Sterling, WA 315:2

Sterlingville, OR 264:1
Stetson, Clinton 199:2
Steunenberg, Albert K.
　23:4
Steunenberg, Frank 43:4
　105:8 106:5 118:3
　127:11 134:2 170:2
　191:2 205:15 252:2
　259:3
Steunenberg, ID 23:2
　102:3
Stevens, Charles 202:3
Stevens, Hazard 27:6
　141:16 155:8 198:2
　220:7 245:8 305:3
Stevens, Henry H. "Har-
　ry" 236:3 238:10
Stevens, Henry L. 191:5
Stevens, Isaac Ingalls
　1:5 6:9 7:7 16:21
　17:13 27:23 31:16
　32:4 39:4 45:6 48:18
　50:8 58:23 76:5 96:3
　103:5 108:8 119:20
　121:5 132:6 133:45
　135:4 141:238 145:11
　150:2 155:32 176:5
　178:10 179:7 181:5
　188:20 198:11 214:5
　220:20 222:23 234:7
　245:26 252:12 257:9
　272:8 301:18 305:18
　306:11
Stevens, James 152:1
　176:2 195:6
Stevens, John H. 150:1
Stevens, Sydney A. 70:4
Stevens, Theodore "Ted"
　54:7 129:1 136:10 241:1
Stevens, Wendall E. 157:2
Stevens Village, AK 66:3
　115:2
Stevenson, Christopher G.
　169:6
Stevenson, E. G. 264:5
Stevenson, Edward A. 29:11
　43:1 87:4 95:10 118:3

Stevenson, George C. 245:5
Stevenson, John C. 41:1
　234:5 244:2
Stevenson, Robert 5:5
Stevenson, WA 152:1 305:1
Stevensville, MT 39:2
　48:3 155:3 181:6
　183:3 247:3 SEE ALSO
　St. Mary's Mission, MT
Steveston, BC 238:4
Stewart, Calvin W. 203:1
Stewart, Carey L. 266:3
Stewart, Charles B. 199:2
Stewart, Daniel 119:5
　199:4
Stewart, David 119:5
　266:1
Stewart, Frank A. 258:4
Stewart, George H. 205:4
Stewart, Hardy T. 258:4
Stewart, James P. 150:2
Stewart, John J. 150:2
　294:1
Stewart, Meredith E. 199:2
Stewart, Peter G. 150:2
Stewart, Samuel V. 214:6
　215:7 247:3 299:9
Stewart, Thomas 241:4
Stewart, BC 275:15
Stibnite, ID 23:1 223:3
Sticklin, Louis J. 266:3
Stiff, Henry C. 133:3
Stikine Village, AK 63:1
Stiles, Charles T. 150:2
Stiles, Theodore L. 150:2
Stillman, E. D. 150:1
Stillwell, William D. 150:3
　179:2
Stilts, George 87:8
Stimple, Bert 148:2
Stimson, Charles D. 69:3
　73:7
Stine, Fred 119:7
Stine, J. H. 300:5
Stinson, Buck 46:3 133:7
　256:14
Stites, Ernest 134:3

STITES                146

Stites, ID  23:3  102:8
  103:2
Stobie, William T.  279:3
Stocking, Fred W.  266:2
Stocklein, Henry J.  266:2
Stoll, William T.  212:8
Stolte, C. E.  2:5
Stolz, Edwin  102:13
Stone, B. F.  119:9
Stonechest, James  173:5
Storey, John C.  199:1
Stork, Alfred  185:6
Story, James L.  150:1
Story, Nelson  1:3  46:2
  48:6  133:5
Stout, James  87:5
Stout, Jonathan L.  150:2
  202:8
Stout, Lansing  145:9
Stout, Tom  215:5
Stowell, Hubbart  252:1
Strahan, Charles  86:7
Strahan, R. S.  150:1
Strahm, John U.  199:2
Strahm, Peter  199:2
Strahorn, Robert Edmund
  279:4  289:5
Strahorn, Robert F.
  133:5  203:1
Straight, Zebulon K.  199:1
Strand, August Leroy  251:4
Stratford, WA  36:1  293:4
Stratton, Charles C.  71:7
Stratton, Howard W.  150:2
Stratton, Owen T.  213:3
Strawberry, MT  308:1
Street, Samuel F.  266:3
Stringer, I. O.  255:3
Stringer, Robert J.  199:1
Strong, Anna Louise
  113:15  178:10  234:11
  276:15  278:2
Strong, C. C.  187:7
Strong, John F. A.  130:9
  161:6  311:1
Strong, Major  268:4
Strong, William H.  119:5

  150:4
Strout, Edwin A.  266:3
Strowbridge, J. A.  150:3
Struthers, William A.
  199:2
Struve, Henry  243:5
Stuart, Elbridge Amos
  41:6
Stuart, Granville  25:3
  46:14  48:16  61:9
  76:18  133:28  155:9
  156:22  181:7  214:9
  215:10  247:5  283:8
  286:15  292:50  298:3
  319:12
Stuart, James  133:22
  188:3  215:7  292:40
  319:11
Stuart, James (a Nez
  Perce)  102:6  103:3
Stuart, John  235:11
Stuart, Robert  272:9
Stuart, ID  102:6  103:2
  SEE ALSO Kooskia, ID
Stubbers, Barney  102:7
Stubblefield, Blaine  114:3
Stuchell, Harry  57:3
Stull, G. C.  227:4
Stump, Jennie Wright
  242:6
Sturdevant, Robert F.
  119:4  150:1
Sturgis, James H.  207:3
Sturgis, Samuel P.  207:5
Sturgis, William P.  199:2
Sublette, William  93:3
  172:4  188:3
Success, WA  267:1
Suffield, E. S.  275:8
Sugar City, ID  23:3
  59:20
Sullivan, Cornelius "Con"
  108:1  172:3  212:3
  311:1
Sullivan, John  266:1
Sullivan, Ward W.  124:11
Sultan, WA  14:1  225:3

305:1
Sulzer, Charles 130:2
Sulzer, AK 130:1
Sumas, WA 14:1
Summers, John W. 293:9
Summit, MT 78:3 319:9
Sumner, Sam R. 116:2
Sumner, Thomas Boyd
  266:3
Sumner, WA 14:1 203:1
  305:2
Sumpter, OR 75:2 225:5
  251:5 264:10 300:2
  308:8
Sun Valley, ID 23:1 118:3
  259:3 261:2
Sundborg, George 241:3
Sunnydale, WA 240:3
Sunnyside, ID 23:1
Sunnyside, WA 82:3 180:2
  191:2 203:1 305:1
Sunrise, MT 78:1 224:2
  319:3
Superior, MT 78:1 224:2
  319:5
Suquamish, WA 305:1
Susanville, OR 225:1 264:2
  308:5
Susitna Station, AK 233:8
Sutherland, Dan A. 130:16
  241:1
Sutherland, J. A. 137:4
Sutherland, John 222:7
Sutherlin, Will H. 48:4
Sutherlin, OR 300:2
Sutico, WA 152:1
Sutton, Alfred E. 266:1
Sutton, Richard P. 67:7
Sutton, Walter 86:7 258:2
Sutton, William J. 38:4
  94:12 289:2
Suzzallo, Henry 32:3 38:8
  58:4 113:1 184:60
  222:4 245:5 257:3
  261:2
Swaim, Moses 199:2
Swain, Bert 113:6

Swalwell, Joseph A. 266:1
  293:6
Swalwell, William G. 266:4
Swan, James Gilchrist 41:1
  50:10 100:6 141:7 150:2
  202:6
Swan, John M. 199:2
Swannell, Frank C. 40:5
Sweeney, Charles 102:10
  106:288 118:1 212:7
  259:2
Sweeney, Robert H. 71:12
Sweeney, Samuel B. 199:2
Sweet, Betty 278:1
Sweet, Mahlon 232:1
Sweet, Willis 95:5 96:3
  117:5 212:2
Sweet, ID 23:3
Sweet Home, OR 152:2
Sweetland, Harold 274:9
Sweetland, Monroe 49:25
  261:2
Sweetman, Maude 245:7
Sweetser, Charles T. 199:1
Swezea, Thomas J. 199:2
Swim, Arthur L. 266:2
Swim, Isaac T. 97:4
Swineford, Alfred P. 55:2
  130:20 149:8 159:4
  160:2 190:6 241:1
  281:2
Swisher, Frank 134:13
Swisher, Perry 95:2
Switzer, Tom 173:12
Switzler, William H.
  207:4
Sybert, William R. 266:2
Sylvanite, MT 319:7
Sylvester, Albert Hale
  116:3
Sylvester, E. O. 149:3
Sylvester, Edmund 32:2
  220:2 245:11 305:2
Symes, George G. 286:5
Synarep, WA 267:1
Syringa, ID 102:4

Tabor, J. B.  150:2
Taft, MT  98:7  99:2
Taghee (Chief)  211:28
Tagish Post, YT  255:6
Tahoe, ID  102:3
Tahsis, BC  165:4
Takotna, AK  137:3  263:5
Talbot, Fred  275:6
Talbot, Guy W.  82:20
Talbot, William C.  9:8
Talbotte, Henry J.  "Cher-
  okee Bob"  102:3  118:2
Talen, Herb  274:8
Talkeetna, AK  63:1  66:2
  137:2  226:4
Talkington, H. L.  103:3
Talmadge, D. H.  300:4
Tanacross, AK  54:5
Tanana, AK  52:2  63:1
  130:3  137:4  309:5
Tannatt, Thomas Redding
  288:4
Tanner, Albert H.  150:2
Tanner, Si  268:10
Tappan, William H.  272:3
  284:5
Tash, Andrew J.  199:2
Tatarrax (Mythical King)
  258:2
Tatlow, Robert Garnett
  253:6
Tatman, Mark  280:2
Tatom, Stanley  130:2
Tauitau (Chief)  4:4
Taylor, Alonzo S.  266:3
Taylor, Arthur J.  150:1
Taylor, Charles M.  199:1
Taylor, Emmette  279:6
Taylor, Glen H.  105:9
  213:4  261:1
Taylor, Harvey  274:10
Taylor, Howard D.  245:14
Taylor, Jacob R.  288:2
Taylor, James  150:2
Taylor, James A.  113:5
Taylor, John A.  199:3
Taylor, Louis D.  236:7  238:4

Taylor, Moulton  41:1
Taylor, Oliver Perry
  266:2
Taylor, Orson D.  305:1
Taylor, Sam F.  95:2
Taylor, Thomas  199:2
Taylor, Til D.  207:6
Taylor, W. D.  202:2
Taylor, W. H.  150:1
Taylor, W. R.  "Jinks"
  207:5
Taylor, Warren A.  241:1
Taylor, Zebulon Bryant
  266:6
Taylor Flats, BC  40:6
Teague, William  5:4
Teal, Joseph N.  42:1
  229:4
Teats, Govnor  266:3
Teeters, Jake  173:6
Teit, James A.  140:1
  189:6
Tekoa, WA  212:1
Telcher, D. H.  103:3
Telford, J. Lyle  236:2
Telkwa, BC  186:3
Teller Station, AK  28:3
  63:1  130:1  148:2  161:8
  190:5
Temple, Isaiah  207:4
Templin, John  266:2
Tendoy (Chief)  164:2
  211:20
Tenino, WA  89:1  152:1
  245:5  305:3
Tennant, J. D.  200:15
Tenney, C. W.  227:4
Ternes, John Benjamin
  266:2
Terrace, BC  186:3
Terreton, ID  23:4
Terrill, William E.  266:3
Terry, Charles C.  31:11
  150:1  276:7  306:19
Terry, Chester N.  51:8
Terry, Frank  266:2
Terry, Lee  80:5

Terwilliger, James  41:1
56:2  210:5  264:3
284:2  285:4
Teske, Lloyd W.  71:5
Tesreau, Elmer  50:2
Teter, Thomas B.  211:7
Tetherow, Andrew Jack-
son  42:4
Tetherow, Solomon S.
56:9  157:3  318:23
Tetlin, AK  63:1
Teton City, ID  23:3  59:6
Tetonia, ID  23:2
Tew, Thomas S.  266:2
Texas Ferry, WA  119:2
Thachek, BC  235:4
Thacher, W. F. G.  232:3
Thayer, Andrew Jackson
150:1
Thayer, Benjamin B.
216:6
Thayer, Elroy M.  266:1
Thayer, William Wallace
150:2  153:1
The Dalles, OR  39:4
42:20  56:29  82:4
87:8  104:13  114:8
147:6  172:6  187:8
193:14  249:5  251:11
296:7  297:21  300:5
302:6  303:12  317:13
318:19  SEE ALSO Dal-
les (The), OR
Theon, WA  119:1
Theophilus, Donald R.
117:54
Thew, W.  235:5
Thews, William B.  95:2
Thoma, Joe  114:3
Thomas, James Albert
157:3
Thomas, Joan K.  278:1
Thomas, John  213:8
Thomas, Joseph A.  150:1
Thomas, Robert Pennell
266:3
Thompson, Alexander  57:5

Thompson, Arthur H.  318:14
Thompson, Carey  232:1
Thompson, Charles William
266:3
Thompson, David  39:19
43:2  50:42  99:3  108:2
155:22  164:3  192:7
198:4  252:8  305:6
Thompson, David P.  43:1
87:4  118:1  210:4  264:1
Thompson, Donald  231:2
Thompson, Edgar I.  266:3
Thompson, Fred R.  191:5
Thompson, H. C.  33:2
Thompson, J. Spencer
238:5
Thompson, James B.  119:4
199:1
Thompson, James P.  57:4
Thompson, John M.  232:2
Thompson, Levant F.  150:3
Thompson, Margaret H.
278:1
Thompson, Robert R.  6:4
119:3  145:7  179:1
229:7
Thompson, William  300:15
Thompson, "Wrong Font"
263:16
Thompson, WA  267:1
Thompson Falls, MT  48:4
76:2  215:6  319:7
Thomson, Lucy (Mrs. Jason
Lee)  44:9
Thomson, Reginald H.  41:1
234:2  240:2  261:2
276:20
Thornburg, Grant  264:3
Thorne, Chester  266:2
Thornhill, Jim  61:30
Thornsbury, Red  175:14
Thornton, Harrison R.
149:2
Thornton, J. Quinn  119:3
198:1  284:2
Thornton, Robert Y.  49:3
Thornton, William M.  133:4

Thornton, ID 59:3
Thorp, Fielden M. 150:1
Thorp, Frank S. 157:2
Thorp, Leonard L. 150:2
Thorp, WA 308:2
Three Mountains (Chief) 39:3
Thurlow, Eugene 246:1
Thurston, Robert F. 294:1
Thurston, Samuel Royal
    145:3 162:3 172:1
    188:3 193:3 198:1
    208:2 249:1 272:2
    284:2 300:8
Tibbals, Henry L. 150:1
Tibbetts, Calvin 44:4
    84:6 162:5
Tibbitts, George W. 150:2
Tichacek, Charles 293:4
Tichenor, William 258:7
Tieje, Ralph E. 94:7
Tiffany, Orrin E. 124:7
Tiffany, Ross K.
    279:5
Tilaukait (Chief) 93:8
    172:5 177:30 252:3
    296:5
Tilco-ax (Chief) 27:5
    212:1
Tillamook, OR 17:4 75:6
    84:1 152:4 195:5
    300:4 303:8
Tillinghast, A. G. 314:3
    315:5
Tilly, Frederick G. 266:2
Tilsley, J. H. 289:2
Tilton, David W. 25:3
    133:3
Timberline Lodge, OR
    239:12
Timentwa, WA 267:1
Timothy (Chief) 4:1 11:1
    27:4 91:4 93:5 280:5
Timson, William 266:2
Tingley, Sam S. 64:3
Tingley, Stephen 5:3 138:3
Tinker, Henry 202:4
Tinkham, Abiel W. 141:4

Tipton, Milton W. 112:9
Tipton, OR 264:3
Titchenal, David J. 157;6
Titlow, Aaron R. 266:2
Tobey, Mark 41:2 69:16
    276:15
Tobin, William J. 136:6
Tod, John 3:15 20:29
    126:5 235:3 253:13
Todd, A. E. 126:4
Todd, J. H. 126:4
Todd, John Y. 42:8 320:2
Todhunter, W. B. 41:1
Tofino, BC 165:12 204:3
Tokeland, WA 203:1 305:1
Toledo, OR 228:5
Toledo, WA 14:1 305:1
Tolman, James Clark
    150:2
Tolmie, Simon Fraser
    238:4 253:14
Tolmie, William Fraser
    3:3 7:7 20:6 50:8
    101:2 131:5 172:3
    177:3 187:20 194:6
    203:2 220:6 222:9
    253:5 272:5 304:2
    305:4
Tomlinson, Robert 10:4
    186:6
Tompkins, Morton 49:3
Tonasket, WA 180:2
    267:1 305:1
Toohoolhoolzote (Chief)
    26:7 SEE ALSO Tu-
    hulhutsut
Tooker, John S. 286:3
Toole, John 181:4
Toole, Joseph K. 60:16
    95:3 133:20 156:3
    214:4 215:7 247:3
    286:25 299:7
Toole, Warren 133:5
Toppenish, WA 82:3
    198:1 305:1
Topping, Eugene S. 107:7
Tornensis, J. S. 281:22

Toroda, WA  39:2  267:1
    SEE ALSO Old Toroda,
    WA
Torrence, E. A.   119:1
Tosi, Pascal  34:2
Toston, Thomas  46:5
Toston, MT  46:3  319:5
Touchet, WA  305:1
Touchette, Felix  112:6
Tower, Charles W.   187:6
    258:4
Tower, MT  308:9
Townsend, John Kirk
    44:10  45:9  101:3
    177:5  187:10  287:11
Townsend, William C.
    199:2
Townsend, MT  46:4  319:8
Toy, Pete  40:13
Tozier, Albert  162:20
Tracy, Charles Howard
    266:2
Tracy, F. P.   193:2
Tracy, Harry  152:3  305:2
Tracy, Tom  252:1
Traeger, Charles  52:10
    290:1
Trail, BC  107:13  151:11
    209:3  253:5
Trapper City, MT   78:2
    319;2
Trask, Egbert  157:3
Trask, Eldridge  37:3
Treacy, William  133:5
Treadwell, Alvah  231:2
Treadwell, David  157:3
Treadwell, John  28:1
    149:5
Treen, Lewis A.  64:5
Treichler, C. Landis
    97:2
Tremblay, Hector  40:8
Tremblay, L. F.   112:5
Trenholme, James D.
    234:2
Trevitt, Victor  179:2
    198:1  264:1

Triem, Eve  278:2
Trimble, Carol  169:5
Trimble, Horace  280:2
Trinidad, WA  293:4
Trinity, WA  225:1
Triplett, Van B.   268:5
Tripp, Tallman  157:2
Troup, James W.   131:20
    198:2  229:4
Troutdale, OR   75:5  152:1
    228:5
Trowbridge, B. C.   264:2
Troy, David S.   184:5
Troy, John Weir   129:9
    130:9  148:2  159:3
    226:4  241:2
Troy, P. M.   245:8  246:1
Troy, Smith  70:8  245:9
    246:1
Troy, ID  23:9  24:13
Troy, MT  319:15
Truax, Henry C.   199:1
Truax, Sewell  119:4
    245:2  280:4
True, M. C.   150:1
Truger, Louis  308:1
Trullinger, John Corse
    68:3  82:4  150:1  295:3
Trumble, R. Edward  157:2
Trumbull, L. J.   303:6
Trutch, John  5:5
Trutch, Joseph William
    3:16  5:9  126:5  238:5
    253:15
Tshimakain Mission  4:5
    91:4  93:9  108:29
    177:25  188:4  252:12
    296:14  305:2
Tslalakun (Chief)  93:4
Tualatin Plains, OR  84:2
    152:1
Tucker, Ernest E.   187:7
Tucker, Horace A.   203:2
Tufts, James  133:33
    286:6
Tugman, William M.   232:4
Tuhulhutsut (Chief)  172:7

SEE ALSO Toohoolhool-
zote
Tukey, John F.  97:2
Tulameen, BC  47:1
Tullis, Amos F.  150:2
Tumalo, OR  42:2
Tumwater, WA  14:1  17:5
  32:4  50:9  172:4  203:1
  222:9  245:7  246:3
  305:4  317:5  SEE ALSO
  Newmarket, WA
Tundra, AK  8:4
Tunin, E. N.  266:2
Tupper, Charles Hibbert
  238:7  253:9
Tupper, Gideon  234:5
Turco, Frank  113:8
Turnbull, Thomas  134:10
Turner, Arthur J.  293:17
Turner, F. P.  102:8
Turner, George W.  39:2
  96:3  106:11  243:6
  245:8  289:3
Turner, Gilbert Lafayette
  266:2
Turner, J. W.  102:4
Turner, John Herbert
  126:4  238:6  253:13
Turner, Joseph H.  207:13
  266:2
Turner, W. B.  38:2
Turnow, John  152:1  195:2
Tussing, Arlon  270:2
Tuttle, Daniel Sylvester
  25:15  43:2  48:5  118:2
  227:4
T'Vault, William G.  51:4
  56:6  97:1  119:4  145:3
  230:3  264:4  300:11
  304:2  317:3  318:7
Tvete, Nels K.  266:1
Twickenham, OR  42:1
Twin Bridges, MT  319:6
Twin Falls, ID  23:14
  24:2  117:5  118:5
  164:2  180:3  259:6
Twisp, WA  267:1

Twitmyer, Edwin B.  38:3
Tye, WA  98:3  SEE ALSO
  Wellington, WA
Tyhee (Chief)  211:15
Tyler, Thomas  266:3
Tyonek, AK  233:6
Tyson, Charles A.  199:1
Tyson, Harry  131:15

Ubet, MT  156:2  319:2
Ucluelet, BC  165:8
Udness, Olaf  266:2
Ugashik, AK  8:5  161:1
Uhlenkott, Henry  102:4
Uhlman, Charles T.  150:1
Uhlman, Wes  178:3  276:2
Ukiah, OR  207:1
Ulbricht, Clem  242:8
Ullman, Albert C.  12:30
  49:3
Uma Howlish (Chief)  147:1
Umapine (Chief)  11:6
Umatilla, OR  34:4  87:7
  118:5  119:10  198:8
  207:15  229:9  264:3
  317:5
Umpqua, OR  230:6  317:2
Umtach (Chief)  222:3
Umtippe (Chief)  4:9  93:3
  177:2
Unalakleet, AK  8:11  52:43
  77:14  137:5  159:3
  161:2  168:3  263:6
  281:4  290:25
Unalaska, AK  8:7  66:3
  77:24  130:8  146:17
  159:10  190:9  281:15
  290:3  311:3
Underwood, Amos  179:1
Underwood, J. Ben  232:10
Underwood, J. J.  293:7
Underwood, John  161:1
Union, WA  225:1  305:1
Union City, MT  46:2  78:3
Union Gap, WA  82:2

Uniontown, WA   119:2
Unionville, MT   78:1   319:6
Unity, ID   23:1
Unity, WA   202:2
Updyke, David   87:6
Upham, Alfred Horatio
   117:42
Upton, John H.   86:6
   300:7
U'Ren, William S.   6:2
   49:2   85:11   86:4   207:1
   244:5   261:6   302:3
Urquhart, James   150:2
Urquhart, William M.
   150:1   266:4
Usibelli, Joe   136:2
Ustick, ID   23:1
Utica, MT   319:3
Utopia, WA   315:3
Utsalady, WA   73:4   100:5
   246:2   314:4
Utter, Frank B.   157:3
Utter, Joseph   203:1
Utter City, OR   258:3


Vader, WA   50:1   152:1
Vail, H. D.   237:4
Valdez, AK   28:3   54:8
   63:2   66:3   115:18   125:7
   130:21   146:6   148:2
   159:8   160:8   233:4
   241:6   263:12   270:4
   309:16   310:6   311:6
Vale, OR   4:1   42:3   56:4
   97:3   134:3   187:2
Valemount, BC   50:5
Valentine, Carl A.   23:5
Valentine, W. D.   289:2
Valentine, WA   280:2
Valsetz, OR   75:4   152:1
   195:6
Van Anda, BC   275:6
Van Asselt, Henry   80:4
   150:4   306:12
Van Bokkelen, J. J. H.   150:2

Van Bronkhorst, Erin   278:1
Van Buskirk, Philip Clay-
   ton   191:5
Vance, Sam   95:2
Vance, Thomas M.   266:2
Vance, Walter D.   185:3
Vance, WA   14:1
Vancouver, WA   15:4   16:11
   41:4   50:14   71:6   73:6
   104:8   151:11   152:4
   163:8   180:6   194:8
   198:9   203:5   210:10
   229:8   252:8   293:4
   305:14   SEE ALSO Fort
   Vancouver
Vanderbilt, John M.   149:4
Vandercook, Wesley   200:12
Vanderhoof, BC   204:2
Van der Pol, John   34:2
Vandervelden, Walter   195:2
Van Duren, William L.
   196:10
Van Dusen, Adam   295:27
Van Dusen, Henry   86:17
Van Eaton, Harold   245:4
Van Epps, Theodore C.   150:1
Van Gorp, Leopold   34:3
   39:4
Van Holderbeke, August
   266:2
Van Horn, WA   315:3
Van Horne, William Cor-
   nelius   151:2   152:2
   238:5
Van Orsdel, W. W.   48:4
   227:25
Vanport, OR   41:2   71:5
   152:6   206:3   210:2
   293:3   303:2
Van Sant, Clara   169:6
Van Scoy, Thomas   71:5
Van Slyke, Willard D.
   237:3
Van Syckle, Ed   195:3
Vantage, WA   198:3   291:3
   305:1
Van Valey, Albert Louis

266:2
Van Valkenburg, Luman G.
266:2
Vanwyck, ID 23:4
Varney, George R. 303:7
Vashon, WA 14:1 305:1
Vassallo, Godfrey 71:16
Vaughn, Hank 36:18 108:2
Veiller, Bayard 234:2
Veniaminov, Ivan 77:13
161:4 269:10
Ventnor, ID 39:2
Vercruysse, Louis 208:9
Verity, Oliver A. 191:10
Vernon, Forbes George
5:5
Vernon, James Mercer
266:4
Verona City, MT 133:1
SEE ALSO Virginia
City, MT
Vert, John 207:6
Vest, George G. 286:5
Vestal, Samuel 203:1
Vey, Tony 207:5
Vickers, Perry 239:3
Victor (Chief) 133:4
141:3 155:7
Victor, Frances Fuller
44:7 45:3 50:15
193:12 302:15 304:10
317:2
Victor, Henry Clay 302:4
Victor, ID 23:2
Victor, MT 319:4
Vienna, ID 223:1 308:4
Villa, Frank 199:1
Villers, Thomas J. 303:9
Vincent (Chief) 27:3
Vincent, Frederick 207:3
Vincent, W. D. 53:11
Vinson, John S. 150:1
Vipond, MT 224:1 319:3
Virginia Bills, WA 267:1
Virginia City, MT 1:3
25:312 36:3 45:3 46:10
48:35 60:4 76:8 78:26

118:4 133:65 155:12
156:8 167:4 181:5
183:7 211:3 214:12
215:22 216:5 224:9
227:9 247:20 256:30
283:4 292:20 308:8
312:5 319:55 SEE AL-
SO Alder Gulch and Ver-
ona City
Virginia City, WA 267:1
Virtue, J. W. 264:3
Vogtlin, George H. 266:2
Volcano, ID 223:1
Vollmer, John P. 23:17
24:6 102:4 192:3
Vollmer, ID 23:3 102:2
Von Boecklin, August 266:2
Von Carnop, John 113:4
Von der Green, Francis O.
258:5
Voorhees, Charles S. 29:8
95:3 133:2 163:10
243:11
Vose, Donald 191:4
Vowell, Arthur Wellesley
5:3
Vrebosch, Aloysius 34:3


Waccan (Boucher, J. B. )
235:9
Waddington, Alfred 3:5
253:4 260:7
Wade, Decius S. 133:9
286:20
Wade, Hugh 130:1
Wade, James M. 116:2
Wadhams, Arthur Edgar
266:2
Wager, John P. 36:2
207:11
Wagner, C. U. 274:15
Wagner, Clinton 87:7
Wagner, E. 157:3
Wagner, John "Dutch"
256:11

Wagner, MT  61:8
Wagontire, OR  152:2
Wagontown, ID  134:4  147:1
  223:1
Wahkiacus, James  242:4
Wahkiacus, WA  242:4
Waiilatpu, WA  17:11  84:3
  93:18  101:7  108:11
  172:9  177:100  187:6
  188:13  198:9  252:16
  257:20  296:50  305:9
  SEE ALSO Whitman Mis-
  sion
Wainwright, AK  63:1
  263:5
Waisbrooker, Lois  191:6
Wait, Aaron E.  150:2
  284:2
Wait, Sylvester M.  119:14
  203:1
Waite, Jack  212:5
Waitsburg, WA  15:2  96:4
  108:1  119:16  203:3
  305:1
Wakefield, William J. C.
  288:3
Wald, Charles  266:1
Walden, Benjamin  318:10
Waldo, Daniel  119:5
  194:5
Waldo, Dwight B.  38:1
Waldo, OR  225:4  264:2
Waldron, Robert  245:4
Waldschmidt, Paul E.
  71:30
Wale, Howard  140:2
Wales, AK  8:3  52:9
  63:1  263:3
Waley, Harmon  50:8
Walhachin, BC  47:1
Walkem, George Anthony
  3:3  126:4  238:17
  253:15
Walker, Charles  80:5
Walker, Courtney Meade
  37:1  119:10
Walker, Cyrus  9:14  32:4

91:2  97:2  195:6  246:4
Walker, Elkanah  4:10  16:9
  27:4  36:2  39:3  91:4
  93:16  108:29  150:1
  177:45  198:2  222:11
  252:11  296:11  305:6
Walker, Frank  266:2
Walker, Louis A.  286:3
Walker, Norman "Doc"
  129:10
Walker, Ramsay  213:4
Walker, Richard E.  266:1
Walker, Robert F.  199:1
Walkerville (Butte), MT
  67:9  167:3  319:7
Wall, E. A.  95:2
Wall, George L.  95:2
Wall, John P.  173:6
Walla Walla, WA  16:11
  17:8  27:15  29:9  36:18
  38:4  39:21  41:9  76:8
  82:8  88:13  96:10  104:10
  108:19  112:7  118:11
  119:488  133:10  142:11
  147:11  152:7  155:11
  163:5  172:7  176:5
  181:5  192:12  198:15
  203:5  215:12  222:20
  228:22  229:6  249:4
  252:11  257:16  280:7
  293:5  296:7  297:12
  305:18
Walla Walla, Jesus  36:16
Wallace, Herbert F.  199:1
Wallace, James  10:7
Wallace, Janet  293:6
Wallace, Lew  49:11
Wallace, Mary C.  278:1
Wallace, Thomas B.  266:2
Wallace, William Henson
  16:2  43:4  87:21  105:8
  118:3  132:1  133:2  139:1
  150:2  234:1  245:7  259:3
Wallace, William R.  118:2
  212:27
Wallace, ID  23:14  24:3
  39:2  96:7  98:50  106:9

107:3  108:5  118:8  164:1
205:6  212:20
Waller, Alvin F.   30:1  44:14
56:3  93:4  150:1  177:3
193:16  208:3  249:2  284:1
318:3
Waller, O. L.   293:8
Wallgren, Monrad C.   16:2
41:3  70:5  88:1  100:3
130:3  169:5  184:4  206:3
234:1  245:8  261:1  293:10
Wallowa, OR  36:7
Wallula, WA  17:4  39:5
41:1  75:3  97:2  108:4
119:3  147:7  151:4  152:2
172:3  198:5  207:2
228:13  229:10  252:2
297:3  305:9
Walsh, D. H.   200:5
Walsh, Ellen L.   169:8
Walsh, Thomas J.   49:2
214:13  215:20  244:2
298:5  299:16
Walter, William  318:8
Walters, Abraham L.   266:1
Walters, Sim  87:4
Walters, Theodore A.   213:12
Walterville, OR  42:1
Walton, Hiram F.   266:3
Walton, Joshua J.   150:2
232:8
Waltz, E. P.   303:9
Walville, WA  152:2
Wampole, Elias  211:4
Wanamaker, Pearl  169:6
245:12
Waneta, BC  107:2
Wanicut, WA  267:1
Wapato, WA  82:1
Waples, William H.   266:2
Wappenstein, Charles W.
41:1  234:8  304:2
Warburton, Stanton  266:3
Ward, Charles  280:4
Ward, Charles Clarence
157:4
Ward, Michael B.   199:4

203:2
Ward, Robert  126:6
Warden, WA  293:9
Wardle, James  5:3
Wardner, George H.   2:11
Wardner, James F.   39:2
95:1  96:3  106:5  107:9
108:10  118:2  192:2
203:1  212:5
Wardner, ID  23:10  24:2
96:4  106:16  108:3
118:6  127:4  152:1
164:1  212:8  223:2
259:4  261:1
Ware, Joel  232:2
Waring, Guy  203:1
Warner, Alexander  108:4
Warner, Floyd  196:5
Warner, Henry H.   266:3
Warren, Albert  266:2
Warren, Felix  118:2
Warren, Frank F.   124:75
Warren, Jack  263:4
Warren, James  118:2
Warren, Joel F.   39:2
95:2  212:4
Warren, Mark  97:2
Warren, Seth  266:2
Warren, ID  23:2  102:22
118:4  192:5  223:3
SEE ALSO Richmond,
ID
Warrenton, OR  187:2
Wasco, OR  75:2  187:2
295:1  300:2
Wascopam, OR  44:5  84:2
177:26  198:1  SEE AL-
SO Dalles Mission
Washakie (Chief)  211:12
Washington, George  266:2
304:1
Washington, Nathaniel  36:1
245:5  252:2  293:16
Washington, ID  102:6  SEE
ALSO Warren, ID
Washougal, WA  198:2
305:1

Wasilla, AK 63:1 226:7 281:4
Waskey, Frank H. 130:3 159:3 241:3
Wasson, George 97:3
Waterbury, Elihu 286:2
Waterhouse, Frank 113:2
Waterhouse, Leonard P. 289:2
Waterman, John Orvis 145:19 284:4
Waters, Walter W. 302:1
Waterville, WA 203:1 293:12 305:1
Watkins, Elton 49:6
Watkins, William Henry 51:45 150:2 187:8
Watkinson, Fred 138:2
Watrous, George H. 266:2
Watson, Alexander R. 266:2
Watson, H. W. 108:1
Watson, J. Howard 96:10 266:3
Watson, James R. 234:2
Watson, Thomas G. 150:1
Watson, William Penn 150:3
Watson, MT 319:2
Watt, Joseph 194:10
Watts, A. E. 294:2
Watts, John W. 51:18
Wauconda, WA 267:2
Waud, John 71:1
Waud, Ralph 274:9
Waugh, DeWitt 25:6
Waughop, John W. 150:1
Wauna, OR 195:5
Waverly, WA 107:4
Wawawa, WA 119:2
Waymire, Frederick 51:50 318:2
Waymire, John 318:9
Weatherford, Alfred H. 150:1
Weatherly, Charlie 230:2
Weaver, Davis 319:3

Weaver, Jacob F. 199:2
Webb, Charles 233:3
Webb, R. P. 157:2
Webb, William B. 286:5
Webber, A. C. 279:6
Webber, H. A. 279:5
Webber's Roadhouse, AK 311:2
Webster, Edgar J. 150:1
Webster, Lionel 110:4
Wedderburn, OR 86:10
Weeden, Robert B. 54:7
Weeks, Arthur F. 2:8
Wegener, O. F. 163:2
Wegner, Frank 173:9
Wehesville, WA 267:1
Weidler, George Washington 73:9 197:4
Weigle, William G. 98:14
Weil, Fred M. 293:6
Weiler, Fred 148:5
Weiner, Ruth F. 278:1
Weippe, ID 23:1 103:4
Weir, Allen 150:2 176:1 245:4 266:3
Weir, George Moir 253:5
Weisbach, Arthur J. 266:2
Weisbach, R. Jacob 234:1
Weiser, ID 23:7 24:2 118:4 164:1 180:6
Weisner, Ira 309:4
Welch, Alvadore 75:3
Welch, Daniel J. 181:4
Welch, Douglass 176:3
Welch, John 2:11
Welcome, George 308:1
Welker, Herman 261:1
Wellcome, John B. 133:11 155:6
Wellington, WA 98:47 305:1
  SEE ALSO Tye, WA
Wellman, Alfred C. 199:3
Wellpinit, WA 91:2
Wells, Alonzo Z. 116:3
Wells, Charles 161:1
Wells, Charles H. 266:2
Wells, George M. 187:6

Wells, Hulet  113:5  276:8
Wells, L. V.  116:2
Wells, Lemuel H.  108:1
Wells, William Benjamin
  150:2
Wells, William V.  266:2
Wells, William W.  230:2
Welsford, Richard A. H.
  275:9
Welsh, John T.  266:3
Welsh, William D.  152:1
Wemme, Henry  239:1
Wenas, WA  203:1
Wenatchee, WA  17:5  41:4
  58:7  96:2  116:399  151:3
  157:100  180:7  198:9
  229:4  243:2  252:7  293:65
  305:9
Wendell, ID  23:7  24:2
Wendling, OR  152:2
West, Calvin Brookings
  230:4
West, Ellsworth  161:1
West, Harry  266:2
West, John  266:2
West, Oswald  12:7  49:30
  114:3  152:7  172:2
  261:4
West Linn, OR  75:4
Westcott, Bob  52:3
Westendorf, Thomas P.
  266:2
Westervelt, Conrad  178:3
  252:1
Westlake, ID  102:3
Weston, David  84:3  162:7
Weston, ID  118:2
Weston, OR  119:5  207:10
  300:2  303:5
Westport, WA  305:1
Westwood, ID  39:1  SEE
  ALSO Rathdrum, ID
Wetzell, William A.  150:1
Weyerhaeuser, John Philip
  203:1
Weythman, James L  157:4
Whaley, Frank  148:6

Whannell, P. B.  3:3
Wharton, Samuel M.  289:2
Wharton, William S.  266:2
Whatcom, WA  14:4  150:2
  191:4  234:2  314:4
  315:2  SEE ALSO Bell-
  ingham, WA
Whealdon, Bon Isaac  97:4
  202:4
Whealdon, William  97:7
Wheatland, OR  68:8  147:1
Wheeler, Burton Kendall
  156:3  214:20  215:35
  244:15  298:10  299:22
Wheeler, Carl  274:16
Wheeler, Charles W.  38:4
  119:5
Wheeler, Cortes H.  187:7
Wheeler, Emerson L.
  199:1
Wheeler, Henry H.  42:7
Wheeler, John W.  134:4
Wheeler, William F.  133:6
Wheeler, William H.  300:3
Wherry, O. T.  2:9
Whidden, Lee M.  266:2
Whistle-Possum (Chief)
  108:1
Whitaker, Robert  303:5
Whitcomb, Lot  172:4
  197:2  229:5  284:14
  297:5
Whitcomb, MT  319:2
White, Aubrey Lee  96:22
  203:1  288:6
White, Benjamin F.  46:3
  286:6
White, Calvin R.  103:3
White, Chester F.  266:1
White, Compton I.  213:7
  293:3
White, Edward  3:4
White, Elijah  4:6  16:5
  44:10  50:7  56:5  84:2
  93:14  119:11  162:7
  177:31  187:14  188:8
  193:16  198:1  202:7

220:6  272:2  318:11
White, F. Wallace  264:6
White, Francis A.  266:4
White, George  181:4
White, Green  95:2
White, Harry  266:4
White, Henry A.  266:2
White, Henry M.  266:2
White, J. C.  99:26
White, John S.  51:7
White, Leonard  229:9
White, Lew  198:2
White, Louis P.  266:2
White, Oliver C.  266:3
White, S. S.  150:1
White, Sam O.  137:10
White, Wallace R.  95:3
White, William Augustus
  108:1
White, William H.  163:5
  243:10  266:3
White Bird (Chief)  11:3
  26:9  27:7  102:5  118:2
  132:4  172:5
White City by the Sea, OR
  9:10
White Knob, ID  223:1
White Mountain, AK  8:4
White Salmon, WA  198:1
  201:6  242:5
White Sulpher Springs, MT
  319:9
White Swan, WA  305:1
Whiteaker, John W.  35:2
  51:4  153:1  232:3  297:3
Whitebird, ID  23:3  97:2
  102:7  164:2
Whited, Kirk  116:2  157:2
Whitefish, MT  1:1  319:2
Whitehall, MT  46:3  319:5
Whitehorse, YT  63:1  115:4
  130:2  137:4  146:11
  159:9  255:9  309:6
Whitehouse, George W.
  199:2
Whiteley, Opal  152:10
Whiteman, Harry  116:1

Whiteside, Fred  133:10
  155:7  156:4  214:3
Whiteson, OR  75:5
Whitfield, William  266:2
Whitford, Ames T.  149:7
Whiting, Ray R.  308:3
Whitlatch, James W.  76:11
  319:4
Whitman, E. B.  119:11
  199:2
Whitman, Marcus  4:325
  6:7  16:23  17:19  27:5
  36:3  41:3  44:10  45:15
  58:17  91:5  93:30
  101:113  108:6  118:8
  119:16  121:7  132:6
  150:2  152:5  153:5
  172:20  176:10  177:398
  179:2  187:32  188:20
  194:4  198:12  208:4
  220:10  222:12  249:8
  252:16  261:4  296:55
  305:10  317:10  318:14
Whitman, Narcissa  4:325
  17:14  33:5  93:20  96:3
  101:113  121:7  172:25
  176:7  177:398  188:10
  198:12  252:11  296:50
  305:4
Whitman, Perrin  91:9
  296:10
Whitman, Stephen G.  199:2
Whitman Mission, WA  4:42
  119:6  153:2  198:4  SEE
  ALSO Waiialatpu
Whitney, Henry James
  231:10
Whitney, Rienzi  315:3
Whitney, OR  225:3  264:2
  308:3
Whitson, Edward  205:3
Whitson, W. C.  87:4
Whitted, Thomas  51:9
Whitten, L. B.  289:2
Whittier, AK  130:5  148:2
Whittlesey, William H.
  150:2

Whitworth, Frederick Har-
 rison 266:2
Whitworth, George F.  38:7
 124:25  266:6  282:3
 305:3  306:4
Whymper, Frederick  161:2
Whyte, Sam  175:16
Whyte, Terry  140:13
Whytecliff, BC  275:6
Wibaux, Pierre  156:1
Wibaux, MT  312:1
Wickersham, James  199:1
Wickersham, James W.
 28:2  55:3  63:3  129:5
 130:43  143:3  159:5
 160:15  161:2  233:14
 241:18  255:4  269:5
 271:4  309:6  311:13
Wickersham, John  199:2
Wickes, MT  46:3  78:2
 319:7
Wickman, Anders G.  266:2
Widby, Edgar J.  116:3
Wien, Fridtjof  137:18
Wien, Noel  137:307  263:23
Wien, Ralph  137:26  263:3
Wien, Sigurd  137:12  263:10
Wiesendanger, Albert K.
 195:5
Wiestling, Joshua Martin
 266:3
Wilber, Hiram  179:3
Wilbur, George R.  49:3
Wilbur, James Harvey
 91:3  150:2  230:3
 305:1
Wilbur, WA  293:10  305:1
Wilcox, A. H.  112:6
Wilcox, Ralph  41:1
Wild, Philip A.  199:2
Wilder, ID  23:3
Wildwood, OR  228:5
Wiley, J. W.  245:9
Wiley City, WA  305:2
Wilkesboro, OR  75:4
Wilkeson, WA  225:1  305:2
Wilkins, Caleb  84:3  162:8

Wilkins, F. M.  232:9
Wilkins, Mitchell  232:3
Wilkins, Thomas H.  266:2
Wilkinson, Starr (Bigfoot)
 134:8
Willamina, OR  75:3  114:3
Willapa, WA  14:1  152:3
 252:1
Willapa Bay, WA  41:6
 109:4
Willard, Carrie  149:4
Willard, Cyrus Field
 191:17
Willard, Fred F.  266:2
Willey, Frank C.  266:3
Willey, Lafayette  266:4
Willey, Norman B.  43:1
 103:2  106:4  212:10
Willey, Samuel  245:5
William (Fort), OR  188:7
 SEE ALSO Fort William
Williams, Dan  40:12
Williams, Edward J.  199:1
Williams, Effie Mae  114:3
Williams, Ervie  251:5
Williams, Gail  176:5
Williams, George H.
 51:110  85:2  87:5  150:4
 197:11  302:2
Williams, Guy  140:3
Williams, Joe  140:3
Williams, Larry  12:11
Williams, Parker  294:2
Williams, Percy  260:4
Williams, Robert W.  266:3
Williams, Vernon  49:3
Williams, Woody  173:8
Williamson, James A.
 266:2
Williamson, John P.  150:1
Williamson, S. B.  150:1
Williamson, Volney D.
 289:3
Williamson, Walter T.
 187:7
Willis, J. E.  266:2
Willis, Margaret  278:1

Williston, Lorenzo P.
133:3  286:3
Williston, R. G.  316:8
Willoughby, R.  18:3
Willson, William Holden
84:4  119:9
Wilmer, F. J.  184:11
Wilmer, BC  151:2
Wilsall, MT  312:1
Wilson, Albert E.  84:3
119:4
Wilson, Alfred V.  119:3
179:14
Wilson, Anthony S.  266:2
Wilson, Asher B.  213:8
Wilson, Dave  114:3
Wilson, Edgar  127:6
Wilson, Elliott M.  266:2
Wilson, Eugene T.  280:2
Wilson, Frank  266:1
Wilson, Fred W.  35:2
Wilson, George Flanders
187:7
Wilson, Holt C.  187:8
Wilson, John L.  96:2
176:1  234:3  243:3
245:5
Wilson, John M.  245:4
Wilson, M. L.  156:3
214:5
Wilson, Mabel Zoe  169:6
Wilson, Norman  114:12
Wilson, Robert Bruce
150:1  187:10
Wilson, Valentine  199:2
Wilson, William  150:2
Wilson, William Edward
38:2  231:32
Wilson, William M.  266:2
Wilson, Zachary T.  266:2
Wilson Creek, WA  293:15
Winans, William P.  119:4
Winchell, Oscar  263:11
Winchester, Harry  266:2
Winchester, ID  23:2
Winchester, OR  145:2
230:1  317:4

Wing, Frederick A.  266:3
Wingard, S. C.  119:6
Wingate, Robert  150:2
Winifred, MT  319:3
Winlock, WA  14:1  89:1
180:2  305:1
Winne, Douglas T.  266:2
Winona, ID  102:5  103:2
SEE ALSO Lowe, ID
Winsor, C. S.  86:10
Winsor, Richard  243:5
Winston, Patrick Henry
96:5
Winston, MT  46:3  319:2
Wintermute, James  163:3
Winters, Jim  61:16
Winthrop, WA  89:1  267:1
Wisdom, Jefferson D.
264:2
Wisdom, MT  319:3
Wise, Odny  278:1
Wise, Stephen S.  304:3
Wiseman, Jonathan T.
199:2
Wiseman, William N.
199:1
Wiseman, AK  115:1  137:6
159:2
Wishram, WA  198:1  305:1
Wiswall, R. D.  203:2
Witherop, John W.  288:3
Witherspoon, Herbert
217:3
Withycombe, James  153:1
Witt, Philander S.  119:1
Witt, Ronald  140:10
Wittenberg, "Papa"  161:4
Wohleb, Joseph  245:5
Wolcott, Allen D.  258:3
Wolf, Charles  195:3
Wolff, Francis  27:4
Wolfle, Conrad  289:3
Wolten, William M.  266:2
Wood, Charles Erskine
Scott  49:5  114:2
285:11  302:2  304:6
Wood, Clark  176:1  207:4

Wood, D. T.  173:12  319:4
Wood, Erskine  114:9
Wood, Frederick J.  266:1
Wood, Fremont  127:25
Wood, Ginny  115:6
Wood, James A.  178:3
Wood, Joseph K.  130:2
Wood, Lyman  150:2
Wood, Merle  274:14
Wood, Morton  52:3
Wood, P. P.  157:2
Wood, Richard  137:5
Wood, Thomas A.  150:1
  179:1
Wood, W. D.  234:1
Wood, William R.  130:1
Woodall, Perry B.  245:7
Woodburn, OR  75:9  300:3
Woodcock, A. C.  232:3
Wooddy, Claiborne A.
  303:25
Woodin, M. D.  306:4
Woodin, Wellington Alfred
  266:3
Woodinville, WA  14:1
Woodland, ID  102:3
Woodruff, Mark  293:39
Woods, Charles Thomas
  5:7
Woods, George L.  153:1
  163:2  197:3
Woods, Joel  199:1
Woods, Ralph  293:7
Woods, Rufus  16:2  36:2
  41:1  58:14  83:3  116:3
  151:3  157:1  172:5
  176:1  198:1  252:3
  293:120
Woods, Ruth  231:2
Woods, Warren W.  157:1
Woods, William  266:2
Woodville, MT  78:3
Woodward, A. P.  150:2
Woodward, Henry H.  150:2
Woodward, Tyler  285:3
Woodwell, A. H.  264:2
Woodworth, Charles  266:2

Woody, Frank H.  133:10
  155:4  181:19
Woody's Landing (Woody-
  ville), OR  68:3
Wool, John Ellis  132:2
  179:2  198:3
Woolard, Alfred E.  266:3
Woolfolk, Alexander  286:3
Woolley, Philip A.  266:2
  314:2
Woolley, WA  314:4  SEE
  ALSO Sedro-Woolley,
  WA
Word, Samuel  133:6  286:3
Worden, Francis  155:24
  181:20  292:11
Worden, Warren A.  266:3
Work, John  3:7  20:8
  39:11  272:8
Work, L. L.  308:1
Worley, ID  23:1
Worsley, John  194:9
Wortley, James T.  194:11
Wortman, J. L. "Jake"
  201:8
Wrangel, Ferdinand Petro-
  vich von  18:2  161:8
Wrangell, AK  18:3  19:11
  28:3  55:2  63:10  128:5
  130:29  131:7  148:2
  159:13  160:5  190:15
  269:11  271:4  290:2
Wright, Albert H.  266:3
Wright, Charles  266:2
Wright, Edgar  242:9
Wright, George  11:9  27:76
  30:1  39:15  43:2  96:2
  108:3  119:13  139:2
  141:6  179:3  198:4
  212:2  252:2  305:7
Wright, John A.  211:7
Wright, Lewis Cass  242:20
Wright, Marcus D.  289:2
Wright, Ora C.  303:15
Wright, Rose Abel  278:1
Wright, Tom  246:6
Wright, W. T.  150:1

Wrinch, H. C.   186:4
Wyatt, Charles A.   266:2
Wyckoff, Lewis   234:5
  306:5
Wyeth, Joseph Henry   187:6
Wyeth, Nathaniel J.   4:4
  6:4   16:5   33:2   43:5
  44:11   45:100   50:6   84:7
  93:14   101:3   118:5
  162:11   177:8   188:13
  194:7   198:4   211:5
  220:5   249:5   259:5
  284:5   287:14   302:3
  305:4   317:10
Wylie, W. W.   133:3
Wyman, Chance   246:3
Wyman, Frank T.   219:4
Wymer, Kenneth   274:6
Wynkoop, Urban G.   266:3


Yacolt, WA   152:1   252:8
Yakima, WA   34:4   41:4
  58:3   82:8   88:55   96:2
  151:4   180:6   198:3   217:4
  243:4   252:7   293:14
  305:10
Yakutat, AK   19:9   63:1
  77:7   130:6   136:3
  159:7   269:5   302:1
Yale, George B.   230:3
Yale, James Murray   3:9
  20:5   235:4   253:5
Yale, Louis J.   39:8
Yale, BC   3:40   5:13
  20:19   123:6   204:2
  238:23   SEE ALSO
  Fort Yale, BC
Yanatco (Chief)   32:3
Yankton, MT   133:4
Yantis, B. F.   27:2   141:2
Yantis, George F.   245:11
Yaquina, OR   75:4   228:15
Yarrow (North Bend), OR
  41:1
Yates, J. Stuart   294:1

Yates, James   3:6   20:5
  253:6
Yates, W. L.   275:10
Yates, William   5:8
Yearsley, Wilbur Simpson
  288:2   293:3
Yeaton, Cyrus F.   39:3
  91:5   108:4
Yeend, James A.   199:1
Yeend, William   199:2
Yelle, Clifford   169:1
  245:11   248:1
Yellow Bird (Chief)   58:3
  SEE ALSO Peopeomox-
  mox
Yellow Jacket, ID   223:1
  308:7
Yellow Serpent (Chief)   177:5
Yellow Wolf (a Nez Perce)
  26:23
Yellowstone City, MT   78:6
Yelm, WA   305:1
Yenney, L. O.   199:1
Yenney, Philip   119:2
  199:1
Yenney, Robert Clark
  187:6
Yenney, W. H.   199:1
Yesler, Henry L.   6:3
  7:8   31:14   32:3   73:11
  80:4   150:3   163:4
  172:18   178:12   195:4
  220:3   222:5   234:11
  243:14   276:10   305:2
  306:15
Yocum, Franklin   30:1
Yocum, Oliver C.   239:3
Yoder, Albert H.   38:3
Yogg, Ed   176:2
Yogo, MT   78:5   319:2
Yoncalla, OR   230:3
Yoran, S. M.   232:1
York, J. B.   102:6
York, Lem A.   24:2
York, MT   319:3   SEE
  ALSO New York, MT
Yorke, Waldo   243:6

Young (Chief) 177:7
Young, Abraham C.  266:2
Young, Angus William
  266:3
Young, Cal M.  232:7
Young, Don  136:7
Young, E. J.  279:5
Young, Ed  137:2  263:13
Young, Edward Thomas
  150:2
Young, Elam  177:6
Young, Ewing  4:5  6:3
  17:7  44:3  50:12
  84:5  114:4  151:4
  162:7  188:13  193:18
  198:6
Young, Frederic G.  261:4
Young, Kenneth B.  106:6
Young, Norris  242:8
Young, Robert  266:2
Young, Samuel P.  199:1
Young, Samuel Hall  63:3
  149:5
Young, Volney C. F.  246:3
Young, William A. G.  3:4
Youngs, Willard O.  169:15
Yunker, William B.  137:14


Zachary, Sarah  150:1
Zagoskin, L. H.  161:8

Zahm, John A.  71:7
Zahren, Herbert  157:1
Zan, James Cullen  187:6
Zatica, Joe  114:5
Zeballos, BC  165:4
Zednick, Victor  184:5
  245:8
Zehntbauer, John A.
  114:11
Zeiszler, Norman  114:8
Zeller, Julius C.  38:1
Zerbinati, Pietro  39:2
Zieber, John S.  145:3
Ziegler, Eustace P.  262:2
Ziegler, Louis  288:7
Zillah, WA  305:1
Zimmer, E. R.  266:2
Zimmerly, Bert  103:5
Zimmerman, Carma Russell  169:18
Zimmerman, Peter  49:7
  266:2
Zincton, BC  47:1
Zioncheck, Marion  41:1
  176:2  234:5  244:5
  245:3
Zittel, Julius A.  288:1
Zollinger, Charles J.  59:4
Zorn, Casper  162:5
Zorn, Henry  162:7
Zortman, MT  61:13  78:2
  224:2  312:1  319:11

Z
1251
N7
D7

Drazan, Joseph Gerald, 1943-
    The Pacific Northwest : an index to
people and places in books / by
Joseph Gerald Drazan. -- Metuchen,
N.J. : Scarecrow Press, 1979.
    xii, 164 p. ; 22 cm.
    Bibliography: p. 1-26.
    ISBN 0-8108-1234-7

    1. Northwest, Pacific--Indexes.
2. Alaska--Indexes.  3. Yukon
Territory--Indexes.  4. Northwest,
Pacific--Biography--Indexes.
5. Alaska--Biography--Indexes.
6. Yukon Territory--Biography--
Indexes.  I. Title.

Z1251.N7D7           979.5/0016
[F851]            79-16683

SUPAT       B/NA A D1-826854       02/01/80